STATE OF CALIFORNIA

THE RESOURCES AGENCY

DEPARTMENT OF FISH AND GAME

FISH BULLETIN 157

GUIDE TO THE COASTAL MARINE FISHES OF CALIFORNIA

by

DANIEL J. MILLER and ROBERT N. LEA
Marine Resources Region

1972

ABSTRACT

This is a comprehensive identification guide encompassing all shallow marine fishes within California waters.

Geographic range limits, maximum size, depth range, a brief color description, and some meristic counts including, if available: fin ray counts, lateral line pores, lateral line scales, gill rakers, and vertebrae are given. Body proportions and shapes are used in the keys and a statement concerning the rarity or commonness in California is given for each species.

In all, 554 species are described. Three of these have not been recorded or confirmed as occurring in California waters but are included since they are apt to appear. The remainder have been recorded as occurring in an area between the Mexican and Oregon borders and offshore to at least 50 miles. Five of California species as yet have not been named or described, and ichthyologists studying these new forms have given information on identification to enable inclusion here. A dichotomous key to 144 families includes an outline figure of a representative for all but two families. Keys are presented for all larger families, and diagnostic features are pointed out on most of the figures. Illustrations are presented for all but eight species.

Of the 554 species, 439 are found primarily in depths less than 400 ft., 48 are meso- or bathypelagic species, and 67 are deepwater bottom dwelling forms rarely taken in less than 400 ft. depth. The deepwater forms included are those taken in commercial trawling gear or that occasionally occur near the surface.

An illustrated glossary is included to facilitate use of the identification keys and species descriptions. A comments section presents in detail reasons for certain taxonomic choices and to acknowledge personal communications.

Original data presented include a ventral sensory pore pattern key for the skates, 170 geographic range limit extensions, and several depth range and maximum size records. Many of the family keys have been revised to incorporate recent taxonomic changes and to clarify previously ambiguous terminology.

TABLE OF CONTENTS

ACKNOWLEDGMENTS

This guide has been made possible through the works and studies of hundreds of fishery researchers and taxonomists, past and present. We cannot thank those of the past whose immortality lies in libraries, but we can credit most of those who have personally aided us. Unfortunately, space does not permit us to fully credit all that has been received from each contributor or to mention all who have helped us.

First, we extend credit to fellow Department colleagues. The meticulously recorded data on range limits, depth, and sizes of California marine fishes offered to us by John Fitch has been of primary importance. John also gave taxonomic advice, offered information on identification, and stimulated us to conduct the museum search for geographic and depth range limit extensions. Dan Gotshall and John Geibel had originally planned to collaborate on this publication but their heavy work loads precluded full collaboration. Dan Gotshall was able to assist in preparing the sections on the eelpouts, poachers, and pricklebacks; and John Geibel assisted in preparing the section on scombrids and printing photographs of some of the fish drawings. Dick Nitsos and Dick Parrish supplied data on depth of bottomfishes, and Paul Gregory and Jack Schott supplied pictures on which some of the fish drawings are based. Dan Collier and his wife Cynthia made photographic prints of most of the fish drawings. Jim Houk spent many hours in the museums searching bottles for pertinent data, and helped in the literature search. Bill Craig and Dick Burge supplied information on ranges, and Pat Powell and the library staff aided in supplying literature and editing the reference section. Nancy Durell and Margaret Hughes typed the manuscript. Herb Frey edited the entire manuscript, and Harold Orcutt offered encouragement and suggestions to undertake this project.

Many fish researchers and taxonomists have given us aid. Geographically, from north to south, we wish to extend our thanks to the following for their suggestions and information so generously offered: Jay C. Quast, National Marine Fish. Service, Auke Bay, Alaska; Sigmund J. Westrheim, Fisheries Research Board of Canada, Nanaimo, B.C.; John L. Hart, Fisheries Research Board of Canada, St. Andrews, N.B.; Alex E. Peden, British Columbia Provincial Museum, Victoria, B.C.; William G. Pearcy, Oregon State University, Corvallis, Ore.; W. I. Follett and Earl S. Herald, California Academy of Sciences, San Francisco; Leonard J. V. Compagno, Systematic Zoology Dept., Stanford University; John S. Stephens, Occidental College, Los Angeles; Boyd W. Walker, University of California at Los Angeles; Robert J. Lavenberg and Camm Swift, Los Angeles County Museum of Natural History; Shelly R. Johnson, University of Southern California; Elbert H. Ahlstrom, National Marine Fisheries Service, La Jolla; Carl L. Hubbs, Laura Hubbs, Richard H. Rosenblatt, Robert L. Wisner, and Layton P. Taylor, Jr., Scripps Institution of Oceanography; and Lo-Chai Chen, California State University at San Diego.

Museum staff members and curators were most cooperative and helpful. Special thanks must be extended to the sage of reference, grammar, and literature, Lillian J. Dempster, California Academy of Sciences, for her enthusiastic search for descriptions and references. The entire staff of the California Academy of Sciences Ichthyology Department, especially Pearl M. Sonoda and William N. Eschmeyer, made it possible to conduct primary museum work in development and testing identification keys. John Bleck, University of California at Los Angeles, and Joe Copp and Donald Dockins, Scripps Institution of Oceanography, gave us much aid in the museum search for range and size extensions.

To all the above and to those not listed, we offer our sincere gratitude for all the help you have given us.

Daniel J. Miller
Robert N. Lea

INTRODUCTION

All the shallow water inshore marine fishes recorded as occurring in California waters between the Oregon and Mexican borders of California are included in this bulletin, as well as most marine fishes introduced into the Salton Sea. In all, 144 families are represented by the 554 species described. Three of these species have not been recorded from California but are included to enable identification since their presence in California waters has not been confirmed. Five California species are undescribed, two in family Stichaeidae, and one each in families Scorpaenidae, Agonidae, and Gerreidae. Of the 554 species, 439 most frequently are found in waters shallower than 400 ft., 48 are primarily meso- or bathypelagic (about ¼ of all California meso- and bathypelagic forms), and 67 bottom dwelling forms rarely taken above 400 ft.

This guide is primarily for identification purposes, using a brief description of color, meristic counts, and body proportions and structures to enable keying out a fish to family and to species within a family. The following additional data are given, if available: geographic range, maximum size, depth range, a comment on rarity, and vertebral counts. A fish is considered *rare* if 20 or less ever have been taken in California; *uncommon* if the fish is seldom seen either because of scarcity or because it is unavailable even though actually present in large numbers; and *common* if it is easily available and appearing frequently in sport or commercial catches or in tide pool, mud flat, or kelp canopy collections.

Illustrations of fish primarily were based on literature, but the origins were not cited because in most cases the published figure was changed. In most cases drawings were compared either with fresh or preserved material, if available. The fish drawings, family key figures, and skate ventral pore patterns were prepared by the senior author. Drawings of some diagnostic characters and all the shark's teeth were prepared by Cathy Short, California Department of Fish and Game.

HOW TO USE THE GUIDE

The Keys

This guide is an accumulation of artificial diagnostic keys based on external features of shape, proportion, color, and numbers of fin rays, gill rakers, lateral line pores, and scales. Internal characters have been avoided except for gill rakers and teeth which can be examined without dissection. The term "artificial" refers to a key based on characters not necessarily indicative of taxonomic or phylogenetic order. Many taxonomic characters are skeletal and internal, and depict evolutionary trends from primitive to more specialized or advanced forms. Even though the keys are not based necessarily on evolutionary criteria, the sequence of families is generally in phylogenetic order; i.e. from the primitive hagfishes to highly specialized molas. The sequence we followed was that of Greenwood et al (1966); however, in several instances closely related families containing only one or several species have been grouped on a single page without adherence to this sequence.

The keys work on the principle of an either/or choice using "a" and "b" alternatives. If a fish does not fit the description of "a" go on to "b", etc. In each case where there is a jump to another section of the key, there is a citation of the section from which you were referred, facilitating backtracking through the key. The key to the families is a collation of features used in keys by Jordan and Evermann (1896–1900), Roedel (1953), Schultz (1936), Wilimovsky (1958), and Clemens and Wilby (1961), with additional characters from Berg (1940). Terminology of key characters is given in the glossary and illustrated glossary.

Measurements and Counts

Measurements, counts, and terminology are essentially that of Hubbs and Lagler (1958), with a few exceptions. Maximum size is in inches (in.) or feet (ft.) and is total length or width; occasionally maximum weights are given. Standard length is for systematic work; i.e., measured from tip of upper jaw or snout to end of hypural (at caudal flexure).

Fin Rays.

Fin ray counts are given for each species of bony fish. These counts were obtained from the literature except for a few species for which we made additional counts. Minimum and maximum fin ray counts represent variation over the entire geographic range of each species, except for worldwide fishes in which the eastern Pacific counts varied significantly from counts in other oceans. Subspecies were not differentiated except for those such as the herring that inhabit several oceans. Fin ray formulas are given to save space. Spines are represented by Roman numerals; soft-rays are in Arabic. When there are two dorsal fins, counts are given for each, separated by a + sign. Fin symbols are: D = dorsal fin; A = anal fin; Pect. = pectoral fin; Pelvic = pelvic or ventral fin. Example of fin formula: QUEENFISH (page 154), D VII–IX + I,18–21. There are two separate dorsal fins, the first with 7 to 9 spines, the second with one spine and from 18 to 21 soft-rays.

Lateral Line.

LLs = scales on the lateral line; LLp = pores on the lateral line. If the lateral line pores continue onto the caudal fin, the count will be divided into those on the body and those on the tail whenever these are differentiated in the literature. When there are no lateral line pores, a count of scales in midbody along the sides is often given, referred to as midlateral scales.

Gill Rakers

Counts are always of the anterior rakers on the first gill arch (see Figure 7). A raker (or rakers) in the angle at the junction of the upper and lower limbs is counted with the lower limb. When only total gill rakers are given (upper and lower limbs combined), the count is preceded by GRt. Rudimentary rakers are included in all counts. Example: KELP BASS (page 142): GR 11–13 + 20–24 = 32–36. There are from 11 to 13 rakers on the upper limb and 20 to 24 rakers on the lower limb totaling from 32 to 36.

Vertebrae (Vert.)

Counts are for all vertebrae, including the hypural. Most of the vertebral counts are from Clothier (1950) and Clothier, Baxter, and Miller (unpublished MS, Calif. Dept. F&G).

Geographic Ranges

Geographic range limits not accompanied by a museum number or a personal communication citation are derived from the literature, but are not cited. Museum symbols are: CAS — California Academy of Sciences, San Francisco; UCLA — University of California at Los Angeles; LACM — Los Angeles County Museum of Natural History; SIO — Scripps Institution of Oceanography, La Jolla; SU — Stanford University Ichthyological Collection (now at CAS).

Depth Ranges

Depths are given in feet and are intended to relate only approximate levels at which a fish may be found. Terminology of the pelagic realm is from Hedgpeth (1957):

Realm	Fathoms*	Meters*	Feet
Epipelagic	0 to 109	0 to 200	0 to 656
Mesopelagic	109 to 547	200 to 1000	656 to 3281
Bathypelagic	547 to 2187	1000 to 4000	3281 to 13,123

* 1 Fathom = 6 ft.; 1 meter = 3.28 ft.

GLOSSARY AND INDEX TO ILLUSTRATED GLOSSARY

ABDOMEN: belly, Figure 1.
ABDOMINAL: pelvic fin placement, Fig. 5a.
ADIPOSE: fin, Figure 6l., fatty.
ANADROMOUS: an ocean fish that spawns in freshwater.
ANAL FIN: Figure 1.
ANTERIOR: toward the head.
ANUS: vent, Figure 1.
AXIL, AXILLA: Figure 3.

BAR: A vertical band.
BARBEL: An elongate, fleshy appendage.
BASE: (of fin) Figure 2.
BEAK: Figure 10d.
BELLY: area covering viscera.
BIFID: with two points.
BRANCHIOSTEGALS: Figure 3.
BREAST: Figure 4a.

CANINE: (teeth) Figure 8c.
CAUDAL FIN: Figure 1.
CAUDAL PEDUNCLE: Figures 1, 2.
CHIN: Figure 1.
CIRRUS: a thin, usually fringed flap. Figure 3.
COMPRESSED: (body form) Figure 9d.
CONCAVE: depressed inward. Figure 9f.
CONVEX: bulging outward. Figure 9d.
CONTIGUOUS: adjoining. Figure 6j.
CONTINUOUS: (fins) Figure 6i.

DEEP, DEPTH: (body form) Figure 9d.
DENTIGEROUS: with small teeth.
DEPRESSED: (body form) Figure 9e; held down, pressed onto body.
DORSAL FIN: Figures 1, 6i,j.

EEL-LIKE: (body form) figure 9a.
ELEVATED: above. Figure 3.
ELONGATE: (body form) Figure 9a, 9b.
EYE: (orbit) Figures 1, 3.

FILAMENTOUS: threadlike. Figure 3.
FIN: (shapes) Figure 6.
FINLET: Figure 6k.
FLAP: a thick extension of skin, Figure 3.
FORKED: (tail shape) Figure 6e.

GILL: rakers, cavity, arch, filaments; Figure 7; membrane Figure 4.

GILL COVER: Figures 1, 3, 4a.
HEAD: Figure 3.
HYPURAL: (bone in tail) Figures 2, 6k.

INCISED: notched. Figure 3.
INCISOR: (teeth) Figure 8d.
INDENTED: (tail form) Figure 6a.
INFERIOR: (mouth form) Figure 10c.
INNER: (fin ray placement) Figure 5c.
INSERTION: posterior attachment of a fin to body. Figure 1.
ISOLATED: not connected by a membrane.
ISTHMUS: Figure 4.

JAWS: Figure 10.

KEEL: Figure 6k.

LATERAL LINE: Figure 1.
LENGTH: Figure 2.
LIPS: Figures 3, 10e,f.
LONGITUDINAL: lengthwise, horizontal.

MANDIBLE: lower jaw. Figure 8b.
MAXILLARY: upper jaw. Figures 3, 8a.
MEMBRANE: thin connective tissue.
MOLARLIKE: (teeth) Figure 8e.
MOUTH: Figures 1, 10.
MULTIFID: With many points.

NAKED: without scales or rays. Figure 6h.
NOSTRIL: Figure 3.

OBSOLETE: nearly gone or missing.
OPERCULUM, OPERCLE: Figs. 3, 7.
ORBIT, ORBITAL: Figure 3.
ORIGIN: anterior attachment of a fin to body. Figure 1.

OVATE: (body form) Figure 9c.
OVERHANGING: (snout form) Figure 10c.

PALATINE: (bone and teeth) Figure 8a.
PAPILLAE: short, broad-based fleshy protuberances.
PECTORAL: (fin and girdle) Figures 1, 5c.
PELVIC: (fin and girdle) Figures 1, 5.
POINTED: (tail form) Figure 6f,g.
PORE: a sensory organ in skin.
POSTERIOR: toward the tail.
PROJECTING: ahead of. Figure 10a.

PYLORIC CAECAE: fleshy append-
ages attached to posterior end of
stomach.

RAKER: (gill) Figure 7.
RAYS: (in fins) Figure 2.
ROUNDED: (tail form) Figure 6b.

SCUTE: thickened, hardened scale on
midline of belly.
SHIELD: thickened, hardened scale on
lateral line or sides.
SHOULDER: (girdle) Figure 5c, pec-
toral.
SIMPLE: not divided.
SNOUT: Figures 3, 10b,c.
SOFT-RAY: Figure 2.
SPINE: Figures 2, 3.
SPINULATED: with minute spines or
hooks.
SQUARE: (tail form) straight. Figure
6d.

STRIATED: with close-set lines or
grooves.
STRIPE: lengthwise or horizontal line.
SUBORBITAL STAY: Figure 3.

TAIL: Figures 1, 6.
TERMINAL: at the end. Figure 10e.
THORACIC: (fin placement) Figure
5b.
TONGUE: Figure 8b.
TRUNCATE: Figure 9c.
TUBULAR: (snout form) Figure 10b.
UNITED: joined. Figure 4b.
UPPER JAW: Figure 8a.

VENT: Figure 1.
VENTRAL: lower surface, pelvic fin.
VERTICAL: upright, as bar or band
on sides.
VOMER: (bone, teeth) Figure 8a.
WIDTH: (body form) Figure 9d.

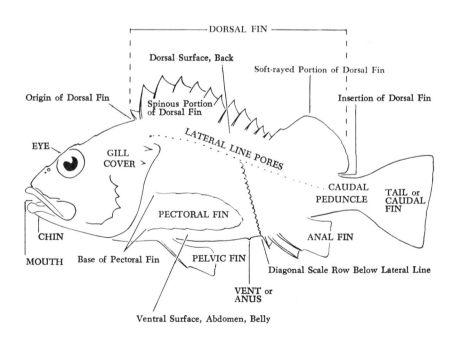

FIGURE 1. A spiny-rayed fish, *Sebastes*, naming fins and general body areas.

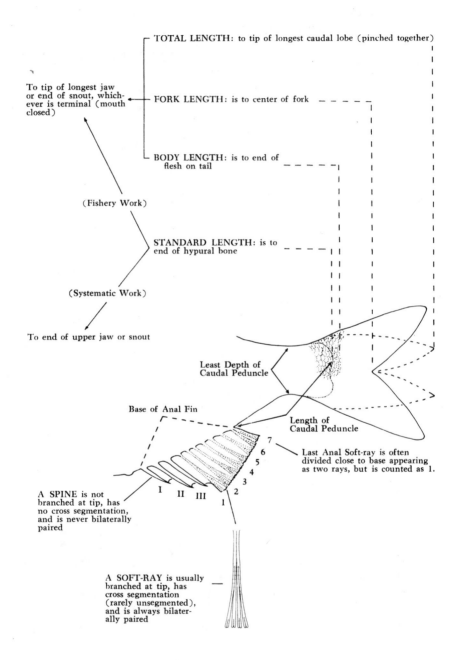

FIGURE 2.   Tail area of a rockfish, *Sebastes*, showing lengths, fin ray construction, and other structures.

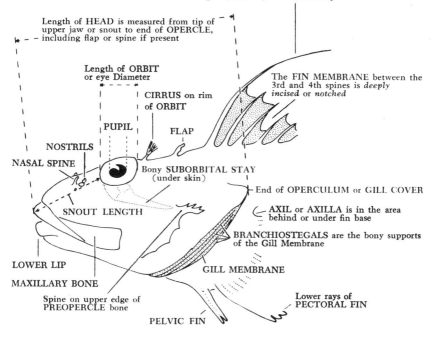

FIGURE 3.   A hypothetical sculpin showing some head and fin structures.

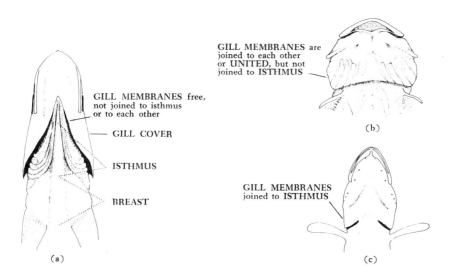

FIGURE 4.   Gill membranes and their attachment (Ventral view of: a, *Spirin-chus starksi;* b, *Clinocottus globiceps;* c, *Anoplarchus purpurescens*).

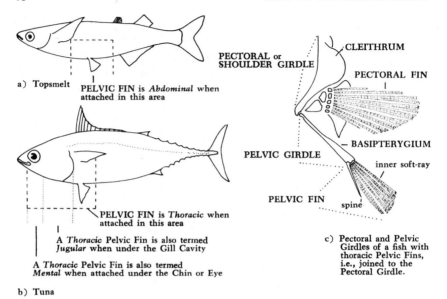

a) Topsmelt

PELVIC FIN is *Abdominal* when attached in this area

PECTORAL or
SHOULDER GIRDLE

CLEITHRUM

PECTORAL FIN

BASIPTERYGIUM

inner soft-ray

PELVIC GIRDLE

PELVIC FIN

spine

PELVIC FIN is *Thoracic* when attached in this area

A *Thoracic* Pelvic Fin is also termed *Jugular* when under the Gill Cavity

A *Thoracic* Pelvic Fin is also termed *Mental* when attached under the Chin or Eye

b) Tuna

c) Pectoral and Pelvic Girdles of a fish with thoracic Pelvic Fins, i.e., joined to the Pectoral Girdle.

FIGURE 5.　Abdominal and thoracic fin placement and construction.

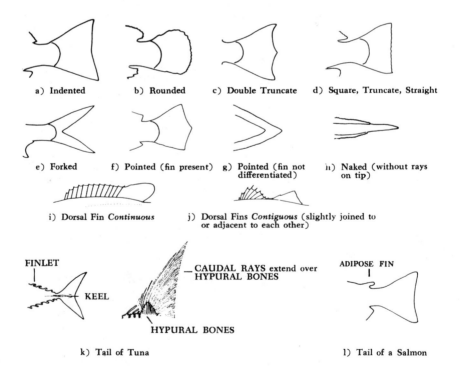

a) Indented　　b) Rounded　　c) Double Truncate　　d) Square, Truncate, Straight

e) Forked　　f) Pointed (fin present)　　g) Pointed (fin not differentiated)　　h) Naked (without rays on tip)

i) Dorsal Fin *Continuous*

j) Dorsal Fins *Contiguous* (slightly joined to or adjacent to each other)

FINLET

KEEL

CAUDAL RAYS extend over HYPURAL BONES

HYPURAL BONES

k) Tail of Tuna

ADIPOSE FIN

l) Tail of a Salmon

FIGURE 6.　Tail and dorsal fin shapes and construction.

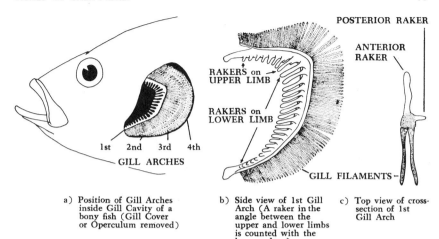

FIGURE 7.   Gill rakers and gill arches of a bony fish.

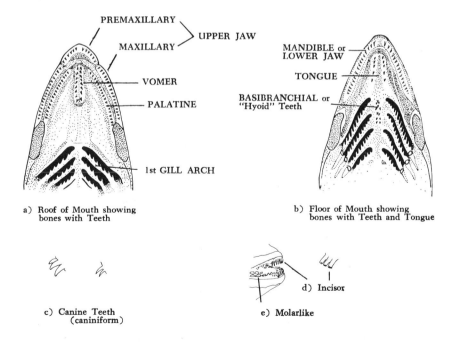

FIGURE 8.   Bones and teeth inside mouth or bucal cavity.

a) Eel-like, greatly elongated, attenuated

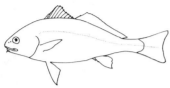

b) Elongate, fusiform, basslike

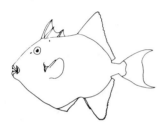

c) Ovate, truncated

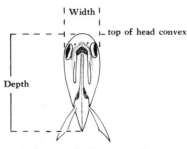

d) Compressed, thin, narrow, deep, or perchlike

e) Body depressed, flattened

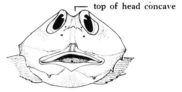

f) Body subcircular, hemispherical

FIGURE 9.   Some body forms of fishes.

a) Lower Jaw *Projecting* beyond Upper Jaw

b) Snout *Tubular* with Jaws at tip

c) Snout *Overhanging* or *Projecting* beyond Mouth, the Mouth is thus *Inferior*

d) Upper Jaw is Prolonged into a swordlike beak

e) Jaws (and Lips) are *Terminal*, i.e., at end of body

f) The Upper Jaw is *Extended* and the Lower Lip is *Inferior* or *Included*

FIGURE 10.   Terminology of mouth and snout forms.

KEY TO THE FAMILIES
Section A

1a No jaws, mouth a sucking
   disc: ....

1b Jaws present 2

2a Gill openings one..................... 4

2b Gill openings 5–7.................... 3

Hagfishes,
lampreys
Page 32

3a Gill openings on sides of
   body; pectoral fins not attached to side of head..............

Sharks
Page 32

underside
of skate

3b Gill openings under body;
   pectorals attached to sides
   of head ....

Skates and
rays
Page 42

4a Eyes on same side of head ......

Flatfishes
Page 199

4b One eye on each side of
   head 5

5a Pelvic fins absent ....

Section B
Page 14

5b Pelvic fins present................. 6

6a Pelvic fins thoracic............... 9

6b Pelvic fins abdominal........... 7

(See Figure 5 for placement and
structure of pelvic fins)

7a Pelvics abdominal; one fin
   on back ....

Section C
Page 17

7b Pelvics abdominal; two fins
   on back 8

8a First dorsal fin with rays,
   the second adipose (no rays).......

Section D
Page 19

8b Both dorsal fins with rays,
   the first with spines, the
   second of soft-rays...................

Section E
Page 20

9a Pelvics thoracic, strongly
   modified forming a cone·
   or sucking disc on belly............

Section F
Page 21

9b Pelvics thoracic and paired,
   not as a cone or sucking
   disc, normal (rays and
   membranes obvious) or
   barbel-like or clublike............ 10 (next page)

sucking disc

—cone

Section A (continued)

10a Pelvics with exactly one
spine and 5 soft-rays...SECTION G
                                                                                          Page 21

10b Pelvics with less than 5
rays, the rays either nor-
mal or as barbel-like or   pelvic fins   SECTION H
clublike structures ....barbel-like   Page 28
                                                           clublike
                                                           pelvics

10c Pelvics with more than 5
soft-rays ....SECTION I
                                                                                          Page 31

Section B: Pelvic Fins Absent

1a Body eel-like (distance
from tip of lower jaw to
base of tail more than 5
times body depth) .... 10 (next page)

1b Body not eel-like (distance
from tip of lower jaw to
base of tail less than 4
times body depth) 2

2a Upper jaw flattened, sword-
like ....   XIPHIIDAE
                                                                                Swordfish
2b Upper jaw not flattened 3   Page 196

3a No caudal fin, body deeply
compressed ....   MOLIDAE
                                                                                Molas
                                                                                Page 210

3b Caudal fin present 4

4a Dorsal fin with spines in
anterior portion .... 8 (next page)

4b Dorsal wholly of soft-rays 5

5a Dorsal fin covering more
than half of dorsal surface   ICOSTEIDAE
(Juvenile has pelvic fins,   Ragfish
see SECTION H, 13a   Pages 184–
page 30)   185

5b Dorsal fin short, in posterior portion of back 6

                                                                                TETRAODONTIDAE
                                                                                Puffers
6a Teeth confluent into two ....   Pages 208–
                                                                                209

                                                                                DIODONTIDAE
                                                                                Porcupine-
6b Teeth confluent into one;   fishes
body covered with spines ....   (burrfish)
                                                                                Pages 208–209

6c Teeth separate, many .... 7 (next page)

Section B: Pelvic Fins Absent (continued)

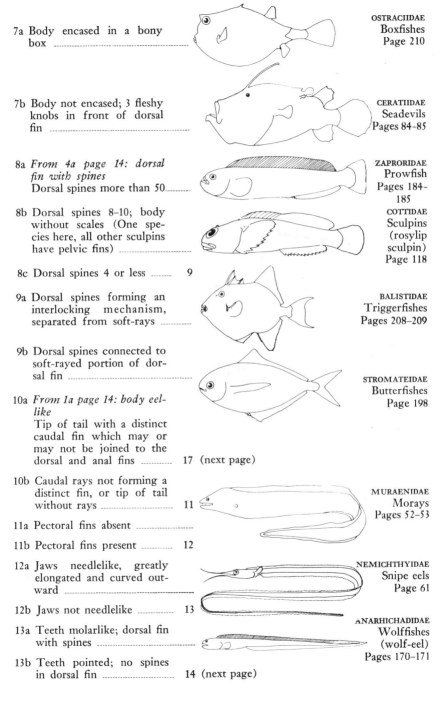

7a Body encased in a bony box ....

OSTRACIIDAE
Boxfishes
Page 210

7b Body not encased; 3 fleshy knobs in front of dorsal fin ....

CERATIIDAE
Seadevils
Pages 84–85

8a *From 4a page 14: dorsal fin with spines*
Dorsal spines more than 50..........

ZAPRORIDAE
Prowfish
Pages 184–185

8b Dorsal spines 8–10; body without scales (One species here, all other sculpins have pelvic fins) ....

COTTIDAE
Sculpins
(rosylip sculpin)
Page 118

8c Dorsal spines 4 or less   9

9a Dorsal spines forming an interlocking mechanism, separated from soft-rays ....

BALISTIDAE
Triggerfishes
Pages 208–209

9b Dorsal spines connected to soft-rayed portion of dorsal fin ....

STROMATEIDAE
Butterfishes
Page 198

10a *From 1a page 14: body eel-like*
Tip of tail with a distinct caudal fin which may or may not be joined to the dorsal and anal fins ....   17 (next page)

10b Caudal rays not forming a distinct fin, or tip of tail without rays   11

MURAENIDAE
Morays
Pages 52–53

11a Pectoral fins absent ....

11b Pectoral fins present   12

12a Jaws needlelike, greatly elongated and curved outward ....

NEMICHTHYIDAE
Snipe eels
Page 61

12b Jaws not needlelike   13

13a Teeth molarlike; dorsal fin with spines ....

ANARHICHADIDAE
Wolffishes
(wolf-eel)
Pages 170–171

13b Teeth pointed; no spines in dorsal fin ....   14 (next page)

16

GUIDE TO THE COASTAL MARINE

Section B: Pelvic Fins Absent (continued)

14a Tip of tail without rays 16

14b Tip of tail with rays 15

15a Origin of dorsal fin more than head length from tip of pectoral fin ----------------------

OPHICHTHIDAE
Snake eels
(worm eel)
Pages 52–53

15b Dorsal fin above pectoral; anterior nostril tubular ------------

CONGRIDAE
Conger eels
Pages 52–53

15c Dorsal fin above pectoral; anterior nostril not tubular-------

ZOARCIDAE
Eelpouts
Page 78

16a Lower jaw longer than upper (Pelvic fins are present on some cutlassfishes as a spine or scale-like structure; caudal fin also present on some. See SECTION H, 14a page 30) ----------

(anterior rays are spines but appear as soft-rays)

TRICHIURIDAE
Cutlass-
fishes
Page 190

16b Lower jaw shorter than upper ----------------------------------

OPHICHTHIDAE
Snake eels
Pages 52–53

17a *From 10a page 15: caudal fin present*
Body encased in bony plates ----------------------------

SYNGNATHIDAE
Pipefishes
(seahorse)
Page 89

17b Body not encased ---------- 18

18a Caudal fin lobes uneven, upper lobe enlarged, fan-shaped; no anal fin (Juveniles of this family have pelvic fins. See SECTION I, 3a page 31) ----------------

TRACHIPTERIDAE
Ribbonfishes
Page 87

18b Caudal fin lobes evenly forked, or rounded; anal fin present ---------------- 19

19a Caudal fin forked; body without scales ----------------

AMMODYTIDAE
Sandlances
Page 184

19b Caudal fin rounded ---------- 20

20a Dorsal fin with spines ------- 22 (next page)

20b Dorsal fin without spines ---- 21

21a Body deeper behind anus (tidepool species) ------------------

SCYTALINIDAE
Graveldiver
Page 184

21b Body deeper before anus; high crest over eyes (deep water species) ----------------

LOPHOTIDAE
Crestfishes
Page 86

Section B: Pelvic Fins Absent (continued)

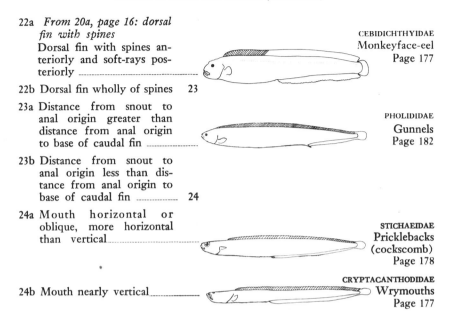

22a *From 20a, page 16: dorsal fin with spines*
Dorsal fin with spines anteriorly and soft-rays posteriorly _____

CEBIDICHTHYIDAE
Monkeyface-eel
Page 177

22b Dorsal fin wholly of spines   23

23a Distance from snout to anal origin greater than distance from anal origin to base of caudal fin _____

PHOLIDIDAE
Gunnels
Page 182

23b Distance from snout to anal origin less than distance from anal origin to base of caudal fin _____   24

24a Mouth horizontal or oblique, more horizontal than vertical_____

STICHAEIDAE
Pricklebacks
(cockscomb)
Page 178

24b Mouth nearly vertical_____

CRYPTACANTHODIDAE
Wrymouths
Page 177

Section C: Pelvic Fins Abdominal; One Dorsal Fin

1a Fin on dorsal surface, adipose (no rays and flabby) _____

ANOTOPTERIDAE
Daggertooth
Pages 68–69

1b Dorsal fin with soft-rays___   2

2a Caudal and dorsal fins broadly rounded _____

CYPRINODONTIDAE
Killifishes
Pages 82–83

2b Caudal fin forked _____   3

3a Tail heterocercal (upper lobe extended); 5 (rarely 7) rows of bony shields on sides and back _____

ACIPENSERIDAE
Sturgeons
Pages 52–53

3b Caudal fin evenly forked or lower lobe elongated; no bony shields on body ___   4

4a Dorsal fin attached posteriorly, much closer to tail than to head _____   9 (next page)

4b Dorsal fin about midbody; dorsal fin origin well in advance of anal fin origin___   5 (next page)

Section C: Pelvic Fins Abdominal; One Dorsal Fin (continued)

5a Lateral line present 8

5b Lateral line absent 6

6a Photophores present ....

6b Photophores absent 7

7a Jaws terminal, even, or lower jaw projecting slightly beyond upper jaw ....

7b Snout overhanging lower jaw ....

8a Mouth horizontal, not reaching to below eye; snout overhanging lower jaw ....

8b Mouth oblique, reaching to behind eye; jaws about equal, or lower jaw slightly projecting ....

9a *From 4a page 17: dorsal fin attached near tail* Photophores present; barbel under chin ....

9b Photophores absent 10

10a Dorsal and anal fins followed by 5 to 7 finlets ....

10b No finlets after dorsal fin.... 11

11a No scales on head; body black ....

11b Head with scales; body silvery 12

12a Tip of pectoral fins extend beyond base of pelvics............

12b Tip of pectoral fins not reaching pelvic base............ 13

13a Lower jaw greatly projecting beyond upper jaw............

13b Both jaws greatly elongated, forming a beaklike, strongly toothed structure............

Section D: Pelvic Fins Abdominal With Two Fins on Back; a Dorsal Fin With Rays, the Other Adipose

1a Photophores present on body or under head .... 9 (next page)

1b Photophores absent 2

2a Dorsal fin base longer than head length.............

ALEPISAURIDAE
Lancetfishes
Page 61

2b Dorsal fin base shorter than head length................. 3

3a A single stout spine at origin of dorsal fin; barbels under chin ....

ARIIDAE
Sea catfishes
Pages 72–73

3b Dorsal fin without a single stout spine at origin; no barbels under chin 4

OPISTHOPROCTIDAE
Spookfishes
(barreleye)
Page 68

4a Eyes bulbous, projecting upwards; nose pointed ....

4b Eyes not projecting upwards 5

5a Dorsal fin origin well in advance of pelvic origin...... 7

5b Dorsal fin origin about opposite or posterior to pelvic fin origin 6

6a Jaws extending to under or slightly beyond eye; jaw teeth few, small ....

OSMERIDAE
Smelts
(eulachon, whitebait)
Page 62

6b Jaws extending to well behind eye; jaw teeth large, caninelike ....

SYNODONTIDAE
Lizardfishes
Pages 68–69

7a Axillary process at base of pelvic fin ....

SALMONIDAE
Trouts
(salmon, steelhead)
Pages 58–60

7b No axillary process at base of pelvic fin 8

8a Branchiostegals 5; scales persistent; jaws not reaching to 2/3 the distance from snout to eye ....

ARGENTINIDAE
Argentines
Pages 64–65

8b Branchiostegals 2–4; scales easily rubbed off; jaws reaching to or nearly to the anterior edge of eye ....

BATHYLAGIDAE
Deepsea smelts
Pages 64–65

Section D: Pelvic Fins Abdominal With Two Fins on Back; a Dorsal Fin With Rays, the Other Adipose (continued)

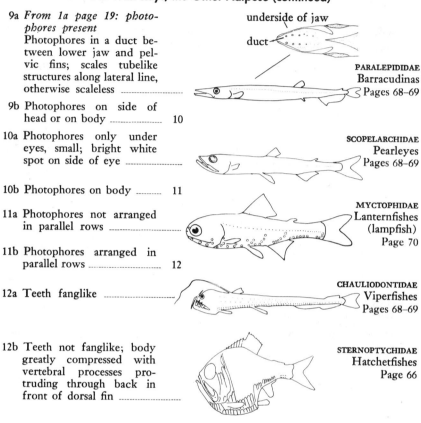

9a *From 1a page 19: photophores present*
Photophores in a duct between lower jaw and pelvic fins; scales tubelike structures along lateral line, otherwise scaleless ....

underside of jaw

duct

PARALEPIDIDAE
Barracudinas
Pages 68–69

9b Photophores on side of head or on body 10

10a Photophores only under eyes, small; bright white spot on side of eye ....

SCOPELARCHIDAE
Pearleyes
Pages 68–69

10b Photophores on body 11

11a Photophores not arranged in parallel rows ....

MYCTOPHIDAE
Lanternfishes
(lampfish)
Page 70

11b Photophores arranged in parallel rows 12

12a Teeth fanglike ....

CHAULIODONTIDAE
Viperfishes
Pages 68–69

12b Teeth not fanglike; body greatly compressed with vertebral processes protruding through back in front of dorsal fin ....

STERNOPTYCHIDAE
Hatchetfishes
Page 66

Section E: Pelvic Fins Abdominal With Two Fins on Back; Both Fins With Rays

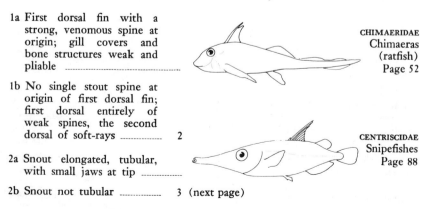

1a First dorsal fin with a strong, venomous spine at origin; gill covers and bone structures weak and pliable ....

CHIMAERIDAE
Chimaeras
(ratfish)
Page 52

1b No single stout spine at origin of first dorsal fin; first dorsal entirely of weak spines, the second dorsal of soft-rays 2

2a Snout elongated, tubular, with small jaws at tip ....

CENTRISCIDAE
Snipefishes
Page 88

2b Snout not tubular .... 3 (next page)

Section E: Pelvic Fins Abdominal With Two Fins on Back; Both Fins With Rays (continued)

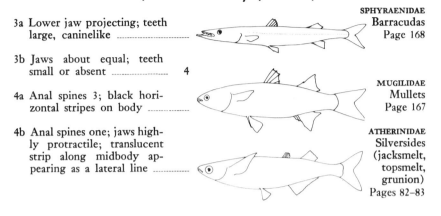

3a Lower jaw projecting; teeth large, caninelike ....

SPHYRAENIDAE
Barracudas
Page 168

3b Jaws about equal; teeth small or absent 4

4a Anal spines 3; black horizontal stripes on body ....

MUGILIDAE
Mullets
Page 167

4b Anal spines one; jaws highly protractile; translucent strip along midbody appearing as a lateral line ....

ATHERINIDAE
Silversides
(jacksmelt,
topsmelt,
grunion)
Pages 82–83

Section F: Pelvic Fins Thoracic, Strongly Modified Into a Cone or Sucking Disc on Belly

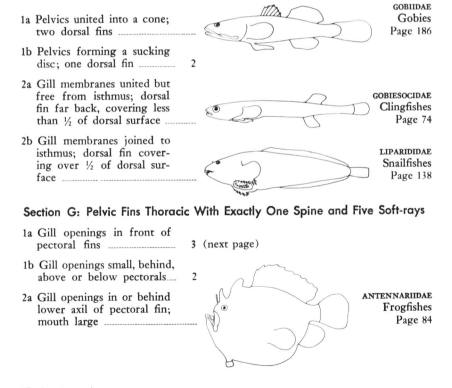

1a Pelvics united into a cone; two dorsal fins ....

GOBIIDAE
Gobies
Page 186

1b Pelvics forming a sucking disc; one dorsal fin 2

2a Gill membranes united but free from isthmus; dorsal fin far back, covering less than ½ of dorsal surface ....

GOBIESOCIDAE
Clingfishes
Page 74

2b Gill membranes joined to isthmus; dorsal fin covering over ½ of dorsal surface ....

LIPARIDIDAE
Snailfishes
Page 138

Section G: Pelvic Fins Thoracic With Exactly One Spine and Five Soft-rays

1a Gill openings in front of pectoral fins .... 3 (next page)

1b Gill openings small, behind, above or below pectorals.... 2

2a Gill openings in or behind lower axil of pectoral fin; mouth large ....

ANTENNARIIDAE
Frogfishes
Page 84

2b (next page)

Section G: Pelvic Fins Thoracic With Exactly One
Spine and Five Soft-rays (continued)

2b Gill openings in or behind upper axil of pectoral; mouth small; body strongly depressed ....

OGCOCEPHALIDAE
Batfishes
Page 84

3a *From 1a page 21 (Sect. G).* First dorsal fin modified into a sucking disc on top of head ....

3b First dorsal not a disc 4

ECHENEIDIDAE
Remoras
(suckerfish, whalesucker)
Pages 144–145

4a Body compressed, ovate, with bony shields along base of dorsal and anal fins ......

4b Body elongate, without bony shields along base of dorsal and anal fins 5

ZEIDAE
Dories
Pages 84–85

5a Dorsal fin followed by one finlet or none 7

5b Dorsal fin followed by 2 or more finlets 6

6a Keels present on caudal peduncle; all except the ESCOLAR have elevated anterior dorsal spines and hypural covered with rays......

SCOMBRIDAE
Mackerels
(tuna, skipjack, bonito, escolar, sierra)
Page 191

6b No keels on caudal peduncle; anterior dorsal spines not elevated and hypural not covered by caudal rays......

GEMPYLIDAE
Snake mackerels
(oilfish)
Page 190

7a Dorsal fin with spines and soft-rays, or wholly of spines .... 10 (next page)

7b Dorsal wholly of soft-rays.. 8

8a Strong spine at upper limit of gill cover; eyes on top of head; mouth vertical ....

URANOSCOPIDAE
Stargazers
Pages 170–171

8b No strong spine on gill cover; eyes normal 9

9a Tail rounded; lateral line straight ....

9b (next page)

BATHYMASTERIDAE
Ronquils
Pages 170–171

Section G: Pelvic Fins Thoracic With Exactly One
Spine and Five Soft-rays (continued)

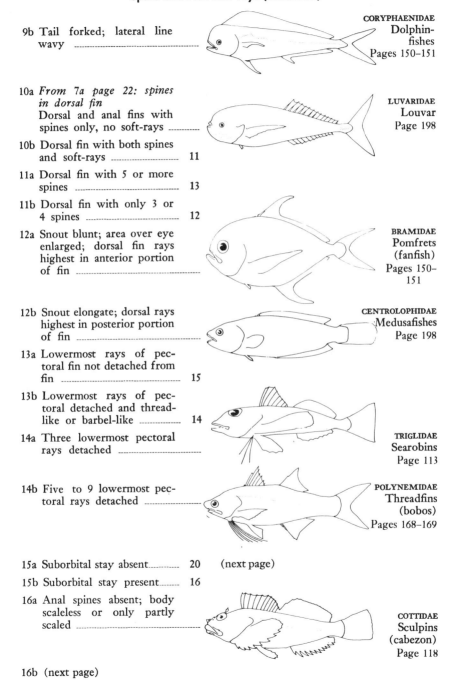

9b Tail forked; lateral line
   wavy ----------------------------------

CORYPHAENIDAE
Dolphin-
fishes
Pages 150–151

10a *From 7a page 22: spines
   in dorsal fin*
   Dorsal and anal fins with
   spines only, no soft-rays ----------

LUVARIDAE
Louvar
Page 198

10b Dorsal fin with both spines
   and soft-rays ---------------------- 11

11a Dorsal fin with 5 or more
   spines ------------------------------ 13

11b Dorsal fin with only 3 or
   4 spines --------------------------- 12

12a Snout blunt; area over eye
   enlarged; dorsal fin rays
   highest in anterior portion
   of fin -----------------------------

BRAMIDAE
Pomfrets
(fanfish)
Pages 150–
151

12b Snout elongate; dorsal rays
   highest in posterior portion
   of fin -----------------------------

CENTROLOPHIDAE
Medusafishes
Page 198

13a Lowermost rays of pectoral fin not detached from
   fin --------------------------------- 15

13b Lowermost rays of pectoral detached and threadlike or barbel-like ------------- 14

14a Three lowermost pectoral
   rays detached ----------------------

TRIGLIDAE
Searobins
Page 113

14b Five to 9 lowermost pectoral rays detached -----------------

POLYNEMIDAE
Threadfins
(bobos)
Pages 168–169

15a Suborbital stay absent............ 20   (next page)

15b Suborbital stay present........ 16

16a Anal spines absent; body
   scaleless or only partly
   scaled -----------------------------

COTTIDAE
Sculpins
(cabezon)
Page 118

16b (next page)

Section G: Pelvic Fins Thoracic With Exactly One
Spine and Five Soft-rays (continued)

16b Three anal spines; body
completely scaled 17

17a Preopercle with 5 spines;
4–11 anal soft-rays ....

17b Preopercle without spines;
11 or more anal soft-rays...... 18

SCORPAENIDAE
Scorpionfishes
(rockfishes,
thornyheads)
Page 90

18a Dorsal fins separated; two
well developed nostrils on
each side of head.................

18b Dorsal fin continuous (may
be deeply notched); only
anterior nostril well de-
veloped 19

ANOPLOPOMATIDAE
Sablefishes
(skilfish)
Page 113

19a First 3 or 4 dorsal fin spines
greatly elongated ....

ZANIOLEPIDIDAE
Combfishes
Page 114

19b Anterior dorsal fin spines
not elongated as in 19a...............

HEXAGRAMMIDAE
Greenlings
(lingcod)
Page 114

20a *From 15a, page 23: suborbital stay absent* Anal fin
without spines; lips pecu-
liarly fringed ....

20b Anal fin with spines; lips
not fringed as above.............. 21

TRICHODONTIDAE
Sandfishes
Page 170

21a Throat with 2 long barbels
placed just behind chin ....

21b Chin without barbels 22

MULLIDAE
Goatfishes
Pages 152–153

22a Three or 4 anal spines ...... 30a page 26 (Rarely a mojarra will have two anal
spines, see 40a page 28)

22b One or 2 anal spines .... 23 (In some families these anal spines are very
weak and may be mistaken for soft-rays)

23a One or 2 anal spines isolated from soft-rayed por-
tion; tail crescent shaped.... 31a page 26 (All carangids have three anal spines
except some very old in which one or two
spines may disappear)

23b All anal spines connected
to soft-rayed portion by
membranes .... 24 (next page)

Section G: Pelvic Fins Thoracic With Exactly One
Spine and Five Soft-rays (continued)

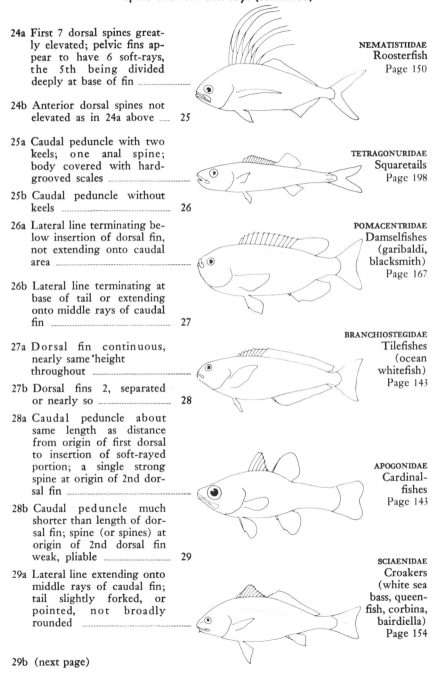

24a First 7 dorsal spines greatly elevated; pelvic fins appear to have 6 soft-rays,
  the 5th being divided
  deeply at base of fin ....

NEMATISTIIDAE
Roosterfish
Page 150

24b Anterior dorsal spines not
  elevated as in 24a above 25

25a Caudal peduncle with two
  keels; one anal spine;
  body covered with hard-
  grooved scales ....

TETRAGONURIDAE
Squaretails
Page 198

25b Caudal peduncle without
  keels 26

26a Lateral line terminating below insertion of dorsal fin,
  not extending onto caudal
  area ....

POMACENTRIDAE
Damselfishes
(garibaldi,
blacksmith)
Page 167

26b Lateral line terminating at
  base of tail or extending
  onto middle rays of caudal
  fin 27

27a Dorsal fin continuous,
  nearly same 'height
  throughout ....

BRANCHIOSTEGIDAE
Tilefishes
(ocean
whitefish)
Page 143

27b Dorsal fins 2, separated
  or nearly so 28

28a Caudal peduncle about
  same length as distance
  from origin of first dorsal
  to insertion of soft-rayed
  portion; a single strong
  spine at origin of 2nd dor-
  sal fin ....

APOGONIDAE
Cardinal-
fishes
Page 143

28b Caudal peduncle much
  shorter than length of dorsal fin; spine (or spines) at
  origin of 2nd dorsal fin
  weak, pliable 29

29a Lateral line extending onto
  middle rays of caudal fin;
  tail slightly forked, or
  pointed, not broadly
  rounded ....

SCIAENIDAE
Croakers
(white sea
bass, queen-
fish, corbina,
bairdiella)
Page 154

29b (next page)

Section G: Pelvic Fins Thoracic With Exactly One
Spine and Five Soft-rays (continued)

29b Lateral line not extending
onto middle rays of caudal
fin; tail broadly rounded ....

ELEOTRIDAE
Sleepers
Pages 184–185

30a *From 22a page 24: 3 or 4
anal spines*
Anal spines 4 (rarely a
surfperch may have 4 anal
spines, see 34a below) ....

PENTACEROTIDAE
Armorheads
Pages 158–159

30b Anal spines three 31

31a *From 30b and 23a*
Two anal spines isolated
from fin, retractable; tail
crescent shaped, with length
of lobes more than 4 times
the depth of the caudal
peduncle ....

CARANGIDAE
Jacks
(scad, pilot-
fish, pompano,
yellowtail,
jack mackerel,
moonfish,
leatherjacket)
Page 146

31b Anal spines connected to
soft-rayed portion; length
of caudal lobes less than
3 times depth of caudal
peduncle 32

CHAETODONTIDAE
Butterfly-
fishes
Pages 158–
159

32a Snout pointed, with small
jaws at tip; teeth very
fine, brushlike ....

32b Snout not pointed as in
32a above 33

33a No sheath of scales ex-
tending out onto dorsal rays 35 (next page)

33b Sheath of scales extending
out onto dorsal fin above
a deep furrow 34

34a Anal soft-rays more than
10; maxillary fully exposed
when mouth is closed ....

EMBIOTOCIDAE
Surfperches
Page 160

34b (next page)

Section G: Pelvic Fins Thoracic With Exactly One
Spine and Five Soft-rays (continued)

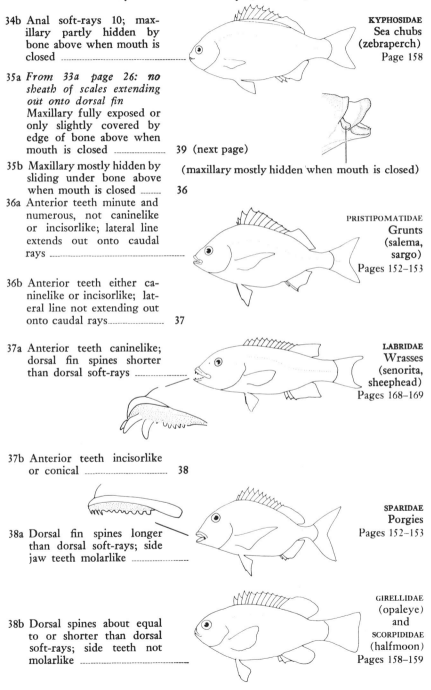

34b Anal soft-rays 10; maxillary partly hidden by bone above when mouth is closed ....

KYPHOSIDAE
Sea chubs
(zebraperch)
Page 158

35a *From 33a page 26: no sheath of scales extending out onto dorsal fin* Maxillary fully exposed or only slightly covered by edge of bone above when mouth is closed ....   39 (next page)

35b Maxillary mostly hidden by sliding under bone above when mouth is closed   36

(maxillary mostly hidden when mouth is closed)

36a Anterior teeth minute and numerous, not caninelike or incisorlike; lateral line extends out onto caudal rays ....

PRISTIPOMATIDAE
Grunts
(salema,
sargo)
Pages 152–153

36b Anterior teeth either caninelike or incisorlike; lateral line not extending out onto caudal rays.............   37

37a Anterior teeth caninelike; dorsal fin spines shorter than dorsal soft-rays ....

LABRIDAE
Wrasses
(senorita,
sheephead)
Pages 168–169

37b Anterior teeth incisorlike or conical   38

38a Dorsal fin spines longer than dorsal soft-rays; side jaw teeth molarlike ....

SPARIDAE
Porgies
Pages 152–153

38b Dorsal spines about equal to or shorter than dorsal soft-rays; side teeth not molarlike ....

GIRELLIDAE
(opaleye)
and
SCORPIDIDAE
(halfmoon)
Pages 158–159

Section G: Pelvic Fins Thoracic With Exactly One
Spine and Five Soft-rays (continued)

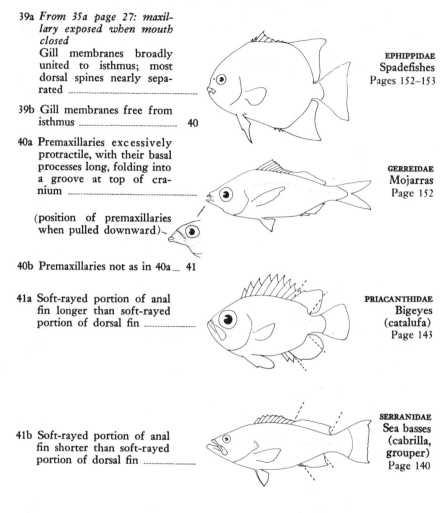

39a *From 35a page 27: maxillary exposed when mouth closed*
Gill membranes broadly united to isthmus; most dorsal spines nearly separated _____

EPHIPPIDAE
Spadefishes
Pages 152–153

39b Gill membranes free from isthmus _____ 40

40a Premaxillaries excessively protractile, with their basal processes long, folding into a groove at top of cranium _____

GERREIDAE
Mojarras
Page 152

(position of premaxillaries when pulled downward)

40b Premaxillaries not as in 40a __ 41

41a Soft-rayed portion of anal fin longer than soft-rayed portion of dorsal fin _____

PRIACANTHIDAE
Bigeyes
(catalufa)
Page 143

41b Soft-rayed portion of anal fin shorter than soft-rayed portion of dorsal fin _____

SERRANIDAE
Sea basses
(cabrilla, grouper)
Page 140

Section H: Pelvic Fins Thoracic With Less Than Five Soft-rays; the Rays Either
Normal or Modified Into Barbel-like or Clublike Structures

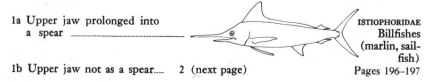

1a Upper jaw prolonged into a spear _____

ISTIOPHORIDAE
Billfishes
(marlin, sailfish)
Pages 196–197

1b Upper jaw not as a spear __ 2 (next page)

Section H: Pelvic Fins Thoracic With Less Than Five Soft-rays (continued)

2a Pelvic fins as long filaments; anterior dorsal fin
rays greatly elevated _____

REGALECIDAE
Oarfishes
Page 86

2b Pelvic fins not as long filaments _____ 3

3a Photophores present on
sides and belly _____

BATRACHOIDIDAE
Toadfishes
(midshipman)
Page 72

3b No photophores on body__ 4

4a Body encased in bony plates __

AGONIDAE
Poachers
Page 134

4b Body not encased in bony
plates _____ 5

5a Dorsal fin preceded by isolated spines _____

GASTEROSTEIDAE
Sticklebacks
(tubesnout)
Page 88

5b No isolated spines in dorsal fin _____ 6

6a Dorsal fin wholly of soft-
rays _____ 12 (next page)

6b Dorsal fin entirely of
spines or of spines and
soft-rays _____ 7

7a Dorsal fin with both soft-
rays and spines _____ 10 (next page)

7b Dorsal fin wholly of spines 8

8a Body not eel-like; anterior
dorsal spines elevated _____

CLINIDAE
Clinids
(reef fin-
spot)
Page 173

8b Body eel-like; dorsal fin
spines about same height__ 9

9a Distance from snout to
anal origin less than distance from anal origin to
base of caudal fin _____

STICHAEIDAE
Pricklebacks
(warbonnet,
whitebarred
blenny)
Page 178

9b Distance from snout to
anal origin greater than
distance from anal origin
to base of caudal fin _____

PHOLIDIDAE
Gunnels
Page 182

Section H: Pelvic Fins Thoracic With Less Than Five Soft-rays (continued)

10a *From 7a page 29: dorsal fin with both soft-rays and spines*
Body partly or wholly without scales; no anal spines ....

COTTIDAE
Sculpins
(Irish lord)
Page 118

10b Body scaled; anal fin with spines **11**

11a Gill membranes free from isthmus; more spines than soft-rays in dorsal fin except for *Chaenopsis* ....

CLINIDAE
Clinids
(kelpfish, fringeheads, pikeblenny)
Page 173

11b Gill membranes attached to isthmus; more soft-rays than spines in dorsal fin ....

BLENNIIDAE
Combtooth
blennies
Page 172

12a *From 6a page 29: dorsal fin wholly of soft-rays*
Gill membranes joined to isthmus; pelvic fins club-like ....

ZOARCIDAE
Eelpouts
Page 78

12b Gill membranes free from isthmus (or slightly joined to isthmus in BROTULI-DAE) **13**

13a Body oblong; dorsal rays less than 60 ....

ICOSTEIDAE
Ragfish
Pages 184–185

13b Body elongate; dorsal rays more than 60 .... **14**

(anterior rays are spines but appear as soft-rays)

14a Pelvic fin soft-rays not barbel-like, appearing as a small scale or spine; tail forked ....

TRICHIURIDAE
Cutlassfishes
Page 190

14b Pelvic fin rays as barbel-like structures; caudal fin rounded (if present) **15**

15a Pelvic fins attached under shoulder girdle; the two pelvic soft-rays completely joined by a membrane ....

BROTULIDAE
Brotulas
Pages 72–73

15b Pelvic fins attached under eyes or on chin; the two pelvic soft-rays joined only at base of fin ....

OPHIDIIDAE
Cusk-eels
Pages 72–73

Section I: Pelvic Fins Thoracic With More Than Five Soft-rays

1a Body elongate, much longer than deep 3

1b Body ovate, compressed 2

2a No spines in fins; tail strongly forked ....

LAMPRIDIDAE
Opah
Pages 84–85

2b Strong spines in dorsal and anal fins; tail rounded ....

OREOSOMATIDAE
Oreos
Pages 84–85

3a Anal fin absent ....

TRACHIPTERIDAE
Ribbonfishes
(king-of-the-salmon)
Page 87

3b Anal fin present 4

4a No spines in anal fin 6

4b One or 2 spines in anal fin 5

5a One dorsal fin ....

MELAMPHAIDAE
Bigscales
Page 86

5b Two dorsal fins (See family NEMATISTIIDAE, 24a page 25)

6a Tail pointed, no caudal fin; barbel present under chin ....

MACROURIDAE
Grenadiers
(rattails)
Page 76

6b Caudal fin present 7

7a Two anal fins; 3 dorsal fins........

GADIDAE
Codfishes
Pages 76–77

7b One anal fin (may be deeply notched); 2 dorsal fins 8

8a Barbel on lower jaw; pelvics filamentous ....

MORIDAE
Codlings
Pages 76–77

8b No barbels under chin; pelvics normal ....

MERLUCCIIDAE
Hakes
Pages 76–77

SPECIES PRESENTATION

HAGFISHES, Family Myxinidae*, and LAMPREYS, Family Petromyzonidae
(Principal sources: Vladykov & Follett, 1958; Clemens & Wilby, 1961; Hubbs, 1967)

BLACK HAGFISH, *Eptatretus deani.* Family MYXINIDAE
Cedros Isl., Baja California (SIO 62–91), to S.E. Alaska, including Guadalupe Isl.
Length to 20 in. Depth 1560 to 3500 ft. Uniform purplish-black. Common in
deep waters.

PACIFIC HAGFISH, *Eptatretus stoutii.* Family MYXINIDAE
Pt. San Pablo, Baja California (SIO 71–164), to S.E. Alaska. Length to 25 in.
Depth 30 to 2400 ft. Light brown to gray, never black; white on rim of pores.
Common.

WHITEFACE HAGFISH, *Myxine circifrons.* Family MYXINIDAE (not illustrated)
In eastern Pacific from near Galapagos Isls. to southern California. Length to
18.5 in. On bottom in deep waters. Body uniform black, head lighter near
mouth. Uncommon. Is separated from other hagfishes by having only one gill
opening on each side.

PACIFIC LAMPREY, *Lampetra tridentata.* Family PETROMYZONIDAE
Pt. Canoas, Baja California, to Bering Sea and Japan. Length to 27 in. Anadromous. Color slate-gray. Common.

WESTERN RIVER LAMPREY, *Lampetra ayresii.* Family PETROMYZONIDAE
San Francisco to Taku River and Lynn Canal, Alaska. Length to 12 in. Anadromous. Dark blue above, silvery below. Uncommon.

head to 1st gill opening 5.4 to 6.6 into total length

BLACK HAGFISH

PACIFIC HAGFISH

head to 1st gill opening 3.6 to 4.5 into total length

mouth with 4   **PACIFIC LAMPREY**
lateral cusps

mouth with 3   **WESTERN RIVER LAMPREY**
lateral cusps

KEY TO THE FAMILIES OF SHARKS
(Principal sources: Bigelow & Schroeder, 1948; Kato, Springer, and Wagner, 1967)

1a Eyes on top of head; body
   skatelike ....

1b Eyes on sides of head 2

2a Gill slits 5 4

2b Gill slits 6 or 7 3

SQUATINIDAE
Angel sharks
Pages 34–35

3a First gill slits continuous (joined
   under throat); snout projecting
   slightly beyond tip of lower jaw.......

CHLAMYDOSELACHIDAE
Frilled shark
Page 34

3b (next page)   * See comments on page 211.

one dorsal fin

3b First gill slits not continuous; tip of lower jaw under eye............

4a *From 2a: gill openings 5* Anal fin absent............

4b Anal fin present............ 5

5a Spine present at origin of each dorsal fin ....

5b No spine at origin of dorsal fins 6

6a Mouth terminal; large white spots on body and fins ....

6b Mouth not terminal, nose projecting well ahead of mouth...... 7

7a Caudal fin greatly elongated, about as long as body............

7b Caudal fin shorter than body...... 8

8a Head flattened; eyes attached to sides of hammer-shaped lobes............

8b Head not flattened laterally........ 9

9a Origin of 1st dorsal fin over or behind origin of pelvic fins............

9b Origin of 1st dorsal fin well ahead of origin of pelvic fins........ 10

10a Length of lower lobe of caudal fin more than ½ length of upper caudal lobe............

10b Length of lower lobe of caudal fin less than ½ length of upper caudal lobe............ 11

11a Gill slits long, extending from well above midbody to middle of throat; teeth small, about 200 in front series of upper jaw............

11b Gill slits not extending onto underside of body; teeth 25–35 in front series of upper jaw............ 12

12a Origin of pectoral fins posterior to 5th gill slit............

12b Origin of pectoral fins under 4th or 5th gill slit............

COW, FRILLED, BULLHEAD, DOGFISH, and ANGEL SHARKS

SEVENGILL SHARK, *Notorynchus maculatus*. Family HEXANCHIDAE
Chile to northern British Columbia, but not in tropics. Length to 8.5 ft. Gray
with dark spotting on back and fins. Common in bays.

FRILLED SHARK, *Chlamydoselachus anguineus*. Family CHLAMYDOSELACHIDAE
Eastern Pacific north to Pt. Arguello. Length to 6.5 ft. Surface to 1650 ft. Rare.

SIXGILL SHARK, *Hexanchus griseus*. Family HEXANCHIDAE
Chile, and from Todos Santos Bay, Baja California, to northern British Columbia,
but not in tropics. Recorded to 11 ft. (reported to 15 ft.), and wt. to 464 lbs.
Shallow bays to 960 ft. Common.

HORN SHARK, *Heterodontus francisci*. Family HETERODONTIDAE
Gulf of California (not at Cape San Lucas) to Monterey Bay, including Guadalupe Isl. Length to 4 ft. Shallow waters to 492 ft. Gray with dark spotting on
body. Common off Southern California.

SPINY DOGFISH, *Squalus acanthias*. Family SQUALIDAE
Temperate and subtropical Atlantic and Pacific; in eastern Pacific in Chile, and
from central Baja California to Alaska and to Japan. Length to 5.2 ft. Shallow
waters to 1200 ft. Dark gray; often with white spotting on sides. Common.

PACIFIC SLEEPER SHARK, *Somniosus pacificus*. Family SQUALIDAE
Southern California to Bering Sea and Japan. Length to 13 ft. Deepwater species,
a California specimen was taken at 750 ft. Light gray above. Uncommon.

PYGMY SHARK, *Euprotomicrus bispinatus*. Family SQUALIDAE
In all warmer seas, north to southern California on our coast. Length to 12 in.
Midwater oceanic species. Uniform brown or black. Rare.

PRICKLY SHARK, *Echinorhinus cookei*. Family SQUALIDAE
Peru to off Moss Landing*. Length to 13.1 ft. Depth 60 to at least 420 ft.
Uncommon.

PACIFIC ANGEL SHARK, *Squatina californica*. Family SQUATINIDAE
Chile, and from Gulf of California to S.E. Alaska. Length to 5 ft., and wt. to 60 lbs.
Shallow waters. Gray to dusky above with dark spotting, white below. Common.

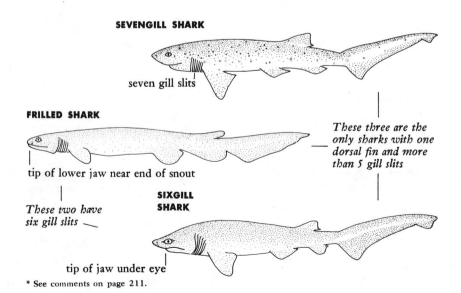

SEVENGILL SHARK

seven gill slits

FRILLED SHARK

*These three are the
only sharks with one
dorsal fin and more
than 5 gill slits*

tip of lower jaw near end of snout

*These two have
six gill slits* —

SIXGILL
SHARK

tip of jaw under eye

* See comments on page 211.

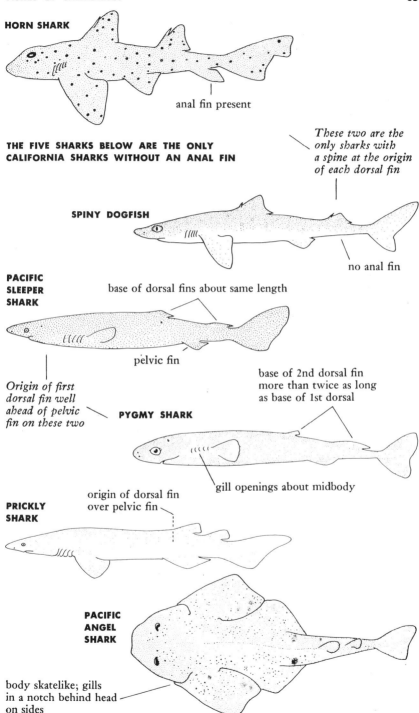

HORN SHARK

anal fin present

**THE FIVE SHARKS BELOW ARE THE ONLY
CALIFORNIA SHARKS WITHOUT AN ANAL FIN**

*These two are the
only sharks with
a spine at the origin
of each dorsal fin*

SPINY DOGFISH

no anal fin

**PACIFIC
SLEEPER
SHARK**

base of dorsal fins about same length

pelvic fin

*Origin of first
dorsal fin well
ahead of pelvic
fin on these two*

base of 2nd dorsal fin
more than twice as long
as base of 1st dorsal

PYGMY SHARK

gill openings about midbody

**PRICKLY
SHARK**

origin of dorsal fin
over pelvic fin

**PACIFIC
ANGEL
SHARK**

body skatelike; gills
in a notch behind head
on sides

THRESHER, HAMMERHEAD, BASKING, WHALE, and CAT SHARKS

COMMON THRESHER, *Alopias vulpinus.* Family ALOPIIDAE
Worldwide in warmer seas, from central Baja California to Strait of Juan de Fuca on our coast. Length to 18 ft., and possibly to 25 ft. Epipelagic. Common.

BIGEYE THRESHER, *Alopias superciliosus.* Family ALOPIIDAE
Worldwide in warm seas; in eastern Pacific north to San Clemente. Length to 18 ft. Depth 510 to 600 ft. Gray above, white below. Rare.

SMOOTH HAMMERHEAD, *Sphyrna zygaena.* Family SPHYRNIDAE
Chile to central California. Length to 11 ft. Epipelagic. Uncommon.

BONNETHEAD, *Sphyrna tiburo.* Family SPHYRNIDAE
Peru to southern California. Length to 4.5 ft. Epipelagic. Uncommon.

SCALLOPED HAMMERHEAD, *Sphyrna lewini.* Family SPHYRNIDAE
Worldwide in tropical seas; in eastern Pacific from Ecuador to southern Baja California (not recorded from California). Length to 12 ft.

BASKING SHARK, *Cetorhinus maximus.* Family CETORHINIDAE
Worldwide in temperate seas; on our coast from Gulf of California to Alaska. Length to 45 ft., but rarely over 32 ft. Epipelagic. Lead-gray above, pale below. Common.

WHALE SHARK, *Rhincodon typus.* Family RHINCODONTIDAE
Worldwide in warm seas; north to Torrey Pines * on our coast. Length to 45 ft., and possibly to 60 ft. Black above, with white spots. One California sighting.

BROWN CAT SHARK, *Apristurus brunneus.* Family SCYLIORHINIDAE
Northern Baja California to British Columbia. Length to 26.75 in. Depth 450 to 1560 ft. Uniform brown; black fin margins. Uncommon.

LONGNOSE CAT SHARK, *Apristurus kampae.* Family SCYLIORHINIDAE
Galapagos Isls. to off San Diego. Length to 18.9 in. Deep water. Uniform gray-black. Rare.

SWELL SHARK, *Cephaloscyllium ventriosum.* Family SCYLIORHINIDAE
Chile to Monterey Bay, including Gulf of California and Guadalupe Isl. Length to 3.3 ft. Shallow waters to 1380 ft. Brownish, with dark spotting. Common.

FILETAIL CAT SHARK, *Parmaturus xaniurus.* Family SCYLIORHINIDAE
Gulf of California to Monterey. Length to 2 ft. Depth 1200 to 1980 ft. Brownish to black. Fairly common in trawl catch.

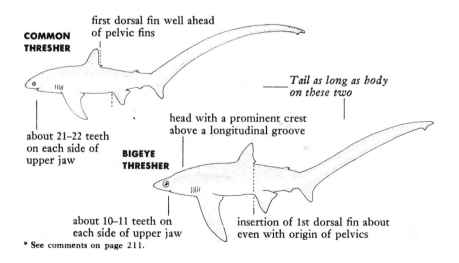

COMMON THRESHER — first dorsal fin well ahead of pelvic fins

Tail as long as body on these two

about 21–22 teeth on each side of upper jaw

head with a prominent crest above a longitudinal groove

BIGEYE THRESHER

about 10–11 teeth on each side of upper jaw

insertion of 1st dorsal fin about even with origin of pelvics

* See comments on page 211.

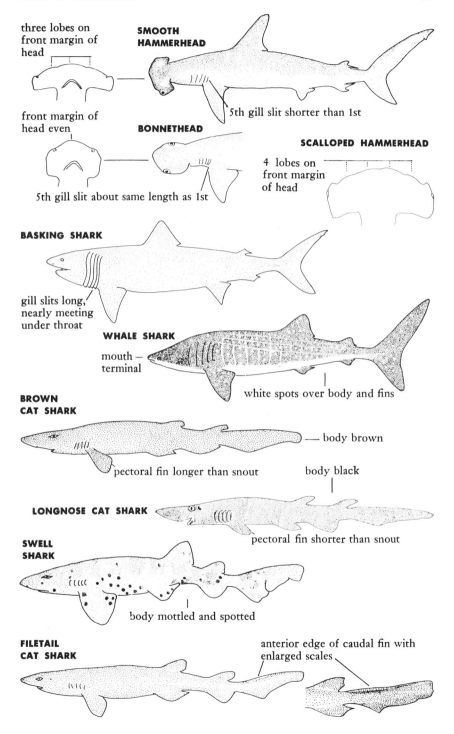

three lobes on front margin of head

SMOOTH HAMMERHEAD

5th gill slit shorter than 1st

front margin of head even

BONNETHEAD

5th gill slit about same length as 1st

SCALLOPED HAMMERHEAD

4 lobes on front margin of head

BASKING SHARK

gill slits long, nearly meeting under throat

WHALE SHARK

mouth — terminal

white spots over body and fins

BROWN CAT SHARK

— body brown

pectoral fin longer than snout

body black

LONGNOSE CAT SHARK

pectoral fin shorter than snout

SWELL SHARK

body mottled and spotted

FILETAIL CAT SHARK

anterior edge of caudal fin with enlarged scales

MACKEREL, SAND, and REQUIEM SHARKS *

WHITE SHARK, Carcharodon carcharias. Family LAMNIDAE
Worldwide in warm seas; in eastern Pacific from Chile to Alaska. Recorded
length to 20 ft., reported to 36 ft. Inshore areas. Slate-gray above, white below.
Uncommon.

BONITO SHARK, Isurus oxyrinchus. Family LAMNIDAE
Worldwide in warm and temperate seas; in eastern Pacific from Chile to
Columbia River, including Gulf of California, but not in tropics. Length to 13
ft., and wt. to 1000 lbs. Epipelagic. Dark gray above, white below. Uncommon.

SALMON SHARK, Lamna ditropis. Family LAMNIDAE
Pt. Dume to Alaska. Length to 10 ft. Epipelagic. Dark gray above, white below.
Uncommon, often taken by salmon gill netters in Pacific Northwest.

RAGGED-TOOTH SHARK, Odontaspis ferox. Family ODONTASPIDIDAE
Two records from southern California and a set of jaws from La Paz, Baja
California. Length to 5.5 ft. Epipelagic. Dark gray above, white below. Rare.

LEOPARD SHARK, Triakis semifasciata. Family CARCHARHINIDAE
Mazatlan, Mexico, to Oregon, including Gulf of California. Length to 6.5 ft.
In bays and along beaches. Dark gray body with black crossbars and spots.
Common.

GRAY SMOOTHHOUND, Mustelus californicus. Family CARCHARHINIDAE
Mazatlan, Mexico, to Cape Mendocino. Length to 64.25 in. Shallow waters to
150 ft. Brown to dark gray above, whitish below. Common.

BROWN SMOOTHHOUND, Mustelus henlei. Family CARCHARHINIDAE
Gulf of California to Humboldt Bay. Length to 3.1 ft. Shallow waters to 210 ft.
Red-brown or bronze above, silvery below. Common.

SICKLEFIN SMOOTHHOUND, Mustelus lunulatus. Family CARCHARHINIDAE
Central America to southern California, including Gulf of California. Recorded
length to 4.6 ft., reported to 5.7 ft. Shallow waters. Plain brown or gray. Rare.

*Lower lobe of caudal fin more than ½ length of upper lobe on the two sharks
below and the* SALMON SHARK *on page 39*

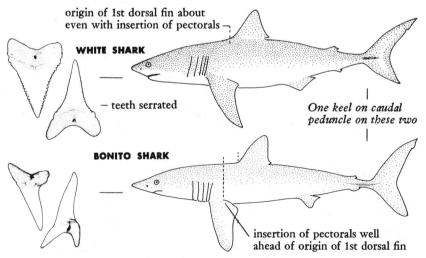

origin of 1st dorsal fin about
even with insertion of pectorals ¬

WHITE SHARK

— teeth serrated

One keel on caudal
peduncle on these two

BONITO SHARK

insertion of pectorals well
ahead of origin of 1st dorsal fin

* Teeth figures are of 2nd tooth from center, upper and lower jaws.

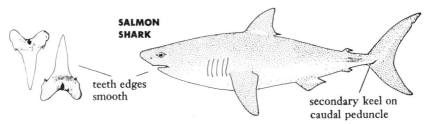

SALMON SHARK

teeth edges smooth

secondary keel on caudal peduncle

Lower lobe of caudal fin less than ½ the length of upper lobe of caudal fin on the sharks below and on pages 40 and 41

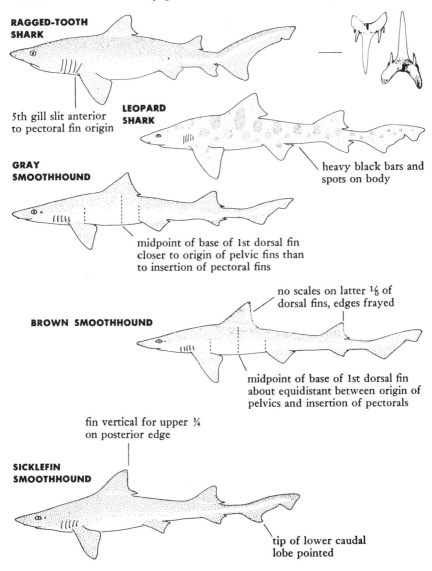

RAGGED-TOOTH SHARK

5th gill slit anterior to pectoral fin origin

LEOPARD SHARK

heavy black bars and spots on body

GRAY SMOOTHHOUND

midpoint of base of 1st dorsal fin closer to origin of pelvic fins than to insertion of pectoral fins

no scales on latter ⅕ of dorsal fins, edges frayed

BROWN SMOOTHHOUND

midpoint of base of 1st dorsal fin about equidistant between origin of pelvics and insertion of pectorals

fin vertical for upper ¾ on posterior edge

SICKLEFIN SMOOTHHOUND

tip of lower caudal lobe pointed

REQUIEM SHARKS, Family Carcharhinidae (continued)

TIGER SHARK, *Galeocerdo cuvier.* Worldwide in warm seas; in eastern Pacific from Peru to southern California. Length to 18 ft. (rare over 14 ft.). Inshore waters. Body gray with darker stripes and blotches. Rare.

SOUPFIN SHARK, *Galeorhinus zyopterus.* Chile and Peru, and from San Juanico Bay, Baja California, to northern British Columbia, but not in tropics. Length to 6.5 ft. Epipelagic. Dark gray above, white below; black on forward edges of dorsal and pectoral fins. Common.

PELAGIC WHITETIPPED SHARK, *Carcharhinus longimanus.* In all warm seas; in eastern Pacific from Revillagigedo Isls., Mexico, to near Cortez Bank,* California. Length to 11 ft. Epipelagic, usually offshore. Body gray, tip of 1st dorsal white. Rare.

BLUE SHARK, *Prionace glauca.* Worldwide in warm seas; in eastern Pacific from Chile to Gulf of Alaska, but not in tropics. Length to 13 ft. Dark blue above, white below. Epipelagic. Common.

PACIFIC SHARPNOSE SHARK, *Rhizoprionodon longurio.* Peru to Long Beach. Length to 3.6 ft. One California record.

DUSKY SHARK, *Carcharhinus obscurus.* Worldwide in tropical and subtropical waters; in eastern Pacific from Revillagigedo Isls., Mexico, to southern California, including Gulf of California. Length to 12 ft. Epipelagic. Rare.

BULL SHARK, *Carcharhinus leucas.* Worldwide in warmer seas; in eastern Pacific from northern Peru to southern California, including Lake Nicaragua (freshwater) and Gulf of California. Rare.

NARROWTOOTH SHARK, *Carcharhinus remotus.* Worldwide in warmer seas; in eastern Pacific from Peru to southern California, including Gulf of California. Length to 5.9 ft. Epipelagic. Rare.

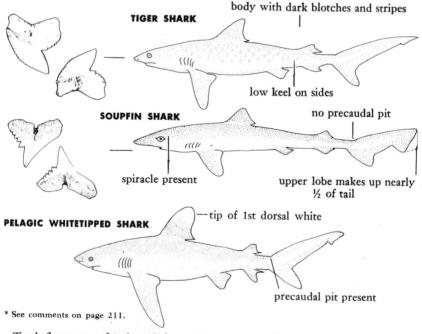

TIGER SHARK — body with dark blotches and stripes — low keel on sides

SOUPFIN SHARK — no precaudal pit — spiracle present — upper lobe makes up nearly ½ of tail

PELAGIC WHITETIPPED SHARK — tip of 1st dorsal white — precaudal pit present

* See comments on page 211.

Teeth figures are of 2nd tooth from center, upper and lower jaws.

All sharks on this page have a precaudal pit

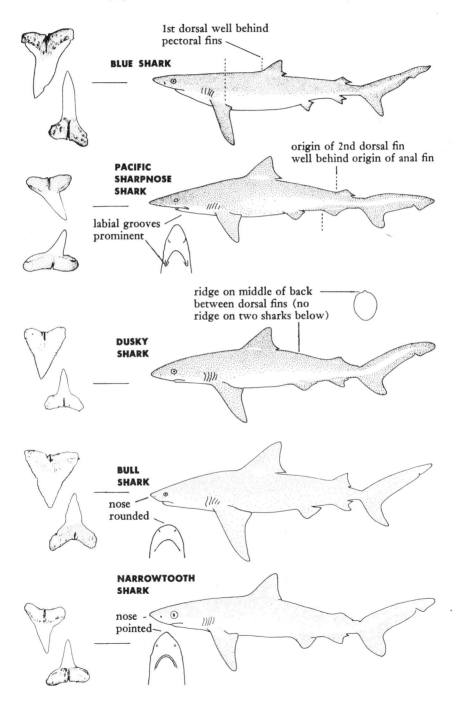

1st dorsal well behind
pectoral fins

BLUE SHARK

origin of 2nd dorsal fin
well behind origin of anal fin

**PACIFIC
SHARPNOSE
SHARK**

labial grooves
prominent

ridge on middle of back
between dorsal fins (no
ridge on two sharks below)

**DUSKY
SHARK**

**BULL
SHARK**

nose
rounded

**NARROWTOOTH
SHARK**

nose -
pointed

KEY TO THE FAMILIES OF RAYS AND SKATES

1a Dorsal fins absent .... **DASYATIDIDAE** Stingrays
1b Dorsal fins present 2   and
2a Two dorsal fins 4   **GYMNURIDAE**
top view of head   Butterfly rays
2b One dorsal fin 3   Pages 50–51
3a No lateral lobes on head ....

MYLIOBATIDIDAE Eagle rays
Pages 50–51

lateral lobe

MOBULIDAE Mantas
3b Lateral lobes present on head ....   (mobula)
Page 50

caudal flap   **RAJIDAE**
4a Caudal fin absent ....   Skates
Pages 44–49

RHINOBATIDAE
caudal fin   Guitarfishes
4b Caudal fin present 5   and
5a Spines or prickles on back and tail .... **PLATYRHINIDAE** Thornback
Pages 42–43

TORPEDINIDAE
5b Body smooth, no spines or prickles .... Electric ray
Pages 42–43

ELECTRIC RAY, THORNBACK, and GUITARFISHES
(Principal sources: Beebe & Tee-Van, 1941; Roedel & Ripley, 1950)

PACIFIC ELECTRIC RAY, Torpedo californica. Family TORPEDINIDAE
Sebastian Viscaino Bay, Baja California, to Queen Charlotte Isls., British Columbia. Length to 4 ft., and weight to 90 lbs. Shallow water to 640 ft. Blue-black to dark gray above; slate-gray below, often with black spotting. Common.

THORNBACK, Platyrhinoidis triseriata. Family PLATYRHINIDAE
1.5 mi. SSE of Thurloe Head, Baja California (LACM 32067), to San Francisco. Length recorded to 2.5 ft., reported to 3 ft. Shallow to 150 ft. Brown on back, white or cream colored below. Common off southern and Baja California.

SHOVELNOSE GUITARFISH, Rhinobatos productus. Family RHINOBATIDAE
Gulf of California to San Francisco (recent records north only to Capitola). Length to 61.5 in., and weight to 40 lbs. Depth, surface to 50 ft. Brownish-gray above, lighter below. Common off southern and Baja California.

BANDED GUITARFISH, Zapteryx exasperata. Family RHINOBATIDAE
Panama to Newport Beach. Length to 3 ft. Taken in shallow bays and to about 70 ft. along coast. Brown on back, lighter below; with blackish transverse bands. Rare.

PACIFIC ELECTRIC RAY

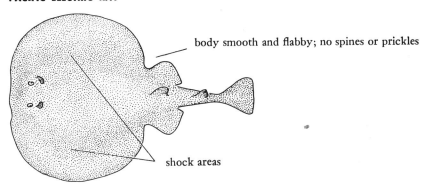

body smooth and flabby; no spines or prickles

shock areas

THORNBACK

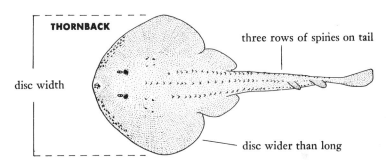

three rows of spines on tail

disc width

disc wider than long

SHOVELNOSE GUITARFISH

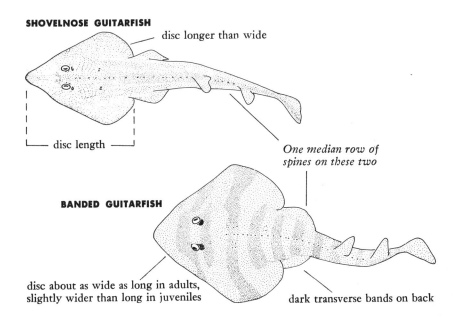

disc longer than wide

disc length

One median row of spines on these two

BANDED GUITARFISH

disc about as wide as long in adults,
slightly wider than long in juveniles

dark transverse bands on back

SKATES, Family Rajidae *[1]

by Dan Miller and Richard Nitsos

(Principal sources: Beebe & Tee-Van, 1941; Roedel &
Ripley, 1950; Carl L. Hubbs *[2])

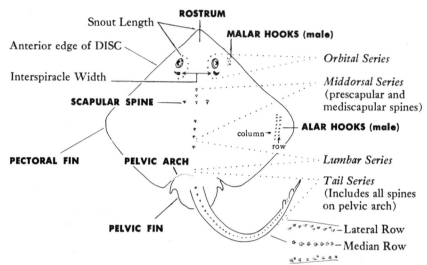

FIGURE 11.   Terminology of dorsal spines and structures of California skates.

SANDPAPER SKATE, *Raja kincaidii*.   Cortez Bank (UCLA W 54-392) to Unalaska
Isl., Alaska. Length to 2 ft. 9 in. Moderate depths, from 180 to 4500 ft. Uniform
dark brown above, white below. Uncommon.

BLACK SKATE, *Raja trachura*.   North of Guadalupe Isl.*[3] to Bering Sea. Length to
32.2 in. Deep water, from 2400 to 4428 ft. Black or slate-gray on both surfaces.
Uncommon.

BIG SKATE, *Raja binoculata*.   San Quintin Bay, Baja California (UCLA W 59-111),
to Bering Sea. Length to 8 ft., but rarely over 6 ft. Depth 10 to 360 ft. Common.

CALIFORNIA SKATE, *Raja inornata*.   Turtle Bay, Baja California, to Strait of Juan
de Fuca. Length to 2.5 ft. Depth 60 to 2200 ft. Olive-brown above, tan below.
Uncommon.

LONGNOSE SKATE, *Raja rhina*.   Pt. Loma to S.E. Alaska. Length to 4.5 ft. Moderate depths, from 180 to 2040 ft. Dark brown above, light brown with darker
blotches below. Common in trawl catch.

KEY TO THE SKATES, Family Rajidae:

1a Ventral surface covered with minute denticles forming a shagreenlike
 surface ....   7 (Page 46)

1b Ventral surface smooth except for patches of prickles under snout and along
 edge of disc on some species 2

2a Orbital spines present ....   4 (next page)

2b Orbital spines absent...................   3 (next page)

* See comments on page 211.

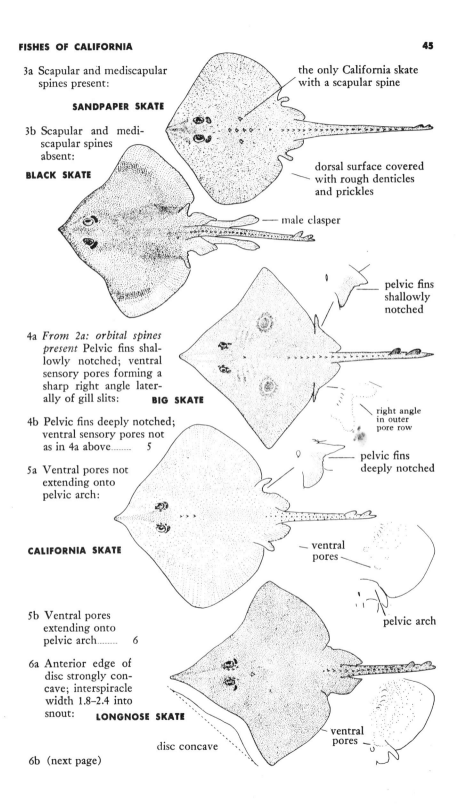

3a Scapular and mediscapular spines present:

SANDPAPER SKATE

the only California skate with a scapular spine

3b Scapular and mediscapular spines absent:

BLACK SKATE

dorsal surface covered with rough denticles and prickles

— male clasper

pelvic fins shallowly notched

4a *From 2a: orbital spines present* Pelvic fins shallowly notched; ventral sensory pores forming a sharp right angle laterally of gill slits: **BIG SKATE**

4b Pelvic fins deeply notched; ventral sensory pores not as in 4a above....... 5

5a Ventral pores not extending onto pelvic arch:

CALIFORNIA SKATE

right angle in outer pore row

pelvic fins deeply notched

— ventral pores

5b Ventral pores extending onto pelvic arch....... 6

6a Anterior edge of disc strongly concave; interspiracle width 1.8–2.4 into snout: **LONGNOSE SKATE**

pelvic arch

disc concave

ventral pores

6b (next page)

SKATES, Family Rajidae (continued)

STARRY SKATE, *Raja stellulata*. Coronado Bank, Baja California (SIO 60-340), to Bering Sea. Length to 2.5 ft. Recorded from 60 to 2400 ft. Light brown or gray-brown above with lighter spotting; often with a large yellowish spot ringed with brown at base of each pectoral fin. Uncommon.

WHITE SKATE, *Bathyraja spinosissima*.* Cocos Isl., Costa Rica, to Waldport, Oregon, including Farallon Isls. (CAS 25617). Length to 3.5 ft. Deep water, from 4200 to 6000 ft. Uniform gray on both sides. Skin surface rough to touch due to fine denticulation on both sides (absent in embryo) forming a shagreenlike or sharklike skin texture. Rare.

DEEPSEA SKATE, *Raja abyssicola*. Three known specimens: 8.6 mi. W of North Coronado Isl. (SIO 62-692); Queen Charlotte Isl., British Columbia (USNM 48623); and in N. Pacific (USNM 73913). Length to 4.5 ft. Depth 4200 to 9528 ft. Uniform whitish-tan on both surfaces. Skin texture shagreenlike on both surfaces as in WHITE SKATE.

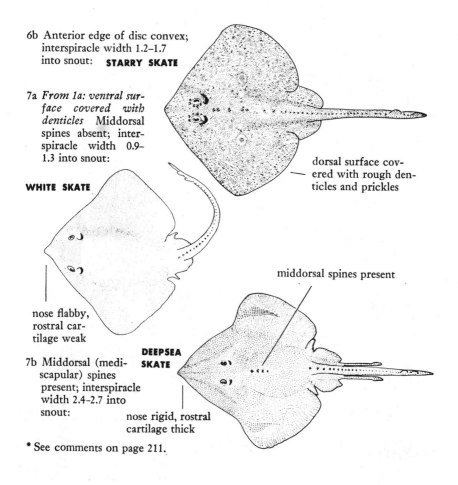

6b Anterior edge of disc convex; interspiracle width 1.2–1.7 into snout: **STARRY SKATE**

7a *From 1a: ventral sur-face covered with denticles* Middorsal spines absent; inter-spiracle width 0.9–1.3 into snout:

WHITE SKATE

dorsal surface cov-ered with rough den-ticles and prickles

nose flabby, rostral car-tilage weak

middorsal spines present

DEEPSEA SKATE

7b Middorsal (medi-scapular) spines present; interspiracle width 2.4-2.7 into snout:

nose rigid, rostral cartilage thick

* See comments on page 211.

KEY TO THE SKATES USING VENTRAL SURFACE CHARACTERS
(Emphasis on Ventral Sensory Pore Patterns):

1a Ventral surface covered with denticles forming a shagreenlike surface........ 7

1b Ventral surface smooth except for patches of prickles under snout and along edge of disc on some species 2

2a Pores not extending onto pelvic arch 4

2b Pores extending onto pelvic arch.... 3

3a Pores laterally of gill slits scattered, extending to more than 70% of distance from rear gill slit to edge of disc; pores on pelvic arch 6–15, extending laterally to or beyond insertion of upper lobe: **LONGNOSE SKATE**

6–15 pores on pelvic arch

3b Pores laterally of gill slits scattered, extending no more than 60% of distance from rear gill slit to edge of disc; pores on pelvic arch 3–6, not extending laterally of insertion of upper lobe: **STARRY SKATE**

3-6 pores on pelvic arch

4a *From 2a: pores not extending onto pelvic arch* Pores laterally of gill slits scattered, not forming longitudinal rows: **CALIFORNIA SKATE**

4b Pores laterally of gill slits forming inner and outer longitudinal rows (the inner row may be absent or represented by one or two pores on one species) 5

pores not reaching pelvic arch

"arch" patterns occ. form a continuous "V"

5a Ventral surface black; less than 15 pores posterior to last gill slit (pores are difficult to see on black surface): **BLACK SKATE**

5b (next page)

THE SKATES, Family Rajidae (continued)

5b Ventral surface white or light tan;
   more than 15 pores posterior to last
   gill slit 6

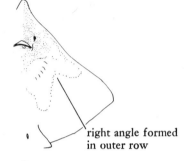

6a Outer pore row forms a distinct
   right angle laterally of the 3rd to
   4th gill slits; pores approach edge
   of disc on rostrum:

                              BIG SKATE

right angle formed
in outer row

outer pore row
remains distant
from edge of disc

6b Outer pore row not forming a right
   angle as in 6a above; pores remain
   distant from edge of disc on rostrum:

                    SANDPAPER SKATE

inner pore row

7a *From 1a page 47: ventral surface
   covered with denticles* Inner pore
   row with no more than 10 pores
   laterally of gill slits:

                         WHITE SKATE

7b Inner pore row with more than 20
   pores laterally of gill slits:

                       DEEPSEA SKATE

TABLE 1.

DORSAL SPINES OF CALIFORNIA SKATES

Species	Spine Series*						Malar hooks
	Orbital	Middorsal	Scapular	Lumbar	Tail (count is of median row)	Alar hooks	
Black Skate, *Raja trachura*	none	none	none	none	20–29; no lateral rows	69–112; 21–23 columns; max. rows 5–8	none
White Skate, *Bathyraja spinosissima*	none	none	none	none	23–29; no lateral rows	not known	not known
Deepsea Skate, *Raja abyssicola*	none	4	none	none	21–25; no lateral rows	74–85; 23–24 columns; max. rows 6	none
Sandpaper Skate, *Raja kincaidii*	none	2–5, occasionally continuous with tail spines	1, occasionally 2	1–8	15–21; no lateral rows	31–78; 17–21 columns; max. rows 2–6	none
Big Skate, *Raja binoculata*	1–2 in post-embryo, 2–3 in adults (occasionally worn off)	1, occasionally none	none	0–4	12–55, usually 13–17; lateral rows often present on largest	6–13; 2–7 columns; max. rows 2–3	11
California Skate, *Raja inornata*	1–10, usually 3–6	0–7	none	0–4	10–66, quite scattered; lateral rows present	9–15, in one row	4–11
Longnose Skate, *Raja rhina*	2–31, increasing in numbers with size	1, often 2	none	none	11–43; lateral rows present in largest	8–12, in one row	14–19
Starry Skate, *Raja stellulata*	2–16	2–11, often continuous with tail spines	none in California specimens	1–15	18–87; lateral rows appear at around 14 inches total length	14–19; 4–11 columns; max. rows 1–2	9–20

* Counts are given for one side of a paired series. See FIGURE 11, page 44, for terminology of spines.

MANTA, MOBULAS, BAT RAY, BUTTERFLY RAY, and STINGRAYS
(Principal sources: Beebe & Tee-Van, 1941; Roedel & Ripley, 1950)

PACIFIC MANTA, *Manta hamiltoni*. Family MOBULIDAE
Worldwide in tropical seas; in eastern Pacific from Tumbez, Peru, to Santa Barbara Isl., including Gulf of California and Guadalupe Isl. Width to 25 ft. Epipelagic. Black to dark brown above, white below. Rare.

SMOOTHTAIL MOBULA, *Mobula lucasana*. Family MOBULIDAE
Costa Rica to Laguna Beach, including Gulf of California and Guadalupe Isl. Width to 4 ft. Epipelagic. Black above, white below. Rare.

SPINETAIL MOBULA, *Mobula japanica*. Family MOBULIDAE
Temperate waters of Pacific to Japan, north to Santa Cruz Isl. on our coast. Width to 7 ft. Epipelagic. Black above, white below. Rare.

BAT RAY, *Myliobatis californica*. Family MYLIOBATIDIDAE
Gulf of California to Oregon. Width to 4 ft., and wt. to 210 lbs. Depth to 150 ft. Dark brown to olive or black above, white below. Common in bays and shallow sandy areas.

ROUND STINGRAY, *Urolophus halleri*. Family DASYATIDIDAE
Panama Bay to Humboldt Bay, including Gulf of California. Length to 22 in. Depth to 70 ft. Brownish above, yellowish below. Common off southern and Baja California.

CALIFORNIA BUTTERFLY RAY, *Gymnura marmorata*. Family GYMNURIDAE
Peru to Pt. Conception, including Gulf of California. Width to 5 ft. Brown to gray above with darker and lighter mottling. Common in shallow bays and along beaches.

DIAMOND STINGRAY, *Dasyatis dipterura*. Family DASYATIDIDAE
Paita, Peru, to Kyuquot, British Columbia. A 5 ft. 9 in. female (38.5 in. width) weighed 113.5 lbs. Shallow areas to 55 ft. Blackish above, white below. Common.

PELAGIC STINGRAY, *Dasyatis violacea*. Family DASYATIDIDAE
Worldwide in tropical seas, north to Pt. Dume on our coast. Width to 32 in. Epipelagic. Dark purplish above, purplish to lead-gray below. Rare.

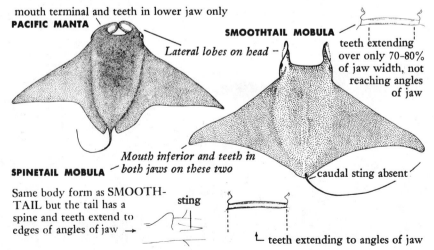

mouth terminal and teeth in lower jaw only
PACIFIC MANTA

SMOOTHTAIL MOBULA

Lateral lobes on head –

teeth extending over only 70–80% of jaw width, not reaching angles of jaw

Mouth inferior and teeth in both jaws on these two

SPINETAIL MOBULA

caudal sting absent

Same body form as SMOOTH-TAIL but the tail has a spine and teeth extend to edges of angles of jaw →

sting

teeth extending to angles of jaw

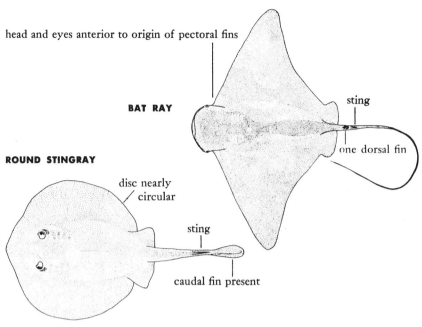

head and eyes anterior to origin of pectoral fins

BAT RAY

sting

one dorsal fin

ROUND STINGRAY

disc nearly circular

sting

caudal fin present

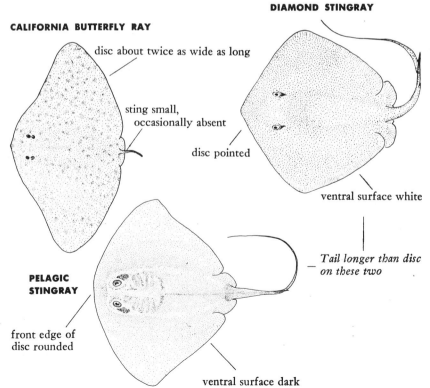

DIAMOND STINGRAY

CALIFORNIA BUTTERFLY RAY

disc about twice as wide as long

sting small, occasionally absent

disc pointed

ventral surface white

Tail longer than disc on these two

PELAGIC STINGRAY

front edge of disc rounded

ventral surface dark

RATFISH, STURGEONS, MACHETE, BONEFISH, MORAY, CONGER EEL and SNAKE EELS

RATFISH, Hydrolagus colliei. Family CHIMAERIDAE
Tiburon Isl., Gulf of California (isolated population), and from Sebastian Viscaino Bay, Baja California,[1] to S.E. Alaska. Length to 3 ft. 2 in. Shallow water to 1200 ft. Body with bronze metallic hues, silvery below with numerous white spots. Common.

GREEN STURGEON, Acipenser medirostris. Family ACIPENSERIDAE
Ensenada to the Bering Sea and Japan. Length to 7 ft., wt. to 350 lbs. Anadromous; to 400 ft. in ocean. Olive-green above, white below; olive stripes on sides. Common. D 33–42; A 22–29; plates: midlateral 23–30; dorsal 8–11; ventral 7–10.

WHITE STURGEON, Acipenser transmontanus. Family ACIPENSERIDAE
Ensenada to Gulf of Alaska. Length to 20 ft. Anadromous; to 400 ft. in ocean. Uniform gray. Common in larger rivers. D 44–48; A 28–31; plates: midlateral 38–48; dorsal 11–14; ventral 9–12.

MACHETE, Elops affinis. Family ELOPIDAE
Peru to Magdalena Bay, Baja California, and in the Salton Sea. Length to 3 ft., wt. to 10 lbs. Body silvery. Uncommon. D 20–27; A 13–16; LLs 110–120; GR 10–12 + 12–20 = 22–32; Vert. 79–82.

BONEFISH, Albula vulpes. Family ALBULIDAE
Worldwide in warmer seas; in eastern Pacific from Panama to San Francisco. Length in eastern Pacific to 17.5 in., and wt. to 1 lb. 13 ounces [2] (world record is 22 lbs.). Gray above, silvery below; base of fins yellowish. Shallow waters. Uncommon along coast, introd. into Salton Sea. D 15–20; A 5–10; LLs 65–75; Vert. 70–74.

CALIFORNIA MORAY, Gymnothorax mordax. Family MURAENIDAE
Magdalena Bay, Baja California (UCLA W 55–112) to Pt. Conception, including Guadalupe Isl. Length to 5 ft. Dark brown to greenish. Common in shallow reef areas. Vert. 143–152.

CATALINA CONGER, Gnathophis catalinensis. Family CONGRIDAE
Gulf of California (SIO 68–91) to Santa Rosa Isl., including Guadalupe Isl. Length to 16.5 in. Depth 30 to 1200 ft. Brownish-gray. Rare. LLp 132.

PACIFIC WORM EEL, Myrophis vafer. Family OPHICHTHIDAE
Peru to San Pedro, including Gulf of California. Length to 18.25 in. Tide pools and shallow areas to 36 ft. Uniform brown. Rare.

YELLOW SNAKE EEL, Ophichthus zophochir. Family OPHICHTHIDAE
Peru to Berkeley Pier, including Gulf of California. Length to about 30 in. Intertidal to about 60 ft. Reddish-olive to yellowish, without spotting. Rare. Pect. 16; LLp 148–149; Vert. 153.

SPOTTED SNAKE EEL, Ophichthus triserialis. Family OPHICHTHIDAE
Peru to Humboldt Bay, including the Galapagos Isls. and Gulf of California. Length to 44 in. Shallow waters to at least 60 ft. Body tan, with large black spots. Rare. Vert. 148.

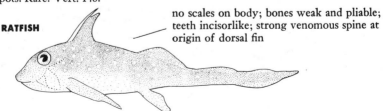

RATFISH — no scales on body; bones weak and pliable; teeth incisorlike; strong venomous spine at origin of dorsal fin

* See comments on page 211.

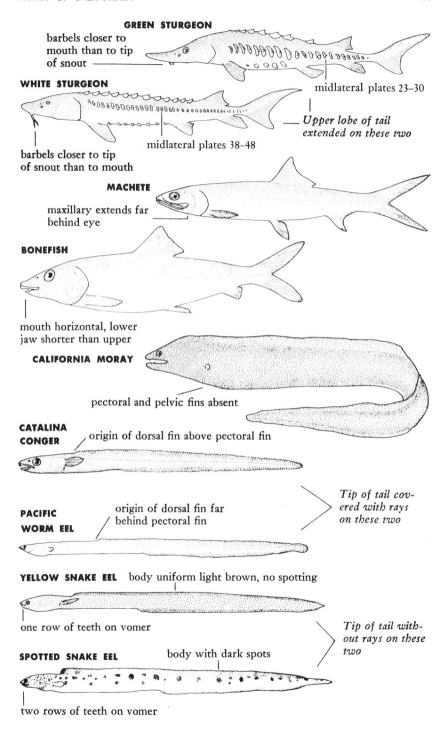

GREEN STURGEON

barbels closer to
mouth than to tip
of snout —————

WHITE STURGEON

midlateral plates 23–30

*Upper lobe of tail
extended on these two*

midlateral plates 38–48

barbels closer to tip
of snout than to mouth

MACHETE

maxillary extends far
behind eye

BONEFISH

mouth horizontal, lower
jaw shorter than upper

CALIFORNIA MORAY

pectoral and pelvic fins absent

**CATALINA
CONGER**   origin of dorsal fin above pectoral fin

**PACIFIC
WORM EEL**

origin of dorsal fin far
behind pectoral fin

*Tip of tail cov-
ered with rays
on these two*

YELLOW SNAKE EEL   body uniform light brown, no spotting

one row of teeth on vomer

*Tip of tail with-
out rays on these
two*

SPOTTED SNAKE EEL   body with dark spots

two rows of teeth on vomer

HERRINGS, Family Clupeidae

(Principal sources: Hubbs, 1925; Svetovidov, 1952; Roedel, 1953)

THREADFIN SHAD, *Dorosoma petenense.* Native to Central America and eastern U.S., introduced into California freshwater lakes. Has been taken in Long Beach Harbor, San Francisco, Drakes and Humboldt Bays. Length to about 9 in. Silvery with a single black spot near operculum. Rare in ocean. D 11–15; A 17–27; midlateral scales 40–48; ventral scutes 15–18 anterior to and 8–12 posterior to pelvic base; Vert. 40–45.

MIDDLING THREAD HERRING, *Opisthonema medirastre.* Peru to Redondo Beach, including Gulf of California. Length to 10.8 in. Inshore pelagic. Bluish dorsally, silver below. Uncommon. D 17; A 19; midlateral scales 48–50; ventral scutes 17–18 anterior to and 14–15 posterior to pelvic base; Vert. 45–47.

ROUND HERRING, *Etrumeus teres.* Worldwide in warmer seas; in eastern Pacific from Chile to Monterey Bay. Length to 12 in. Inshore pelagic. Dark blue above, white below. Uncommon. D 18–20; A 10–19; midlateral scales 48–55; Vert. 53–55.

PACIFIC HERRING, *Clupea harengus.* Pacific subspecies, *C. h. pallasii,* from northern Baja California to arctic Alaska and Japan. Length to 18 in. An inshore schooling species; spawns in inter- and subtidal zones. Dark green above, white below. Common. D 15–21; A 13–20; midlateral scales 38–54; GR 20 + 45 = 65; Vert. 46–55.

PACIFIC SARDINE, *Sardinops sagax caeruleus.* Guaymas, Mexico, to Kamchatka. Length to about 16 in. Epipelagic. Blue-green above, white below; series of black spots on back (occ. absent). Common. D 17–20; A 17–20; midlateral scales 52–60; Vert. 48–54.

AMERICAN SHAD, *Alosa sapidissima.* Todos Santos Bay, Baja California, to Alaska and Kamchatka. Intro. from Atlantic. Length to 30 in. Dark blue above, white below; black spots on back. Anadromous; taken to 600 ft. Common. D 15–19; A 19–23 (18–24 in Atlantic); midlateral scales about 60; ventral scutes 21–22 anterior to and 16–17 posterior to pelvic base; GR 14–25 + 28–47 = 42–72; Vert. 55–58 (53–59 in Atlantic).

FLATIRON HERRING, *Harengula thrissina.* Peru to La Jolla Cove, including Gulf of California. Length to 7.25 in. Inshore, pelagic. Bluish above, silver below. Rare. D 16–19; A 14–17; midlateral scales 37–42; ventral scutes 16–17 anterior to and 12–14 posterior to pelvic base; GR 9–18 + 24–31 = 33–49.

KEY TO THE HERRINGS, Family Clupeidae:

1a Last dorsal soft-ray shorter than 1st dorsal soft-ray........ 3

1b Last dorsal soft-ray greatly elongated, threadlike........ 2

2a No scales on dorsal midline anterior to dorsal fin: **THREADFIN SHAD**

2b Scales present on dorsal midline anterior to dorsal fin:

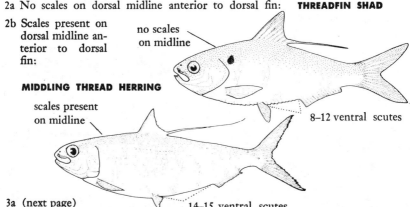

no scales on midline

MIDDLING THREAD HERRING

scales present on midline

8–12 ventral scutes

3a (next page)

14–15 ventral scutes

* See comments on page 212.

3a Origin of pelvic fins posterior to or even with insertion of dorsal fin:

ROUND HERRING

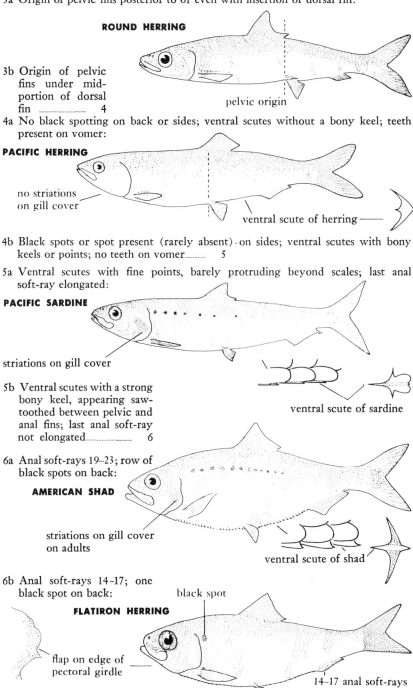

3b Origin of pelvic
   fins under mid-
   portion of dorsal
   fin 4

pelvic origin

4a No black spotting on back or sides; ventral scutes without a bony keel; teeth
   present on vomer:

PACIFIC HERRING

no striations
on gill cover

ventral scute of herring ———

4b Black spots or spot present (rarely absent) on sides; ventral scutes with bony
   keels or points; no teeth on vomer........ 5

5a Ventral scutes with fine points, barely protruding beyond scales; last anal
   soft-ray elongated:

PACIFIC SARDINE

striations on gill cover

5b Ventral scutes with a strong
   bony keel, appearing saw-
   toothed between pelvic and
   anal fins; last anal soft-ray
   not elongated.............. 6

ventral scute of sardine

6a Anal soft-rays 19–23; row of
   black spots on back:

AMERICAN SHAD

striations on gill cover
on adults

ventral scute of shad

6b Anal soft-rays 14-17; one
   black spot on back:

black spot

FLATIRON HERRING

flap on edge of
pectoral girdle ___

14–17 anal soft-rays

ANCHOVIES, Family Engraulididae
(Principal sources: Hildebrand, 1943; Roedel, 1953;
Howard, 1954; Peterson, 1956)

ANCHOVETA, Cetengraulis mysticetus. Sechura Bay, Peru, to Los Angeles Harbor, but rare north of Magdalena Bay, Baja California. Length to about 7 in. Greenish above, silvery below. Its occurrence off California may be the result of inadvertent introductions by American tuna bait boats returning from tropical waters. D 13–17; A 18–26; Pect. 15; midlateral scales 42–52; GRt 63–145 (number increasing with size); Vert. 39–43.

NORTHERN ANCHOVY, Engraulis mordax. Cape San Lucas, Baja California (one record from La Paz, inside the Gulf), to Queen Charlotte Isls., British Columbia. Length to 9 in. but rarely over 7 in. Back metallic blue to green, silver below. Body roundish and scales easily rubbed off. By far the most abundant anchovy in California. D 14–19; A 19–26; Pect. 13–20; midlateral scales about 41–50; GR 28–41 + 37–45 (number increasing with size); Vert. 43–47.

SLIM ANCHOVY, Anchoviella miarcha. Panama Bay to Mazatlan, Mexico, and the Galapagos Isls. Only one California record from San Diego Bay. (This record has been questioned.) Length to 4 in. Found in estuaries and may enter freshwater. Greenish above; brownish dots on top of head and in opercular region. D 11–15; A 12–20; Pect. 13–14; midlateral scales about 38; GR 12–18 + 18–23; Vert. 43–44.

DEEPBODY ANCHOVY, Anchoa compressa. Todos Santos Bay, Baja California, to Morro Bay. Length to 6.5 in. A schooling fish occasionally along shoreline but primarily in bays and estuaries. Brownish to green above, silvery below; body deep, strongly compressed. Common. D 12–14; A 29–33; Pect. 13–14; midlateral scales about 45; GR 19–22 + 24–27 = 43–48; Vert. 39–41.

SLOUGH ANCHOVY, Anchoa delicatissima. Magdalena Bay, Baja California, to Belmont Shores, Long Beach Harbor (UCLA W 51–81). Length to 3.7 in. Greenish above, white below with a bright silvery lateral band. Common in estuaries and backwaters of bays, occasionally near shore outside of bays. D 13–15; A 23–26; Pect. 12–13; midlateral scales about 43; GR 18–21 + 26–32; Vert. 39–41.

KEY TO THE ANCHOVIES, Family Engraulididae:

1a Gill membranes broadly united:

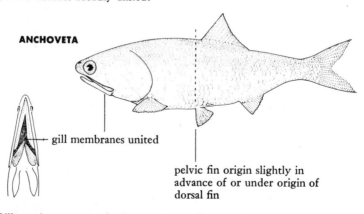

ANCHOVETA

gill membranes united

pelvic fin origin slightly in
advance of or under origin of
dorsal fin

1b Gill membranes not united .... 2 (next page)

2a Origin of anal fin anterior to middle of dorsal fin base.. 4

2b Origin of anal fin under or posterior to last few soft-rays of dorsal fin........ 3

3a Body depth 5.0–5.9 into standard length; pectoral axillary scale more than
½ length of pectoral fin:

NORTHERN ANCHOVY

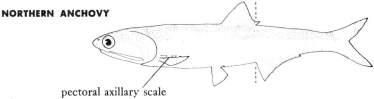

pectoral axillary scale

3b Body depth 7.0–8.0 into
standard length; pectoral
axillary scale less than ½
length of pectoral fin:

SLIM ANCHOVY   brownish dots

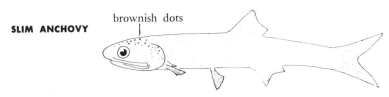

4a *From 2a: origin of anal fin anterior to middle of dorsal fin base* Anal fin base
more than two times length of dorsal fin base; 29–33 anal soft-rays:

DEEPBODY ANCHOVY

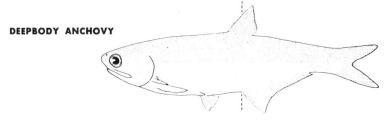

4b Anal fin base less than two times length of dorsal fin base; 23–26 anal soft-rays:

SLOUGH ANCHOVY

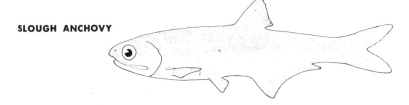

TROUTS and SALMON, Family Salmonidae
(Principal sources: Clemens & Wilby, 1961; Rounsefell, 1962; Hallock & Fry, 1967)

CUTTHROAT TROUT, *Salmo clarkii.* Eel River to S.E. Alaska. Length to 2.5 ft., and wt. to 17 lbs. (anadromous form). Freshwater and anadromous. Dark olive above, with a red stripe on sides in adult; black spotting on upper parts and fins. Rarely taken in ocean in California. D 10–13 (8–11) *; A 11–13 (8–12) *; LLs 116–126; scales in row above LL 120–208; GRt 14–21; Vert. 61–64.

RAINBOW TROUT, *Salmo gairdnerii.* (A sea-run RAINBOW TROUT is a STEELHEAD). Northern Baja California to Bering Sea and Japan. Weight to over 30 lbs. Anadromous. Color similar to CUTTHROAT TROUT. Common. D 12–15 (10–12)*; A 13–16 (8–12)*; LLs 119–138; scales in row above LL 115–164; GRt 16–22; Vert. 63–65.

CHUM SALMON, *Oncorhynchus keta.* Del Mar to Arctic Alaska and to Honshu, Japan. Length to 40 in. Anadromous. Metallic blue above, silvery below; white tips on fins of mature fish. Uncommon. D 13–16 (10–13) *; A 16–20 (13–17) *; LLs 124–153; scales in row above LL 130–153; GRt 18–26; pyloric caecae 140–186; Vert. 59–68.

SOCKEYE SALMON, *Oncorhynchus nerka.* Sacramento River system to Bering Sea and Japan. Length to 33 in. Anadromous. Bluish-green above, silvery below; no spots on back. Rare in ocean off California. D 12–18 (11–16) *; A 15–21 (12–18) *; LLs 122–150; scales in row above LL 124–146; GRt 28–40; pyloric caecae 60–115; Vert. 56–67.

PINK SALMON, *Oncorhynchus gorbuscha.* La Jolla to Arctic Alaska and Japan. Length to 2.5 ft., and wt. to 12 lbs. Anadromous. Dark green above; large black oval spots on back and tail. Uncommon. D 13–16 (10–15) *; A 16–20 (13–17) *; LLs 147–205; scales in row above LL 169–232; GRt 24–35; pyloric caecae 165–196; Vert. 60–69.

KING SALMON, *Oncorhynchus tshawytscha.* San Diego to Bering Sea and Japan. Length to 4 ft. 10 in., and wt. to 126.5 lbs. Anadromous. Dark blue above, silvery below; black spots on back. Common south to Avila. D 13–17 (10–16) *; A 16–22 (13–20) *; LLs 130–165; scales in row above LL 131–158; GRt 18–31; pyloric caecae 140–185; Vert. 64–72.

SILVER SALMON, *Oncorhynchus kisutch.* Chamalu Bay, Baja California, to Bering Sea and Japan. Length to 3 ft. 2.5 in., and wt. to 30 lbs. Anadromous. Color similar to KING SALMON. Common south to Santa Barbara. D 12–15 (9–13) *; A 15–19 (13–16) *; LLs 121–144; scales in row above LL 118–147; GRt 19–25; pyl. cae. 45–83; Vert. 58–66.

* Dorsal and anal fin counts in ( ) do not include rudimentary soft-rays, and are counts most commonly given in literature and keys.

KEY TO ADULT SALMON AND TROUT, Family Salmonidae
(see page 60 for juveniles):

1a Lining of mouth cavity black or with black blotches; anal soft-rays 15–22 3

1b Lining of mouth cavity bright white; anal soft-rays 10 - 16 2

2a Basibranchial teeth present; red mark on mandible in adult (occ. absent in sea-run fish): **CUTTHROAT TROUT** (not illustrated, same body form as 2b below)

(see Figure 8b, page 11 showing placement of basibranchial teeth)

RAINBOW TROUT

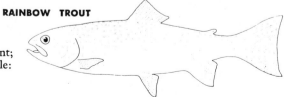

2b Basibranchial teeth absent; no red mark on mandible:

3a (next page)

3a Large black spots on back and tail........ 5

3b No large black spots on back and tail (some fine speckling may be present) 4

4a Gill rakers 18–26:   **CHUM SALMON**

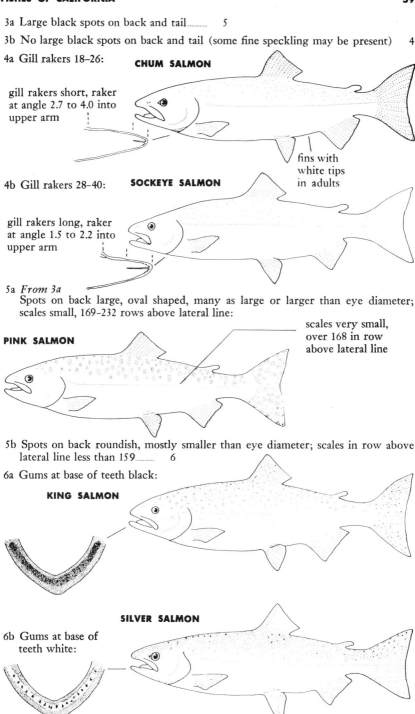

gill rakers short, raker
at angle 2.7 to 4.0 into
upper arm

fins with
white tips
in adults

4b Gill rakers 28–40:   **SOCKEYE SALMON**

gill rakers long, raker
at angle 1.5 to 2.2 into
upper arm

5a *From 3a*
   Spots on back large, oval shaped, many as large or larger than eye diameter;
   scales small, 169–232 rows above lateral line:

PINK SALMON

scales very small,
over 168 in row
above lateral line

5b Spots on back roundish, mostly smaller than eye diameter; scales in row above
   lateral line less than 159........ 6

6a Gums at base of teeth black:

   KING SALMON

6b Gums at base of
   teeth white:

SILVER SALMON

JUVENILE TROUTS and SALMON, Family Salmonidae
(Principal source: Forrester & Pritchard, 1944)

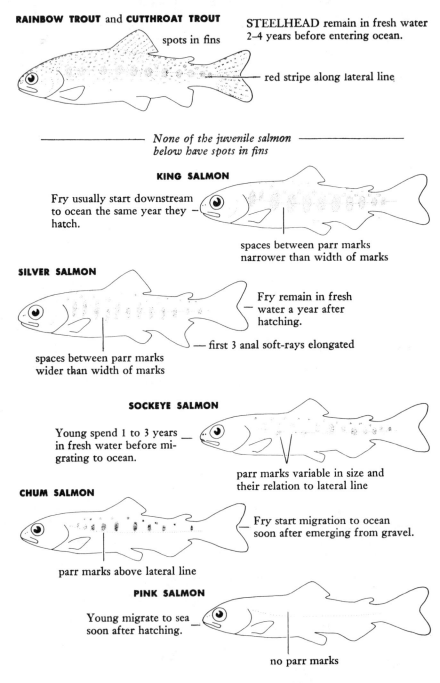

RAINBOW TROUT and **CUTTHROAT TROUT**

spots in fins

STEELHEAD remain in fresh water 2–4 years before entering ocean.

red stripe along lateral line

*None of the juvenile salmon
below have spots in fins*

KING SALMON

Fry usually start downstream to ocean the same year they hatch.

spaces between parr marks narrower than width of marks

SILVER SALMON

Fry remain in fresh water a year after hatching.

first 3 anal soft-rays elongated

spaces between parr marks wider than width of marks

SOCKEYE SALMON

Young spend 1 to 3 years in fresh water before migrating to ocean.

parr marks variable in size and their relation to lateral line

CHUM SALMON

Fry start migration to ocean soon after emerging from gravel.

parr marks above lateral line

PINK SALMON

Young migrate to sea soon after hatching.

no parr marks

LANCETFISH, SLICKHEAD, and SNIPE EEL
(Principal source: Fitch & Lavenberg, 1968)

LONGNOSE LANCETFISH, Alepisaurus ferox. Family ALEPISAURIDAE
Worldwide in warmer seas; in eastern Pacific from Chile to Dutch Harbor, Unalaska Isl., Alaska. Length to 6 ft. Depth, surface to 6000 ft. Uniform blackish, with silvery and brassy overtones. Uncommon. D XXX–XLIII; A 15–17; Pect. 13; Pelvic 8–10; scales absent; GR $2-6 + 16-24 = 20-30$; Vert. 48–52.

CALIFORNIA SLICKHEAD, Alepocephalus tenebrosus. Family ALEPOCEPHALIDAE
An eastern Pacific species, north to Bering Sea. Length to 2 ft., and wt. to 3 lbs. Depth 150 to 18,000 ft. Uniform dark brown. Uncommon. D 17; A 17; Pect. 10; lateral line tubes 55; scales absent on head.

SLENDER SNIPE EEL, Nemichthys scolopaceus. Family NEMICHTHYIDAE
Found in all warmer seas; north to Alaska on our coast and over to Japan. Length recorded to 57 in., reported to 60 in. Depth 300 to 6000 ft. Uniform dusky. Uncommon.

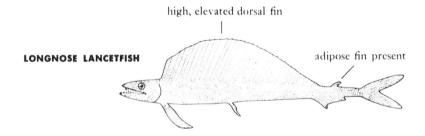

high, elevated dorsal fin

LONGNOSE LANCETFISH

adipose fin present

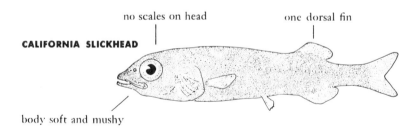

no scales on head

one dorsal fin

CALIFORNIA SLICKHEAD

body soft and mushy

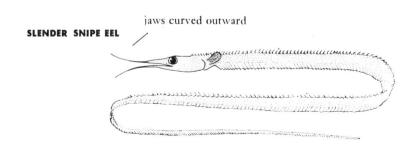

jaws curved outward

SLENDER SNIPE EEL

SMELTS, Family Osmeridae
(Principal sources: Clemens & Wilby, 1961; McAllister, 1963)

SURF SMELT, *Hypomesus pretiosus.* Eastern Pacific subspecies, *H. p. pretiosus,* from Long Beach to Prince William Sound, Alaska. Length to 10 in. Spawns in surf in daytime. Sides silver with purplish hue, back light green. Common. D 8–11; A 12–17; Pect. 14–17; LLp 4–12; midlateral scales 66–76; GR 10–13 + 20–25 = 30–36; Vert. 62–70.

DELTA SMELT, *Hypomesus transpacificus.* Found only in portions of brackish and fresh water of Sacramento and San Joaquin River systems. Length to about 4.5 in. Silvery-tan with faintly speckled lateral band. Common. D 9–10; A 15–17; Pect. 10–12; LLp 8–9; midlateral scales 53–58; GR 8–10 + 19–23 = 27–33; Vert. 53–56.

EULACHON, *Thaleichthys pacificus.* Bodega Head to Bering Sea. Length to about 12 in. Taken to 600 ft. in ocean. Spawns in rivers from Mad River north. Silvery on sides, bluish-brown on back with fine speckling. Common. D 10–13; A 18–23; Pect. 10–12; LLp 70–78; GR 4–6 + 13–18 = 17–23; Vert. 65–72.

WHITEBAIT SMELT, *Allosmerus elongatus.* San Pedro to Strait of Juan de Fuca, British Columbia. Length to 9 in. From surface to 180 ft. Spawning behavior not known. Sides silver, back greenish. Uncommon. D 9–10; A 14–17; Pect. 12–14; LLp about 20; midlateral scales 62–68; GR 10–13 + 23–28 = 33–41; Vert. 65–67.

NIGHT SMELT, *Spirinchus starksi.* Pt. Arguello to Shelikof Bay, Alaska. Length to 5.5 in. Surface to 420 ft. Spawns in surf at night. Sides silver, brownish-green on back. Common. D 8–11; A 15–21; Pect. 10–11; LLp 16–24; midlateral scales 60–66; GR 8–13 + 24–32 = 32–45; Vert. 60–65.

LONGFIN SMELT, *Spirinchus thaleichthys.* San Francisco Bay, Humboldt Bay, and Eel River in California, north to Hinchinbrook Isl., Prince William Sound, Alaska. Length to about 6 in. Surface to 66 ft.; ascends rivers to spawn. Sides silver, brownish dorsally. Common. D 8–10; A 15–22; Pect. 10–12; LLp 14–21; midlateral scales 54–65; GR 10–13 + 26–34 = 38–47; Vert. 54–61. (Clemens & Wilby have D minimum 6, GRt 36).

KEY TO THE SMELTS, Family Osmeridae:

1a Maxillary extends beyond middle of eye........   3 (next page)

1b Maxillary not extending beyond middle of eye........   2

2a Longest anal soft-ray 2.6–3.5 in head length; midlateral scales 66–76:

SURF SMELT

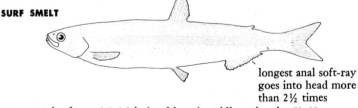

longest anal soft-ray
goes into head more
than 2½ times

2b Longest anal soft-ray 2.0–2.3 in head length; midlateral scales 53–58:

DELTA SMELT

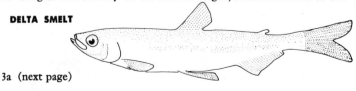

3a (next page)

3a *From 1a: maxillary extends beyond middle of eye* Striations on gill cover; lateral line complete with 70-78 pores:

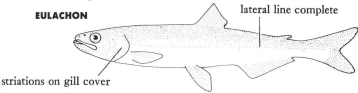

EULACHON

lateral line complete

striations on gill cover

3b No striations on gill cover; lateral line incomplete or obsolete, if present, with less than 25 pores 4

4a One to 3 large canine teeth on vomer; pectoral rays 12-14; eye diameter 4/5 or more (usually about equal) to depth of caudal peduncle:

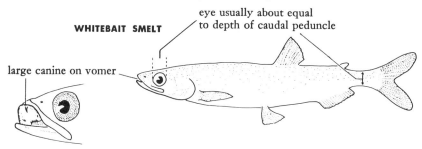

WHITEBAIT SMELT

eye usually about equal to depth of caudal peduncle

large canine on vomer

4b No large canines on vomer; pectoral rays 10-12; eye diameter 4/5 or less of depth of caudal peduncle 5

5a Angle of jaw at 54°-65° to top of snout; midlateral scales 60-66; longest anal soft-ray 2.2-3.1 into head:

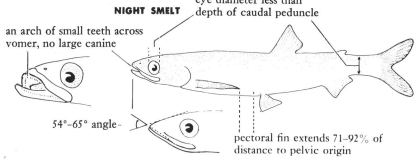

NIGHT SMELT

eye diameter less than depth of caudal peduncle

an arch of small teeth across vomer, no large canine

54°-65° angle

pectoral fin extends 71-92% of distance to pelvic origin

5b Angle of jaw at 68°-90° to top of snout; midlateral scales 54-65; longest anal soft-ray 1.4-2.2 into head:

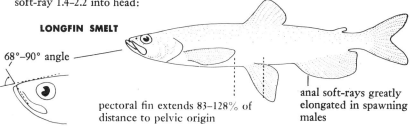

LONGFIN SMELT

68°-90° angle

pectoral fin extends 83-128% of distance to pelvic origin

anal soft-rays greatly elongated in spawning males

LIGHTFISHES, ARGENTINE, and DEEPSEA SMELTS
(Principal sources: Bolin, 1938; Cohen, 1956, 1958, 1966; Clemens & Wilby, 1961)

BENTTOOTH BRISTLEMOUTH, *Cyclothone acclinidens*. Family GONOSTOMATIDAE
Pacific, Atlantic and Indian Oceans; in eastern Pacific from Peru-Chile Trench to off Oregon. Length to 2.8 in. Mesopelagic, 180 to over 3412 ft. Body grayish-brown, abdomen black. Photophores small. Abundant but uncommonly taken. D 13–15; A 18–20; Pect. 9–10; Pelvic 6–7; GR 7–9 + 13–15 (2 rakers at angle); Vert. 31.

BIGEYE LIGHTFISH, *Danaphos oculatus*. Family GONOSTOMATIDAE
Pacific and Indian Oceans; in eastern north Pacific from Gulf of Panama to Oregon. Length to 2.25 in. Mesopelagic, to over 1200 ft. Body whitish; large serial photopores ventrally. Uncommon. D 6; A 24–25; GR 2 + 11–13 = 13–15; Vert. 38.

PACIFIC ARGENTINE, *Argentina sialis*. Family ARGENTINIDAE
Cape San Lucas, Baja California, to off coast of Oregon, including Gulf of California. Length to 8.25 in. Adults near bottom, 36 to 900 ft.; larvae pelagic. Body silvery to light brown; scales large. Uncommon. D 10–13; A 12–15; Pect. 15–18; Pelvic 10–12; LLs 48–51; GR 7–9 + 15–21; branchiostegals 5; Vert. 47–50.

CALIFORNIA SMOOTHTONGUE, *Leuroglossus stilbius*. Family BATHYLAGIDAE
North Pacific Ocean from off Colombia, South America, to Bering Sea and Sea of Okhotsk, including Gulf of California. Length to 6 in. Mesopelagic, from near surface to 2264 ft. Silvery to brassy, darker above. Abundant in offshore waters, uncommonly taken. D 9–12; A 11–14; Pect. 8–9; Pelvic 8–10; GR 7–9 + 14–17 = 21–26; branchiostegals 2; Vert. 39–52.

SNUBNOSE BLACKSMELT, *Bathylagus wesethi*. Family BATHYLAGIDAE
Eastern North Pacific Ocean from central Baja California to off Oregon. Length to 4.3 in. Mesopelagic, from approximately 130 to 3281 ft. Dark brown above; sides silvery to whitish with black spots. Uncommon. D 12–13; A 14–16; Pect. 10–11; Pelvic 9–11; GR 8 + 16–17 = 24–25; branchiostegals 2; Vert. 43–46.

POPEYE BLACKSMELT, *Bathylagus ochotensis*. Family BATHYLAGIDAE
North Pacific Ocean from northern Baja California to Bering Sea and Sea of Okhotsk. Length to 7.1 in. Mesopelagic, 160 to 2953 ft. Body color gray-brown; scale pockets evident. Uncommon. D 9–12; A 12–15; Pect. 6–10; Pelvic 10–12; midlateral scales 40; GRt 28; Vert. 48.

ROBUST BLACKSMELT, *Bathylagus milleri*. Family BATHYLAGIDAE
North Pacific Ocean from Cortez Bank, California, to Bering Sea, Sea of Okhotsk, and Kuril-Kamchatka Trench. Length to 8.5 in. Mesopelagic, 197 to over 3280 ft. Uniform black to blackish-brown. Uncommon. D 6–9; A 20–28; Pect. 11–16; Pelvic 6–8; midlateral scales 23–27; GRt 25–27; Vert. 50–54.

PACIFIC BLACKSMELT, *Bathylagus pacificus*. Family BATHYLAGIDAE
Southern California to Bering Sea and Kuril-Kamchatka Trench. Length to 7.5 in. Mesopelagic, 490 to over 3280 ft. Uniform black to blackish-brown. Uncommon. D 8–13; A 15–22; Pect. 7–11; Pelvic 7–10; midlateral scales 37–42; GRt 28–32; Vert. 44–48.

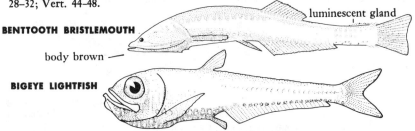

luminescent gland

BENTTOOTH BRISTLEMOUTH

body brown —

BIGEYE LIGHTFISH

PACIFIC ARGENTINE

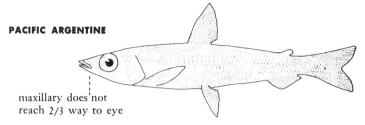

maxillary does not
reach 2/3 way to eye

KEY TO THE DEEPSEA SMELTS, Family Bathylagidae:

1a Snout pointed, greater than eye diameter:

CALIFORNIA SMOOTHTONGUE

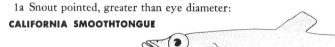

1b Snout rounded, less than eye diameter in length........ 2

2a Gill openings not reaching halfway up side of body........ 4

2b Gill openings extending at least half way up side of body........ 3

3a Anal fin base longer
   than length of
   caudal peduncle:

SNUBNOSE BLACKSMELT

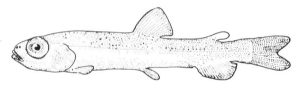

3b Anal fin base equal
   to or shorter than   \
   length of caudal   *Body silver or gray*
   peduncle: *on these two*
                                /
   POPEYE BLACKSMELT

4a *From 2a: gill openings not extending half way up side*
   Approximately 25 scale pockets along midline; 11–16 pectoral rays:

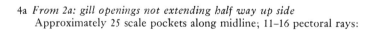

ROBUST BLACKSMELT   body black

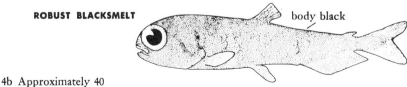

4b Approximately 40
   scale pockets along
   midline; 7–11 pec-
   toral rays: PACIFIC BLACKSMELT (body shape same as in 4a)

HATCHETFISHES, Family Sternoptychidae
(Principal sources: Schultz, 1961; Berry & Perkins, 1966; Baird, 1971)

DOLLAR HATCHETFISHES, *Sternoptyx spp.* This complex is composed of three species, all very similar. To identify to species see Baird, 1971. All three are reported to occur in the mesopelagic zone off California. Largest reach a little over 2 in. Bright silver, darker above. Uncommon. Counts are inclusive for the three species: D, blade + 8–11; A 14-16; Pect. 10–11; GRt 7–9; Vert. 28–31.

SLENDER HATCHETFISH, *Argyropelecus affinis.* Atlantic, Indian, and Pacific Oceans; in eastern Pacific north to off Oregon. Length to about 4 in. Mesopelagic, normally from 330 to 2000 ft. Silvery, black above. Uncommon, but the most common of our hatchetfishes. D 9; A 11–13; Pect. 10–11; GRt 18–22; Vert. 38–40.

SPURRED HATCHETFISH, *Argyropelecus hemigymnus.* In all warm and temperate seas; in eastern Pacific north to off Oregon. Length a little less than 2 in. Mesopelagic, from 330 to 2400 ft. Uncommon. D 8–9; A 11; Pect. 9–11; GRt 18–25; Vert. 35–38.

SILVERY HATCHETFISH, *Argyropelecus sladeni.* Found in all warmer seas; in eastern north Pacific from southern Baja California to British Columbia. Length to over 3 in. Mesopelagic, from 330 to 2000 ft. Uncommon. D 9–10; A 12–13; Pect. 10–11; GRt 17–21; Vert. 35–37.

SILVER HATCHETFISH, *Argyropelecus lychnus.* An eastern Pacific species; from Chile to Pt. Conception. Length to over 3 in. Mesopelagic, normally between 650 and 1300 ft. Uncommon. D 9; A 12; Pect. 10–11; GRt 16–19; Vert. 35–37.

KEY TO THE HATCHETFISHES, Family Sternoptychidae:

1a Abdominal photophores 10; eyes normal, not telescopic:

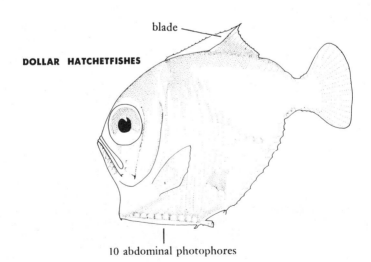

blade

DOLLAR HATCHETFISHES

10 abdominal photophores

1b Abdominal photophores 12; eyes telescopic........ 2 **(next page)**

2a Supra-abdominal, preanal, anal, and subcaudal photophores in a nearly continuous straight line:

SLENDER HATCHETFISH

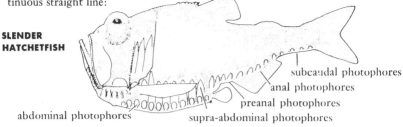

subcaudal photophores
anal photophores
preanal photophores
abdominal photophores   supra-abdominal photophores

2b Supra-abdominal, preanal, anal, and subcaudal photophores not in a continuous straight line 3

3a Postabdominal spine single, serrated; dorsal soft-rays 8–9:

SPURRED HATCHETFISH

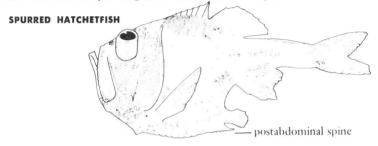

— postabdominal spine

3b Postabdominal spines 2, smooth; dorsal soft-rays 9–10........ **4**

4a Upper preopercular spine usually curved dorsally, never ventrally; dark well developed pigment spots form a line along posterior midline:

SILVERY HATCHETFISH

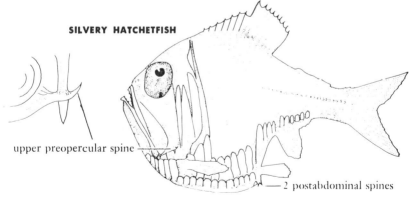

upper preopercular spine

— 2 postabdominal spines

4b Upper preopercular spine usually curved ventrally, never dorsally; pigment spots minute along posterior midline: **SILVER HATCHETFISH**

(same body form as in 4a above)

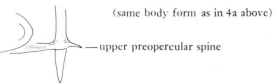

—upper preopercular spine

BARRELEYE, DRAGONFISHES, VIPERFISH, DAGGERTOOTH, BARRACUDINA, PEARLEYE, and LIZARDFISH
(Principal sources: Clemens & Wilby, 1961; Fitch & Lavenberg, 1968)

PACIFIC BARRELEYE, *Macropinna microstoma.* Family OPISTHOPROCTIDAE
Northern Baja California to Kuril-Kamchatka Trench. Length to 6.3 in. Depth 324 to 2940 ft. Adult dark brown; young light brown, with bars on sides. Uncommon. D 11–12; A 14; Pect. 17–19; Pelvic 9–10; LLs 23–26.

HIGHFIN DRAGONFISH, *Bathophilus flemingi.* Family MELANOSTOMIATIDAE
Central Baja California to British Columbia. Length to 6 in. Mesopelagic, from 600 to 2000 ft. Uniform black. Uncommon. D 15–16; A 16–17; Pect. 5–7; Pelvic 15–17; LL absent; scales absent; photophores in ventrolateral row 27–28; Vert. 44–46.

LONGFIN DRAGONFISH, *Tactostoma macropus.* Family MELANOSTOMIATIDAE
Southern California to Alaska and Japan. Length to 13.5 in. Depth 102 to 1800 ft. Uniform black. Uncommon. D 14–16; A 19–22; Pect. absent; Pelvic 8–10; GR 13–18 + 32–34 = 47–50.

PACIFIC VIPERFISH, *Chauliodus macouni.* Family CHAULIODONTIDAE
Southern California north to Alaska and Japan. Length to 9 in. Depth 240 to 5000 ft. Blackish to dark brown; sides spotted. Uncommon. D 5–7; A 10–12; Pect. 12–13; Pelvic 7–8; LL absent; midlateral scales 56; GR 3 + 8 = 11; Vert. 60.

DAGGERTOOTH, *Anotopterus pharao.* Family ANOTOPTERIDAE
Worldwide in temperate seas; north to Bering Sea and to Japan. Length to 4 ft. 9.5 in., and wt. to 3 lb. 10 oz. Mesopelagic. Silvery to dusky, caudal fin dark. Uncommon. D (adipose fin only); A 14–17; Pect. 12–16; Pelvic 9–11; LLp 75–83; GR none; Vert. 77–83.

SLENDER BARRACUDINA, *Lestidium ringens.* Family PARALEPIDIDAE
Cedros Isl., Baja California, to British Columbia. Length to 8 in. Mesopelagic. Light olivaceous above, silvery on sides. Uncommon. D 9–12; A 28–33; Pect. 11–12; Pelvic 8–9; scales absent.

NORTHERN PEARLEYE, *Benthalbella dentata.* Family SCOPELARCHIDAE
In eastern Pacific from California into Gulf of Alaska. Length to 7 in. Mesopelagic. Brown above, paler below; a bright silvery area on outer margin of eye. Uncommon. D 6–7; A 17–21; Pect. 22–25; Pelvic 9; LLs 56–58.

CALIFORNIA LIZARDFISH, *Synodus lucioceps.* Family SYNODONTIDAE
Guaymas, Mexico, to San Francisco. Length to 25.17 in. Depth 5 to 150 ft. Uniform brown above, tan to whitish below. Uncommon. D 11–13; A 12–14; Vert. 60–63.

PACIFIC BARRELEYE

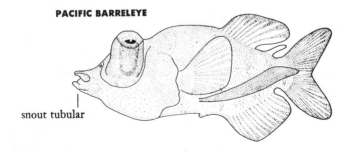

snout tubular

HIGHFIN DRAGONFISH

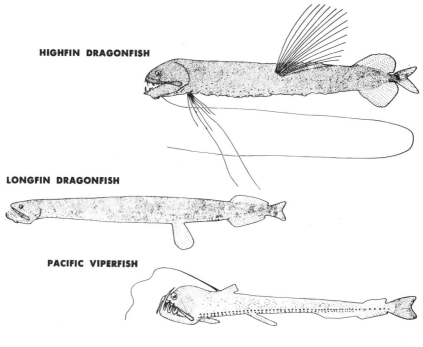

LONGFIN DRAGONFISH

PACIFIC VIPERFISH

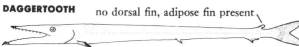

DAGGERTOOTH no dorsal fin, adipose fin present

SLENDER BARRACUDINA

NORTHERN PEARLEYE

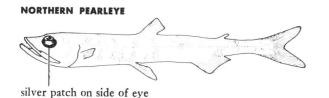

silver patch on side of eye

CALIFORNIA LIZARDFISH

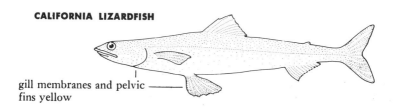

gill membranes and pelvic
fins yellow

LANTERNFISHES, Family Myctophidae*
(Principal sources: Bolin, 1939; Paxton, 1967; Moser & Ahlstrom, 1970)

CALIFORNIA HEADLIGHTFISH, *Diaphus theta.* North Pacific from N. Baja California to Gulf of Alaska and Japan. Length to 4.5 in. Mesopelagic, surface to 2600 ft., usually below 600 ft. D 11–15; A 12–14; Pect. 9–12; Pelvic 7–8; LLs 34–38; GR 5–7 + 12–16; Photophores: VO 5 (3 on same level), AO 4-6 + 4-7, Prc 4; Vert. 34–36.

CALIFORNIA FLASHLIGHTFISH, *Protomyctophum crockeri.* California Current System from S. Baja California to Oregon, and a separate population off Japan. Length to 2.5 in. Mesopelagic, to 1640 ft., rarely at surface. D 11–13; A 20–23; Pect. 14–17; Pelvic 8; GR 4–6 + 13–18 = 17–24; Photophores: VO 4, AO 13–15, Prc 2; Vert. 36–38.

NORTHERN LAMPFISH, *Stenobrachius leucopsarus.* California Current System from northern Baja California to Bering Sea and Japan. Length to 5 in. Mesopelagic, from near surface to 9500 ft. D 12–15; A 14–16; Pect. 8–11; Pelvic 8–10; LLs 35–38; GR 5–6 + 12–15 = 17–20; Photophores: VO 3–5, AO 5–8 + 6–8, Prc 4; Vert. 35–38.

BLUE LANTERNFISH, *Tarletonbeania crenularis.* California Current System from central Baja California to off British Columbia. Length to 5 in. Mesopelagic, from surface at night to 2730 ft. D 11–14; A 17–19; Pect. 11–15; Pelvic 7–8; midlateral scales 45–50; GR 4–6 + 10–12 = 15–18; Photophores: VO 5–7, AO 9–12 + 3–5, Prc 1; Vert. 39–42.

CALIFORNIA LANTERNFISH, *Symbolophorus californiensis.* California Current System from Cedros Isl., Baja California, to Alaska and Japan. Length to 4.5 in. Mesopelagic, from surface at night to 2500 ft. D 13–15; A 19–22; Pect. 16–20; Pelvic 8; LLs 38–42; GR 6–7 + 15–17; Photophores: VO 4, AO 6–7 + 8–10, Prc 2; Vert. 37–40.

MEXICAN LAMPFISH, *Triphoturus mexicanus.* Northern Chile to San Francisco, rare north of Pt. Conception. Length to about 4 in. Mesopelagic, 150 to below 3060 ft. D 13–16; A 14–17; Pect. 8–10; Pelvic 7–9; Photophores: VO 5 (appear as 3), AO 4-6 + 4-6, Prc 4 (continuous with AO series); LLs 35–38; GR 4 + 11–14 = 15–18; Vert. 33–35.

BROADFIN LAMPFISH, *Lampanyctus ritteri.* California Current System from southern Baja California to Bering Sea. Length to 7.5 in. Mesopelagic, from 165 to 3600 ft. D 12–15; A 16–19; Pect. 10–13; Pelvic 8–9; LLs 37–38; GR 4 + 10 = 14; Photophores: VO 4, AO 6–8 + 8–9, Prc 4; Vert. 35–37.

KEY TO THE LANTERNFISHES, Family Myctophidae:

1a Pair of well developed "headlight" photophores present between eyes:

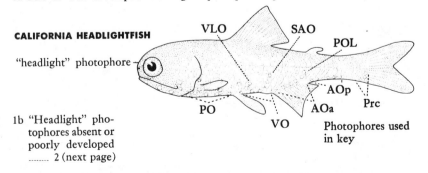

CALIFORNIA HEADLIGHTFISH

"headlight" photophore

1b "Headlight" photophores absent or poorly developed
.... 2 (next page)

Photophores used in key

* Includes 7 of the 32 California members of Family Myctophidae.

2a AO in a continuous series; POL absent:

**CALIFORNIA
FLASHLIGHTFISH**

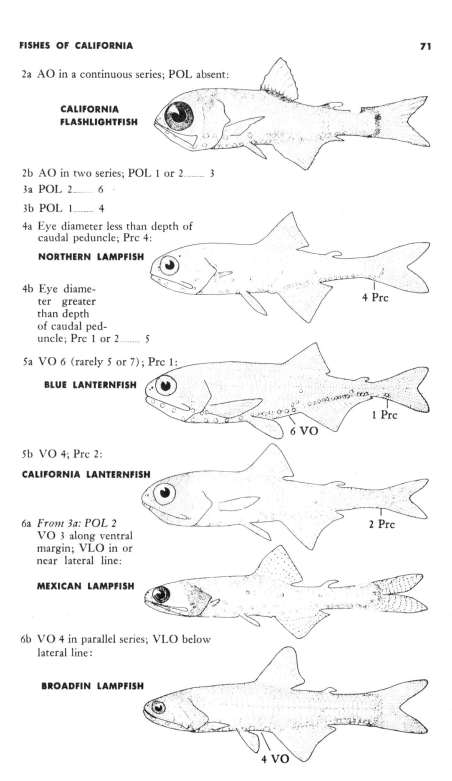

2b AO in two series; POL 1 or 2........ 3

3a POL 2........ 6 ·

3b POL 1........ 4

4a Eye diameter less than depth of
caudal peduncle; Prc 4:

NORTHERN LAMPFISH

4 Prc

4b Eye diame-
ter greater
than depth
of caudal ped-
uncle; Prc 1 or 2........ 5

5a VO 6 (rarely 5 or 7); Prc 1:

BLUE LANTERNFISH

6 VO

1 Prc

5b VO 4; Prc 2:

CALIFORNIA LANTERNFISH

2 Prc

6a *From 3a:* POL 2
VO 3 along ventral
margin; VLO in or
near lateral line:

MEXICAN LAMPFISH

6b VO 4 in parallel series; VLO below
lateral line:

BROADFIN LAMPFISH

4 VO

TOADFISHES, CUSK-EELS, BROTULAS, and CHIHUIL
(Principal sources: Hubbs & Schultz, 1939; Follett, 1970)

SPECKLEFIN MIDSHIPMAN, *Porichthys myriaster.* Family BATRACHOIDIDAE
Magdalena Bay, Baja California (SIO 60–388), to Pt. Conception. Length to 19 in. Shallow to 414 ft. Dark gray to brownish above, pale below; pectoral fins heavily spotted. Common. D II + 36-40; A 33–39; Pelvic I,2; GR lower limb 17; Vert. 46-49.

PLAINFIN MIDSHIPMAN, *Porichthys notatus.* Family BATRACHOIDIDAE
Gulf of California, and from Gorda Bank, Baja California,* to Sitka, Alaska. Length to 15 in. Near surface to 1000 ft. Dark gray to olive-green above, yellowish below. Common. D II + 33–38; A 28–34; Pelvic I,2; GR 1 + 14-16; Vert. 42-45.

SPOTTED CUSK-EEL, *Chilara taylori.* Family OPHIDIIDAE
San Cristobal Bay, Baja California, to N. Oregon. Length to 14.25 in. Depth 4 to over 800 ft. Light brown to cream colored; fish over 4 in. with dark blotches on upper parts. Common. D 198–216; A 156–170; GR 1-4 + 5-9 = 6-12; Vert. 86-91.

BASKETWEAVE CUSK-EEL, *Otophidium scrippsi.* Family OPHIDIIDAE
North of Guaymas, Mexico (LACM 6519), to Pt. Arguello. Length to 10.75 in. Depth 9 to 230 ft. Brownish to olive above, tan below. Uncommon. D 136–153; A 113–119; Vert. 67-69.

RED BROTULA, *Brosmophycis marginata.* Family BROTULIDAE
Ensenada Bay, Baja California, to Petersburg, Alaska. Length to 18 in. Depth 10 to 840 ft. Dark red body with bright red fins. Uncommonly seen, but common in 60 to 80 ft. in rocky areas. D 92–107; A 72–81; Pelvic 2; scales over LL 170; Vert. 63-65.

PURPLE BROTULA, *Oligopus diagrammus.* Family BROTULIDAE
Panama to San Clemente Isl., including Galapagos Isls., Gulf of California, and Guadalupe Isl. Length to 8 in. Depth 18 to 60 ft. Deep purplish-black or slate. Rare. D 95–115; A 76–91; Pect. 24-29; scales in row above LL 97–115.

CHIHUIL, *Bagre panamensis.* Family ARIIDAE
Peru to off Santa Ana River, including Gulf of California. Length to about 20 in. Frequents inshore, shallow areas. Gray above, white below. One California record. D II,6-7; A 27–30; Pect. I,13; Pelvic 6; GR 5-6 + 13-15 = 18-21; Vert. 55-56.

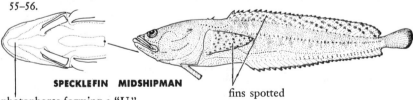

SPECKLEFIN MIDSHIPMAN
photophores forming a "U"   fins spotted

photophores forming a sharp "V"

PLAINFIN MIDSHIPMAN

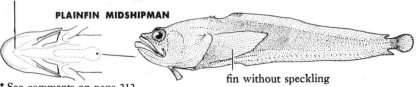

* See comments on page 212.   fin without speckling

SPOTTED CUSK-EEL more than 190 dorsal soft-rays

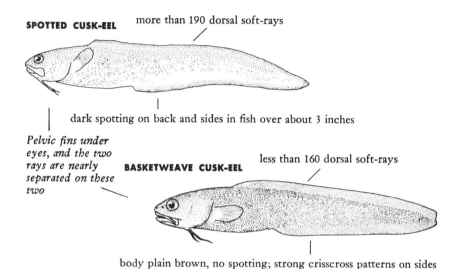

dark spotting on back and sides in fish over about 3 inches

Pelvic fins under eyes, and the two rays are nearly separated on these two

BASKETWEAVE CUSK-EEL less than 160 dorsal soft-rays

body plain brown, no spotting; strong crisscross patterns on sides

lateral lines contiguous

RED BROTULA caudal fin distinct, separate from dorsal and anal fins

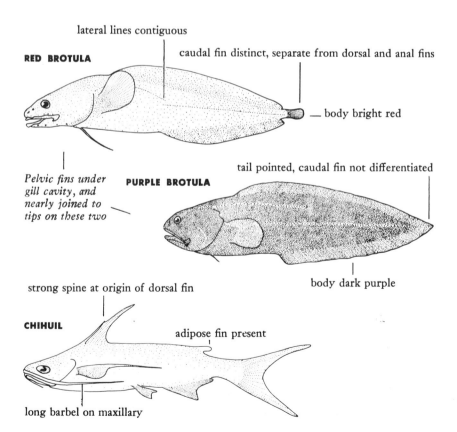

— body bright red

Pelvic fins under gill cavity, and nearly joined to tips on these two

PURPLE BROTULA tail pointed, caudal fin not differentiated

body dark purple

strong spine at origin of dorsal fin

CHIHUIL adipose fin present

long barbel on maxillary

CLINGFISHES, Family Gobiesocidae
(Principal sources: Briggs, 1955; Greenfield & Wiley, 1968)

BEARDED CLINGFISH, Gobiesox papillifer. Panama Bay to San Pedro. Length to 2.25 in. Intertidal. Light brown to gray, often with darker spotting. Uncommon. D 14-15 (12-13) *; A 9-11 (7-9) *; Pect. 23-25.

CALIFORNIA CLINGFISH, Gobiesox rhessodon. San Bartolome Bay, Baja California, to Santa Cruz Isl. (LACM 20623) and Gaviota on the mainland (SIO 60-509), including Guadalupe Isl. Length to 2.5 in. Depth, surface to 35 ft. Gray to brown, with darker brown spotting. Uncommon. D 12-14 (10-12) *; A 11-12 (9-10) *; Pect. 18-21.

NORTHERN CLINGFISH, Gobiesox maeandricus. Between Guadalupe Isl. and mainland of Baja California (on drift kelp), to Mud Bay, Revillagigedo Isl., Alaska (CAS 13632). Length to 6.5 in. Intertidal and in kelp canopy. Uniform gray-brown, translucent on underparts. Common, but rare south of Pt. Conception. D 14-16 (12-14) *; A 13-15 (11-13) *; Pect. 21-23; Vert. 32-34.

LINED CLINGFISH, Gobiesox eugrammus. Guadalupe Isl., and on mainland from south side of Pt. Banda, Baja California, to Bird Rock, San Diego Co. Length to 2.25 in. Depth 30 to 270 ft. Translucent cream; orange to red markings on upper parts and head; dorsal and caudal fins black with white margin; eye with red outer and yellow inner rings around black pupil. Rare. D 14-15 (11-13) *; A 11-13 (8-10) *; Pect. 21-26; Vert. 26-29.

SLENDER CLINGFISH, Rimicola eigenmanni. Arroyo Mesquital, San Juanico Bay, Baja California, to Palos Verdes Peninsula. Length to 2.25 in. Intertidal. Uniform tan, but variable with surroundings including bright green to red, brown, olive, or yellow. Uncommon. D 5-8; A 5-8; Pect. 17-19; Vert. 33-35.

KELP CLINGFISH, Rimicola muscarum. Pt. Banda (S. side NW of Pt. Arbolitos), Baja California (SIO 59-305), to Goose Isl., British Columbia. Length to 2.34 in. Kelp canopy, rarely in tidepools. Variable in color, from green to various shades of brown. Uncommon. D 6-8; A 6-8; Pect. 14-17; LL absent.

SOUTHERN CLINGFISH, Rimicola dimorpha. San Benito Isls., Baja California, to northern Channel Islands. Length to 1.35 in. Life color not known. Rare. D 6-7; A 6-8; Pect. 15-16.

---

* Dorsal and anal fin counts in ( ) do not include hidden soft-rays. See comment on page 212.

KEY TO THE CLINGFISHES, Family Gobiesocidae:

1a Dorsal fin with 5-8 soft-rays and widely separated from caudal fin: disc small, length 5.4-6.6 into standard length; upper lip about same width at front as at sides......... 5 (next page)

1b Dorsal fin with 10-16 soft-rays and contiguous to caudal fin; disc large, length 2.6-3.9 into standard length; upper lip broad, wider at front of snout than at sides......... 2

2a Rim of snout with numerous barbel-like papillae:

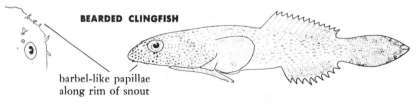

BEARDED CLINGFISH

barbel-like papillae
along rim of snout

2b Rim of snout without barbel-like papillae......... 3 (next page)

3a Free posterior margin of fleshy pectoral pad complete, extending dorsally to a point opposite upper gill membrane attachment; lower incisors trifid:

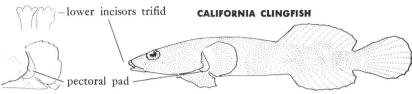

— lower incisors trifid   **CALIFORNIA CLINGFISH**

pectoral pad

3b Free posterior margin of fleshy pectoral pad incomplete, not extending dorsally as far as upper gill membrane attachment; lower incisors rounded with a single cusp........ 4

4a Eye small, 5.5–8.3 into head length and 1.2–1.9 into bony interorbital space; posterior nostril just in front of anterior edge of eye:

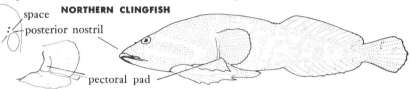

space   **NORTHERN CLINGFISH**

posterior nostril

pectoral pad

4b Eye large, 3.7–5.1 into head length and 0.8–1.4 into bony interorbital space; posterior nostril directly above anterior edge of eye:

LINED CLINGFISH

posterior nostril
on edge of eye

5a *From 1a: dorsal fin widely separated from caudal fin*
The 2 pairs of pores near tip of snout arranged approximately parallel; caudal peduncle deep, its least depth 1.7–2.6 into its length; pectoral rays 17–19:

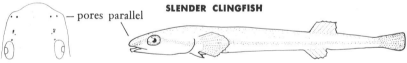

— pores parallel   **SLENDER CLINGFISH**

5b The inner pore of each pair near tip of snout lies posterior to the outer; caudal peduncle shallow, its least depth 2.8–4.2 into its length; pectoral rays 14–17........ 6

6a Eye into bony interorbital 1.2–1.8; males with a small genital papilla:

inner pore   **KELP CLINGFISH**
posterior
to outer

6b Eye into bony interorbital 1.0–1.2; males with a large genital papilla:

SOUTHERN CLINGFISH

genital papilla

GRENADIERS, CODLINGS, HAKE, and CODFISHES
(Principal sources: Svetovidov, 1948; Clemens & Wilby, 1961; Fitch & Barker, 1972)

CALIFORNIA RATTAIL, *Nezumia stelgidolepis*. Family MACROURIDAE
Cedros Isl., Baja California, to west of Trinidad Head (CAS 17168). Length to
17.5 in. Depth 200 to 2000+ ft. Uniform black to dusky. Uncommon. D II,
8–11 + 138–153; A 123–135; GR 0–2 + 7–8; Vert. 86–90.

PACIFIC RATTAIL, *Coryphaenoides acrolepis*. Family MACROURIDAE
Guadalupe Isl. (LACM 31428) to Alaska and to Japan. Length to about 2 ft.
Mesopelagic, 2300 to 6000 ft. Uniform dusky. Uncommon. D II,8–11 + 109–111;
A 103–105; Pect. 20; Pelvic 10; GR 0 + 6–7 = 6–7; Vert. 86.

HUNDRED-FATHOM CODLING, *Physiculus rastrelliger*. Family MORIDAE
Panama to Eureka. Length to 8 in. Depths around 1000 ft. Uniform dusky. Uncommon. D 8–11 + 52–62; A 56–63; Pect. 24–28; Pelvic 7; LLp 99–105; GR 7–9
+ 18–22 = 26–30.

FINESCALE CODLING, *Antimora microlepis*. Family MORIDAE
Worldwide; in eastern Pacific from Chile to Bering Sea and Japan. Length to at
least 26 in. Depth 1200 to 10,000 ft. Uniform dusky. Uncommon. D 4–5 + 50–55;
A 37–42; Pect. 20; Pelvic 6–7; GR 5 + 15 = 20; Vert. 57–58.

PACIFIC HAKE, *Merluccius productus*. Family MERLUCCIIDAE
Gulf of California (isolated population), and from Magdalena Bay, Baja California, to Alaska and Asiatic coast. Length to 3 ft. Depth, from near surface to
3000 ft. Uniform gray to dusky brown, with brassy overtones. Common. D 10–13
+ 37–43; A 37–44; Pect. 14–16; Pelvic 6–8; LLs 130–135; GR 4–5 + 14–17 = 18–
21; Vert. 52–55.

PACIFIC COD, *Gadus macrocephalus*. Family GADIDAE
Santa Monica Reef to Bering Sea and into Yellow Sea. Length to 45 in. Depth
40 to 1200 ft. Gray to brown above, pale below; brown spots on upper parts.
Uncommon. D 11–16 + 14–21 + 14–21; A 16–25 + 14–22; Pelvic 6–7; GR 18 +
23–24 = 41–42; Vert. 51–56.

PACIFIC TOMCOD, *Microgadus proximus*. Family GADIDAE
Pt. Sal to Unalaska Isl., Alaska. Length to 12 in. Depth, near surface to 720 ft.
Uniform brown to olive-green above, white below. Common. D 11–15 + 16–21
+ 18–22; A 20–29 + 18–24; Pelvic 6–7; GR 3–5 + 18–23 = 22–28; Vert. 53–60.

WALLEYE POLLOCK, *Theragra chalcogramma*. Family GADIDAE
Carmel to Bering Sea and Japan. Length to 3 ft. Depth, near surface to 690 ft.
Brownish to olive-green with faint mottling above, whitish below. Rare. D 10–13
+ 12–18 + 14–20; A 15–22 + 15–21; Pelvic 6–7; GRt 34–40, 5–7 on upper limb;
Vert. 50.

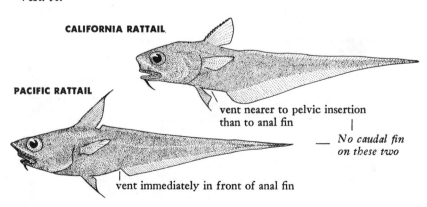

CALIFORNIA RATTAIL

PACIFIC RATTAIL

vent nearer to pelvic insertion
than to anal fin

— *No caudal fin
on these two*

vent immediately in front of anal fin

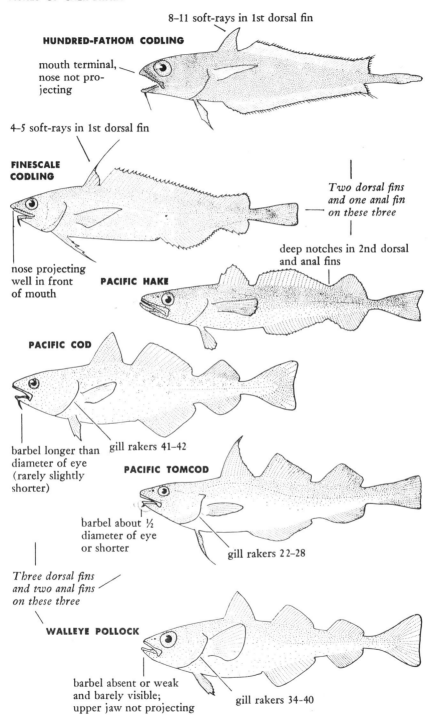

8–11 soft-rays in 1st dorsal fin

HUNDRED-FATHOM CODLING

mouth terminal, nose not projecting

4–5 soft-rays in 1st dorsal fin

FINESCALE CODLING

Two dorsal fins and one anal fin on these three

deep notches in 2nd dorsal and anal fins

nose projecting well in front of mouth

PACIFIC HAKE

PACIFIC COD

barbel longer than diameter of eye (rarely slightly shorter)

gill rakers 41–42

PACIFIC TOMCOD

barbel about ½ diameter of eye or shorter

gill rakers 22–28

Three dorsal fins and two anal fins on these three

WALLEYE POLLOCK

barbel absent or weak and barely visible; upper jaw not projecting

gill rakers 34–40

EELPOUTS, Family Zoarcidae * [1]
(Principal sources: Schultz, 1936; Shmidt, 1950; Bayliff, 1959;
Clemens & Wilby, 1961; Shelly Johnson* [2])

BEARDED EELPOUT, Lyconema barbatum.   San Quintin Bay, Baja California, to Mack Arch, Oregon. Length to 6.7 in. Depth 270 to 1224 ft. The only eelpout with dark brown spots on sides. Uncommon. D 103; A 90; Pect. 15.

BLACK EELPOUT, Lycodes diapterus.   San Diego to Bering Sea and Sea of Japan. Length to 12.5 in. Depth 180 to 3456 ft. Belly black; pelvic, pectoral, and anal fins blue-black. Common in trawls. D 104-117; A 94-107; Pect. 18-25; Pelvic 3; Vert. 121-125.

FLATCHEEK EELPOUT, Embryx crotalina.   Santa Barbara Isl. to Shumagin Isls., Alaska. Length to 15.25 in. Depth 2800 to 4110 ft. Dark brown with light colored, non-overlapping scale pockets. Rare. D 120-122; A 111-114; Pect. 15-17.

BIGFIN EELPOUT, Aprodon cortezianus.   San Diego to Queen Charlotte Sound, British Columbia. Length to 19.5 in. Depth 300 to 2034 ft. Common in trawls. D 105-108; A 89-90; Pect. 20-21; Pelvic 3; GR 2 + 11 = 13; Vert. 105-115.

BLACKBELLY EELPOUT, Lycodopsis pacifica.   Ensenada to Afognak Isl., Alaska. Length to 14 in. Depth 30 to 1308 ft. Gray to reddish-brown; black spot in anterior part of dorsal fin. Common. D 90-107; A 70-90; Pect. 16-19; Pelvic 3; GR 0-2 + 8-12 = 8-12; Vert. 97-108.

MIDWATER EELPOUT, Melanostigma pammelas.   San Diego to between Vancouver Isl. and Queen Charlotte Isl., British Columbia. Length to 4.2 in. Depth 314 to 7200 ft. The only pelagic California eelpout. Intense black on head and abdomen, lighter on rest of body. Uncommon. D 73-88; A 64-75; Pect. 6-8; Vert. 87-90.

TWOLINE EELPOUT, Bothrocara brunneum.   Los Coronados Isls., Baja California, to Sea of Okhotsk, USSR. Length to 25.4 in., the largest California eelpout. Depth 654 to 4536 ft. Common. D 107-112; A 92-96; Pect. 14-17; GR 3-5 + 14-15 = 18-19.

SOFT EELPOUT, Bothrocara molle.   Ensenada to Avacha Bay, USSR. Length to 5.5 in. Depth 2900 to 5900 ft. Body brown, dorsal and anal fins edged with black. Uncommon. D 100-107; A 89-95; Pelvics absent.

BLACKMOUTH EELPOUT, Lycodapus fierasfer.   San Diego to Bering Sea. Length to 6 in. Depth 162 to 6486 ft. Body pearly with fine black speckling, jaws and lining of mouth jet-black. Rare. D 82-85; A 70-74; Pect. 6-8; Pelvics absent.

PALLID EELPOUT, Lycodapus mandibularis.   Port Hueneme to Ratz Pt., Alaska. Length to 6.75 in. Depth 192 to 1758 ft. Pale tan with fine speckling. Rare. D 86-88; A 76-78; Pelvics absent.

KEY TO THE EELPOUTS, Family Zoarcidae:

1a Pelvic fins absent................   6 (next page)

1b Pelvic fins present................   2

2a Fringe of minute barbels or cirri on underside of lower jaw:

BEARDED EELPOUT

cirri under jaw

2b Underside of lower jaw without cirri........   3

3a Pectoral fin deeply notched; vomer with a patch of teeth:

BLACK EELPOUT

3b (next page)

pectoral fin notched

* [1] Includes 10 of the 18 California members of this family.
* [2] See comments on page 212.

3b Pectoral fin not notched; vomer without teeth........ 4

4a Scales present on operculum:

   FLATCHEEK EELPOUT

                    scales covering 1st ⅓ of fin rays`

4b No scales on operculum........ 5

5a Palatine teeth present:

      BIGFIN EELPOUT

5b Palatine teeth absent:

   BLACKBELLY EELPOUT

6a *From 1a: pelvic fins absent*   `belly black`
   Opercular opening a small round hole above pectoral fin base:

   MIDWATER EELPOUT

       opercular opening ____

6b Opercular openings extending onto ventral surface 7

7a Gill membranes free from isthmus 9

7b Gill membranes attached to isthmus........ 8

8a Lateral line in two segments, the lowermost extending to caudal fin; gill rakers
   short, blunt: lateral line discontinuous

TWOLINE EELPOUT

8b Lateral line continuous but not reaching past middle of body; gill rakers long,
   pointed:
      SOFT EELPOUT

9a *From 7a: gill membranes free from isthmus*
   Six or more teeth on vomer; top of head concave in side view:

   BLACKMOUTH EELPOUT

9b One or 2 teeth
   on vomer; top   top of head flat to convex ___
   of head convex
   or flat in side view: **PALLID EELPOUT**

FLYINGFISHES, Family Exocoetidae, and HALFBEAKS, Family Hemiramphidae
(Principal sources: Meek & Hildebrand, 1923–1928; Bruun, 1935;
Fitch & Lavenberg, 1971)

SHARPCHIN FLYINGFISH, *Fodiator acutus*. Family EXOCOETIDAE
Worldwide in warmer seas; in eastern Pacific from Peru to Goleta, including the
Galapagos Isls. Length to 9.25 in. Dark blue above, silver below. Rare north of
San Diego. D 9–10; A 9–11; predorsal scales 24–26; GR 7–8 + 21–26; Vert. 39–41.

BLACKWING FLYINGFISH, *Hirundichthys rondeletii*. Family EXOCOETIDAE
Tropical waters of Atlantic and Pacific, north to about 150 mi. SW of San
Diego. Not recorded in California. D 10–12; A 11–13; Pect. 16–18; Pelvic 6; pre-
dorsal scales 27–32; Vert. 43.

BLOTCHWING FLYINGFISH, *Cypselurus heterurus*. Family EXOCOETIDAE
Worldwide in tropical seas; north on our coast to Santa Catalina Isl. Length to
about 16 in. Pectorals with a light band in center bordered by dusky-gray, black
posteriorly. Uncommon. D 12–14; A 8–10; Pect. 15–16; GR 5–7 + 15–17; predorsal scales 28–41; Vert. 47–49.

CALIFORNIA FLYINGFISH, *Cypselurus californicus*. Family EXOCOETIDAE
Cape San Lucas, Baja California, to Astoria, Oregon. Length to 19 in. Epipelagic.
Pectorals uniform dusky with a clear edge. Common in southern California, rare
north of Pt. Conception. D 9–13; A 9–12; Pect. 15; Pelvic 6; predorsal scales
47–50; midlateral scales 64–70; GR 8 + 13 = 21; Vert. 48–51.

RIBBON HALFBEAK, *Euleptorhamphus longirostris*. Family HEMIRAMPHIDAE
Worldwide in tropical seas; in eastern Pacific from Galapagos Isls. to S. California. Length to 18 in. Greenish above, silver below. Rare. D 21–25; A 21–23;
Pect. 8–9; Pelvic 6–9; predorsal scales 53–72; GR 6–8 + 18–23 = 25–31; Vert.
70–74.

LONGFIN HALFBEAK, *Hemiramphus saltator*. Family HEMIRAMPHIDAE
Ecuador to California, including the Galapagos Isls. Length to 18 in. Dusky-
brown above, sides silver. Rare. D 13–14; A 11–12; midlateral scales 53–61; GR
26–27 on lower limb.

CALIFORNIA HALFBEAK, *Hyporhamphus rosae*. Family HEMIRAMPHIDAE
Mazatlan * to Santa Ana River (CAS 37984). Length to 6 in. Back greenish with
silvery stripes along sides. Rare. D 14; A 14; midlateral scales 58–65.

SILVERSTRIPE HALFBEAK, *Hyporhamphus unifasciatus*. Family HEMIRAMPHIDAE
Peru to San Diego, including the Galapagos Isls. Length to 12 in. Near surface,
shallow waters. Greenish above, silver below. Rare. D 13–16; A 15–17; midlateral scales 52–59; GR 8–12 + 20–30; Vert. 51–52.

KEY TO THE FLYINGFISHES, Family Exocoetidae, and HALFBEAKS, Family Hemiramphidae:
1a Tip of pectoral fins do not reach pelvic fin base........ 5 (Halfbeaks, next page)
1b Tip of pectoral fins extend beyond base of pelvic fins........ 2 (Flyingfishes)

2a Pectoral fins not extending beyond insertion of
    dorsal fin; snout longer than eye diameter:

SHARPCHIN FLYINGFISH

2b Pectoral fins extend well
    beyond insertion of dorsal
    fin; snout shorter than eye diameter........ 3   juveniles
                                                      with beak
* See comments on page 212.

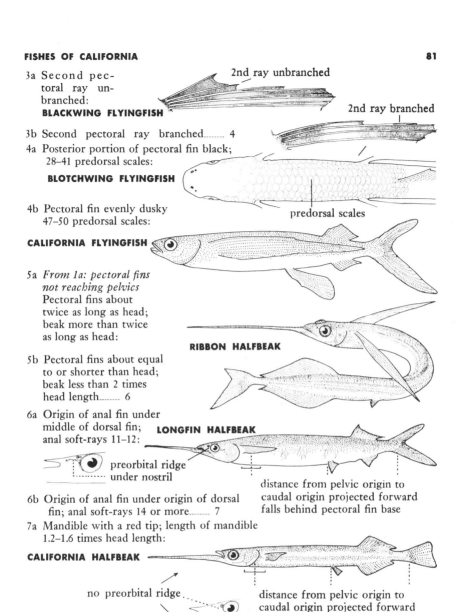

3a Second pec-
   toral ray un-
   branched:
   BLACKWING FLYINGFISH

2nd ray unbranched

2nd ray branched

3b Second pectoral ray branched........ 4

4a Posterior portion of pectoral fin black;
   28–41 predorsal scales:

   BLOTCHWING FLYINGFISH

4b Pectoral fin evenly dusky
   47–50 predorsal scales:

predorsal scales

CALIFORNIA FLYINGFISH

5a *From 1a: pectoral fins
   not reaching pelvics*
   Pectoral fins about
   twice as long as head;
   beak more than twice
   as long as head:

   RIBBON HALFBEAK

5b Pectoral fins about equal
   to or shorter than head;
   beak less than 2 times
   head length........ 6

6a Origin of anal fin under
   middle of dorsal fin;   **LONGFIN HALFBEAK**
   anal soft-rays 11–12:

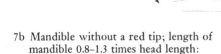

preorbital ridge
under nostril

distance from pelvic origin to
caudal origin projected forward
falls behind pectoral fin base

6b Origin of anal fin under origin of dorsal
   fin; anal soft-rays 14 or more........ 7

7a Mandible with a red tip; length of mandible
   1.2–1.6 times head length:

CALIFORNIA HALFBEAK

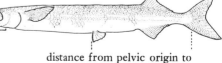

no preorbital ridge

distance from pelvic origin to
caudal origin projected forward
falls between pectoral base and
preoperculum

7b Mandible without a red tip; length of
   mandible 0.8–1.3 times head length:

SILVERSTRIPE HALFBEAK

distance from pelvic origin to
caudal origin projected forward
falls between preopercle and
mouth

NEEDLEFISH, SAURY, KILLIFISH, and SILVERSIDES

CALIFORNIA NEEDLEFISH, *Strongylura exilis.* Family BELONIDAE
Peru to San Francisco, including the Galapagos Isls. Length to 3 ft. Shallow
water to about 300 ft. Greenish-blue above, silver on sides and belly; teeth green.
Common south of central Baja California. D 0-I,12–16; A 0-I,15–20; GR none;
Vert. 68–74.

PACIFIC SAURY, *Cololabis saira.* Family SCOMBERESOCIDAE
Revillagigedo Isls., Mexico (LACM 6823), to Gulf of Alaska and Japan. Length
reported to 14 in., but largest measured is 13.5 in. Epipelagic. Bright blue on
back, metallic silver on sides. Common offshore. D 9–12 + 4–6 finlets; A 12–
15 + 4-7 finlets; Pect. 7–14; Pelvic 6; scales above midline 120–129; Vert. 63–67.

CALIFORNIA KILLIFISH, *Fundulus parvipinnis.* Family CYPRINODONTIDAE
Almejas Bay, Baja California (UCLA W 52–249), to Morro Bay. Length to 4.25
in. Olive-green above, yellowish-brown below; males dark brown on back during breeding time. Common in bays of southern California. D 12–15; A 11–13;
midlateral scales 31–37; GR 0-1 + 7–10 = 7–11; Vert. 34–37.

CALIFORNIA GRUNION, *Leuresthes tenuis.* Family ATHERINIDAE
Magdalena Bay (UCLA W 55-115), to San Francisco. Length to 7.25 in. Spawn on
sandy beaches at high tides, taken to 60 ft. Greenish above, silver on sides with
a lateral stripe. Common south of Pt. Conception. D V-VII + I, 9–10; A I,
21–24; midlateral scales 75; GR 5–7 + 24–29 = 30–35; Vert. 47–50.

JACKSMELT, *Atherinopsis californiensis.* Family ATHERINIDAE
Santa Maria Bay, Baja California, to Yaquina, Oregon. Length reported to 22
in., largest measured is 17.5 in. Greenish-blue above, silvery on sides with a
midline stripe. Common throughout the inshore area and in bays. D V–IX +
I,11–14; A I,21–26; midlateral scales about 75; Vert. 50–54.

TOPSMELT, *Atherinops affinis.* Family ATHERINIDAE
Gulf of California to 4 mi. W of Sooke Harbour, Vancouver Isl., B. C.,
including Guadalupe Isl. Length to 14.4 in. Bright green above, silvery below
with a midline stripe. Common in bays, sloughs, and in kelp beds. D V–IX +
I,8–14; A I,19–25; Pect. 13; midlateral scales 63–65; GR 4-8 + 21–34 = 27–41;
Vert. 45–52.

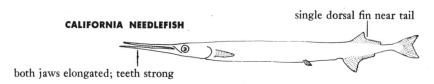

CALIFORNIA NEEDLEFISH   single dorsal fin near tail

both jaws elongated; teeth strong

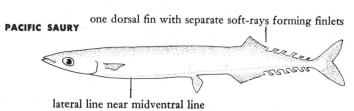

PACIFIC SAURY   one dorsal fin with separate soft-rays forming finlets

lateral line near midventral line

CALIFORNIA KILLIFISH   one dorsal fin   dorsal and caudal
                                                                      fins rounded

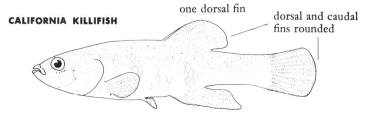

KEY TO THE SILVERSIDES, Family Atherinidae:

1a No teeth on jaws, or teeth minute:

premaxillaries   7–9 scales between dorsal fins
pulled downward   **CALIFORNIA GRUNION**

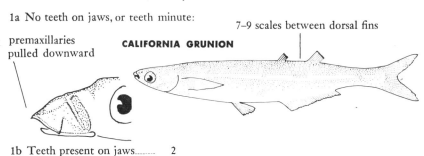

1b Teeth present on jaws........ 2

2a Bands of unforked teeth on jaws; 10–12 scales between dorsal fins:

JACKSMELT

teeth not forked,   10–12 scales between dorsal fins
arranged in several
bands on each jaw

premaxillaries
pulled downward

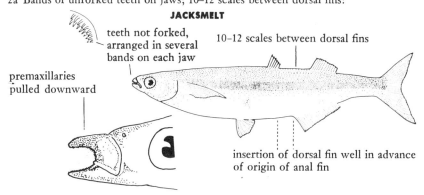

insertion of dorsal fin well in advance
of origin of anal fin

2b A single row of forked teeth present on jaws; 5–8 scales between dorsal fins:

5–8 scales between dorsal fins

TOPSMELT

teeth forked, in one
row on each jaw

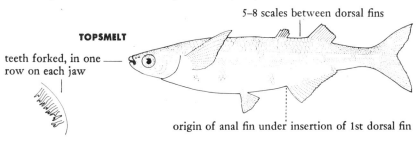

origin of anal fin under insertion of 1st dorsal fin

FROGFISH, BATFISH, SEADEVIL, OREO, DORY, and OPAH
(Principal source: Fitch & Lavenberg, 1968)

ROUGHJAW FROGFISH, *Antennarius avalonis.* Family ANTENNARIIDAE
Peru to Santa Catalina Isl., including Gulf of California. Length to 13.5 in.
Depth, near surface to 360 ft. Brown to gray, with dark brown spotting. Rare.
D III,12–14; A 8–9; Pect. 13; Pelvic I,5; GR rudimentary.

SPOTTED BATFISH, *Zalieutes elater.* Family OGCOCEPHALIDAE
Peru to Pt. Conception. Length to 6 in. Depth 60 to 372 ft. Light olive to tan,
with dark brown spotting. Rare.

WARTED SEADEVIL, *Cryptopsaras couesii.* Family CERATIIDAE
Found in all oceans; north to Santa Cruz on our coast. Length to 8 in. Depth
1440 to 5000 ft. Uniform black. Rare. D I + I (embedded) + 4–5; A 4; Pect. 16.

OXEYE OREO, *Allocyttus verrucosus.* Family OREOSOMATIDAE
Gorda Pt., Mendocino Co., to Japan. Length to 15 in. Moderate depths to 1800
ft. Dark brown to tan. Rare. D VI,30–34; A II–III,28–33; Pelvic I,6; LLs 88–90.

MIRROR DORY, *Zenopsis nebulosa.* Family ZEIDAE
Found in most warm seas; taken along California coast from Ventura to Santa
Cruz. Length to 19 in. Depth 100 to 1000+ ft. Uniform blackish. Rare. D VIII–
IX + 25–27; A III,25–26; Pect. 12–13; Pelvic I,5.

OPAH, *Lampris regius.* Family LAMPRIDIDAE
Worldwide in warm seas; in eastern Pacific from Cape San Lucas, Baja California,
to Ice Bay, Alaska, and over to Japan. Length recorded to 4.5 ft., and wt. to 160
lbs., reported to 6 ft. Depth, surface to 1680 ft. Body blue with white spots; fins
red; eye yellow. Uncommon. D O–II,46–50; A O–I,33–39; Pect. 20–22; Pelvic
14; LLs approx. 86; GR 2–3 + 13–14 = 15–16; Vert. 43–45.

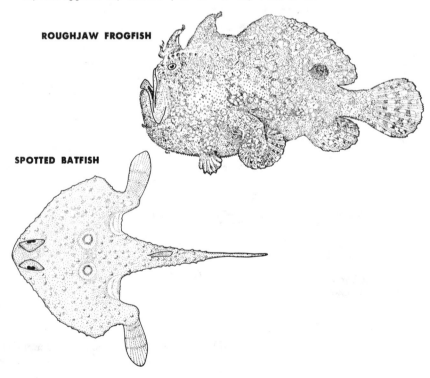

ROUGHJAW FROGFISH

SPOTTED BATFISH

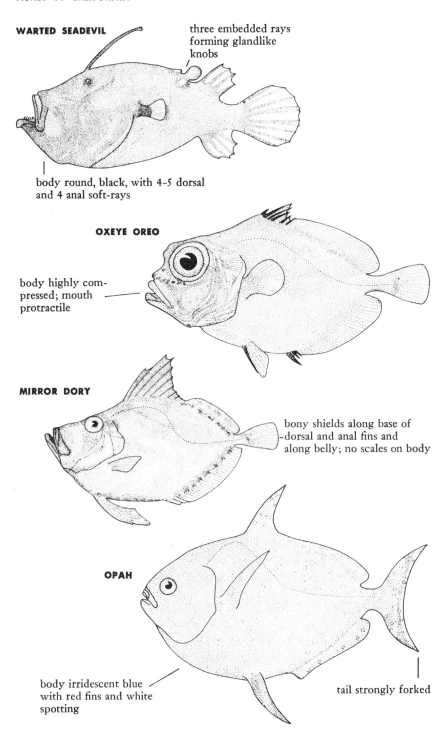

WARTED SEADEVIL

three embedded rays
forming glandlike
knobs

body round, black, with 4-5 dorsal
and 4 anal soft-rays

OXEYE OREO

body highly com-
pressed; mouth
protractile

MIRROR DORY

bony shields along base of
dorsal and anal fins and
along belly; no scales on body

OPAH

body irridescent blue
with red fins and white
spotting

tail strongly forked

BIGSCALES, CRESTFISH, and OARFISH

CRESTED BIGSCALE, *Poromitra crassiceps*.   Family MELAMPHAIDAE
Atlantic and Pacific oceans; in eastern Pacific from Chile to Gulf of Alaska. Length to about 5.5 or 6 in. Mesopelagic, to depths of 6000 ft. Uniform black. Uncommon. D III,12–13; A I–II,9; Pect. 14; Pelvic I,7–8; midlateral scales approx. 23–28; GR about 15 on lower limb.

TWOSPINE BIGSCALE, *Scopelogadus mizolepis*.   Family MELAMPHAIDAE
Eastern Pacific subspecies, *S. m. bispinosus*, from northern Chile to northern California. Length to 5 in. Mesopelagic, from 390 to 4800 ft. Black with lighter scale pockets. Uncommon. D II,10–12; A I + 7–9; Pect. 14–15; Pelvic I,7; midlateral scales less than 15; GR 6–9 + 15–18; Vert. 24–26.

HIGHBROW CRESTFISH, *Lophotus cristatus*.   Family LOPHOTIDAE
Worldwide in warmer seas; in eastern Pacific north to Pt. Dume.* Length to almost 40 in., and wt. to 6 lbs. Depth, surface to 300 ft. Body silvery; dorsal, anal, and caudal fins red. Rare.

OARFISH, *Regalecus glesne*.   Family REGALECIDAE
Worldwide in lower latitudes; in eastern Pacific from Chile to Topanga Canyon, Santa Monica Bay. Length to 35 ft., and wt. to 500 lbs. Depth, surface to 1350 ft. Body silvery with darker bands and blotches; dorsal fin red. Rare. D 340+; Pect. 12; Pelvic 1; Vert. 136+.

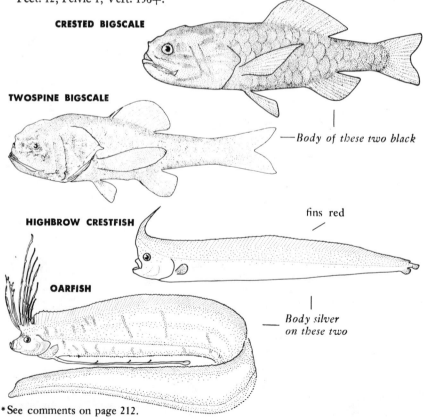

CRESTED BIGSCALE

TWOSPINE BIGSCALE

—*Body of these two black*

fins red

HIGHBROW CRESTFISH

OARFISH

— *Body silver on these two*

*See comments on page 212.

RIBBONFISHES, Family Trachipteridae
(Principal sources: Fitch, 1964, 1967)

SCALLOPED RIBBONFISH, *Zu cristatus*. All tropical seas; in eastern Pacific from Galapagos Isls. to Newport Beach. Length to 40 in., and wt. to 6 lbs. Shallow water to 300 ft. Body silver with about six dark vertical bars. Rare. D 6 + 115–138; A absent; Pect. 11–12; Pelvic 5–6; LLs 114–118; GRt 8–11; Vert. 63.

POLKADOT RIBBONFISH, *Desmodema polysticta*. Worldwide in warm seas; in eastern Pacific from Ecuador to off Monterey. Mesopelagic. Silvery with numerous round spots in young, fading in larger fish. Rare. D 187–215; A absent; Pect. 12–14; Pelvic 9–10; LLs 262–306; GRt 11–14; Vert. 104–109.

KING-OF-THE-SALMON, *Trachipterus altivelis*. Chile to Alaska. Length to about 6 ft. Surface to 1800 ft. Body silvery to dusky with spotting in young fish. Uncommon. D 3–6 + 160–185; A absent; Pect. 10–11; Pelvic 6–7; LLs 106–122; GR 3–5 + 9–11 = 12–16; Vert. 90–94.

TAPERTAIL RIBBONFISH, *Trachipterus fukuzakii*. Chile to Alamitos Bay. Length to about 56 in. Epipelagic and mesopelagic. Body metallic silver with several dark blotches on sides. Rare. D 5–6 + 157–168 (Fitch, 1967 has total dorsal rays 153–172 in additional specimens); A absent; Pect. 11–13; Pelvic 5; LLs 91–105; Vert. 69–72.

SCALLOPED RIBBONFISH

belly scalloped

caudal rays
parallel
to body axis

POLKADOT RIBBONFISH

KING-OF-THE-SALMON

*Caudal rays nearly
vertical on these
two*

TAPERTAIL RIBBONFISH

body narrows here

STICKLEBACKS and SNIPEFISH
(Principal source: Miller & Hubbs, 1969)

TUBESNOUT, *Aulorhynchus flavidus*. Family GASTEROSTEIDAE
Pt. Rompiente, Baja California (LACM 32052), to Sitka, Alaska. Length to 7 in. Surface to 100 ft. Light tan with dark cross bars. Uncommon. D XXIII to XXVI free spines + 9–11; A I,9–10; Pelvic I,4; GRt 25–31; Vert. 54–56.

THREESPINE STICKLEBACK, *Gasterosteus aculeatus*. Family GASTEROSTEIDAE
Rio Rosario, Baja California, to Japan; anadromous form ranges from about Monterey northward. Length to 4 in. Surface to 90 ft. Olive to dusky above, silver below; male blackish with coppery head in springtime. Common. D II–III free spines + I,10–13; A I,7–12; Pect. 17–23; Pelvic I,0–2; GR 4–8 + 12–18 = 18–23; Vert. 30–33.

SLENDER SNIPEFISH, *Macrorhamphosus gracilis*. Family CENTRISCIDAE
Worldwide in warm seas; in eastern Pacific north to Santa Monica Bay. Length to 4.25 in. (6 in. in South Africa). Surface to 700 ft. Silvery, with reddish or greenish, darker on back. Common. D IV–VIII + 11–13; A 18–19; Vert. 23.

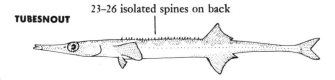

TUBESNOUT — 23–26 isolated spines on back

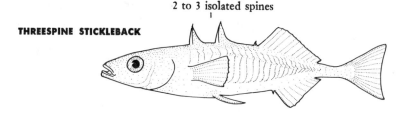

THREESPINE STICKLEBACK — 2 to 3 isolated spines

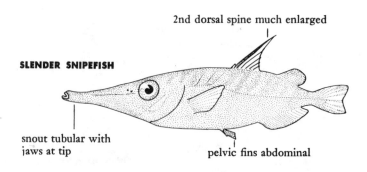

SLENDER SNIPEFISH — 2nd dorsal spine much enlarged — snout tubular with jaws at tip — pelvic fins abdominal

SEAHORSE and PIPEFISHES, Family Syngnathidae * [1]
(Principal sources: Herald, 1940, 1941; Hubbs & Hinton, 1963)

PACIFIC SEAHORSE, *Hippocampus ingens*. Northern Peru to San Diego (a provisional record to San Francisco), including Galapagos Isls. and Gulf of California. Length to 12 in. Shallow areas. Body blackish, with white spotting. Rare. D 18–21; A 4-5; Pect. 15–17; body rings 11–13; tail rings 36–40.

KELP PIPEFISH, *Syngnathus californiensis*. Santa Maria Bay, Baja California (UCLA W 51-264), to around San Francisco. Length to 19.5 in. Green to brown, matching habitat background. Common; found primarily in kelp beds. D 36–47; A 3–5; Pect. 12–14; body rings 17–22; tail rings 44–50; Vert. 65–74.

BAY PIPEFISH, *Syngnathus leptorhynchus*.* [2] Black Warrior Lagoon, Baja California (UCLA W 59-94), to Sitka, Alaska. Length to 13 in. Pale olive-green to dark green or brown. Common in eelgrass beds of bays. D 28–44; A 3–5; Pect. 11–13; body rings 17–20; tail rings 36–46; Vert. 56–64.

SNUBNOSE PIPEFISH, *Syngnathus arctus*. Mazatlan, Mexico, to Tomales Bay, including Gulf of California. Length to 4.25 in. Shallow bays to 45 ft. Pale brown; double row of spots on sides. Uncommon. D 20–23; body rings 15; tail rings 39.

BARRED PIPEFISH, *Syngnathus auliscus*. Panama to Pt. Conception, including Gulf of California. Length to 6.7 in. Shallow areas, usually in eelgrass. Brown to green, matching surroundings. Uncommon. D 26–34; body rings 14–15; tail rings 35–38.

KEY TO THE PIPEFISHES, Family Syngnathidae:

1a Caudal fin absent; head at a right angle
   to main axis of body: **PACIFIC SEAHORSE**

1b Caudal fin present; head on same axis as body........ 2

2a Body rings 14–15............ 4

2b Body rings 17–22............ 3

3a Tail rings 44–50; dorsal soft-rays 36–47; primarily
   found in kelp beds, rarely entering bays: KELP PIPEFISH
   (not illustrated, same body form as 3b below)

3b Tail rings 36–46; dorsal soft-rays 28–44; found in
   eelgrass beds in bays: **BAY PIPEFISH**

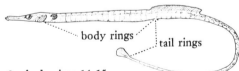

body rings   tail rings

4a *From 2a: body rings 14-15*
   Body depth at 5th body ring greater than snout length;
   body compressed; dorsal soft-rays 20–23; head into
   standard length 10.0–12.3; double row of spots along
   side of body: **SNUBNOSE PIPEFISH**

no caudal fin,
tail prehensil

4b Body depth at 5th body ring less than snout length; body not noticeably compressed; dorsal soft-rays 26–34; head into standard length 7.0–10.5; no double row of spots along side of body:

                          BARRED PIPEFISH

* See comments on page 212.

SCORPIONFISHES, Family Scorpaenidae

The family Scorpaenidae contains the largest number of California marine species, comprising four genera and 62 species known to California. These are among the most difficult of our marine fish to identify. The principal literature sources are Phillips (1957), Barsukov (1964), and Chen (1971). The key to the rockfishes (genus *Sebastes*) on page 92 relies heavily on color with additional meristic counts and body proportions given. Because diagnostic color may disappear in preserved material this key may not be applicable for some museum specimens. As in Phillips' work, this key may not apply to some juvenile forms under 4 to 6 in., since color pattern, shape and number of head spines, and body proportions may change considerably with size.

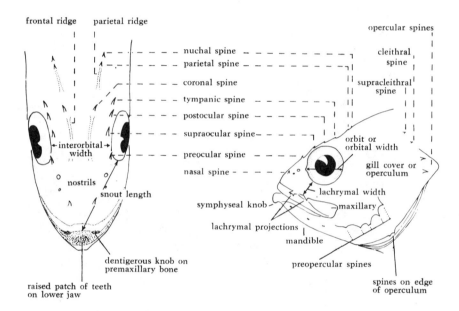

FIGURE 12.   Head structures and spines of rockfish.

KEY TO THE GENERA OF FAMILY Scorpaenidae:

1a Dorsal spines 15–17; lateral ridge from preorbital to preoperculum with 5 to 10 strong spines; pectoral fin with a deep notch forming upper and lower lobes in fish over 100 mm total length.......... *Sebastolobus* (next page)

1b Dorsal spines 11–14; lateral ridge, if present, with no more than 6 spines; pectoral fin not deeply notched.......... 2

2a Dorsal soft-rays 11–17; lateral ridge absent; usually 13 dorsal spines (rarely 11, 12, or 14); palatine teeth present.......... *Sebastes* (page 92)

2b Dorsal soft-rays 8–10; lateral ridge present; 12 or 13 dorsal spines; palatine teeth present or absent.......... 3

3a Dorsal spines 12; palatine teeth present.......... *Scorpaena* (next page)

3b Dorsal spines 13; palatine teeth absent.......... *Scorpaenodes* (next page)

THORNYHEADS and SCORPIONFISHES, Family Scorpaenidae

SHORTSPINE THORNYHEAD, *Sebastolobus alascanus.* N. Baja California to Bering Sea and Commander Isls. Length to 29.4 in. Depth 84 to 5000 + ft. Red with some black in fins; gill cavity pale; dark blotch inside operculum. Common. D XV–XVII,8–10; A III,4–5; Pect. 20–23; LLp 29–33 + 2 on tail; GR 5–8 + 12–17 = 18–24; Vert. 29–31.

LONGSPINE THORNYHEAD, *Sebastolobus altivelis.* Cape San Lucas, Baja California, to Aleutian Isls. Length to 15 in. Depth 1090 to 5000 ft. Red with black blotches in fins; lining of gill cavity dark gray or black. Uncommon. D XV–XVI,8–10; A III,4–6; Pect. 22–24; LLp 28–32 + 2 on tail; GR 7–9 + 14–17 = 21–26; Vert. 29.

SCULPIN or SPOTTED SCORPIONFISH, *Scorpaena guttata.* Gulf of California (isolated population); near Uncle Sam Bank, Baja California (LACM 30317), to Santa Cruz, California, including Guadalupe Isl. Length to 17 in. Shallow to 600 ft. Red to brown, with dark spotting over body and fins. Common south of Pt. Conception. D XII,8–10; A III,5–6; Pect. 17–19; LLp 24–26; LLs 50; GRt 16–17; Vert. 24.

RAINBOW SCORPIONFISH, *Scorpaenodes xyris.* Peru to San Clemente Isl., including the Galapagos Isls., Gulf of California, and Guadalupe Isl. Length to 5 in. Depth 60 to 84 ft. Dark to light brown, with darker spotting over body and fins. Rare. D XIII,10–11; A III,5–6; Pect. 17–19; LLs 44–50; GR 6 + 14 = 20; Vert. 24 (rarely 25).

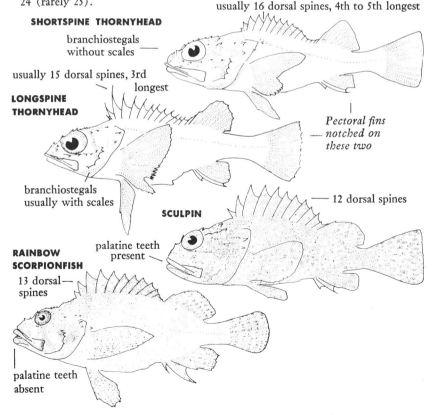

usually 16 dorsal spines, 4th to 5th longest

SHORTSPINE THORNYHEAD

branchiostegals without scales

usually 15 dorsal spines, 3rd longest

LONGSPINE THORNYHEAD

Pectoral fins notched on these two

branchiostegals usually with scales

SCULPIN

12 dorsal spines

palatine teeth present

RAINBOW SCORPIONFISH

13 dorsal spines

palatine teeth absent

ROCKFISHES, Family Scorpaenidae

COPPER ROCKFISH, *Sebastes caurinus*, and WHITEBELLY ROCKFISH, *Sebastes vexillaris*. There are no certain diagnostic features to distinguish these two nominal species. The COPPER ranges from Monterey to Kenai Penn., Alaska, the WHITEBELLY from San Benito Isls., Baja California, to Crescent City. The COPPER reaches 22.5 in. in length and the WHITEBELLY 20 in. The COPPER is dark brown to olive on back, while the WHITEBELLY is dull yellow and olive-pink on back. Both are found near the surface to 600 ft., and are common. Meristic counts for both are: D XIII,11–14; A III,5–7; Pect. 16–18; LLp 37–45; GRt 26–32.

CALICO ROCKFISH, *Sebastes dallii*. Sebastian Viscaino Bay, Baja California, to San Francisco. Length to 8 in. Depth 60 to 840 ft. Yellowish-green with irregular darker blotches and bars; brown streaks on tail. Common in southern California. D XIII,12–14; A III,6; Pect. 16–17; LLp 38–44; GRt 31–34; Vert. 27.

SILVERGRAY ROCKFISH, *Sebastes brevispinis*. Santa Barbara Isl. to Bering Sea. Length to 28 in. Depth 300 to 780 ft. Dark gray above, silvery-gray on sides, white below; lower portions of pectoral, anal, and pelvic fins pinkish. Rare. D XIII,14–17; A III,7–8; Pect. 16–18; LLp 44–53; GRt 33–36.

TREEFISH, *Sebastes serriceps*. Cedros Isl., Baja California, to San Francisco. Length to 16 in. Depth shallow to 150 ft. Olive to yellowish with five to six vertical black bars on sides. Common in southern California. D XIII,13–15; A III,5–7; Pect. 17–18; LLp 44–50; GRt 27–29.

CHINA ROCKFISH, *Sebastes nebulosus*. San Miguel Isl. (Milton Love, UCSB,pers. comm.),to S.E. Alaska. Length to 17 in. Depth 36 to 420 ft. Black with yellow and white mottling; a broad yellow stripe from about 3rd dorsal spine along lateral line to tail. Common. D XIII,12–14; A III,6–8; Pect. 17–19; LLp 37–42; GRt 26–31; Vert. 26.

KEY TO THE ROCKFISHES (Genus *Sebastes*), Family Scorpaenidae:

1a Body color bright red, pink, or red-orange, often with bars, stripes, blotches, or spotting overlaying the basic reddish color........ 20 (page 98)

1b Body color shades of black, blue, dark gray, green, olive, or brown, with no red on body other than small orange spotting and flecking on some, or with an occasional reddish flush on belly around base of pectoral or pelvic fins........ 2

2a Mandibles covered with scales, rough to touch........ 13 (page 95)

2b Mandibles smooth to touch, without scales or with only small patches of fine scales present........ 3

3a Latter ⅔ of lateral line in a clear whitish or pinkish zone:

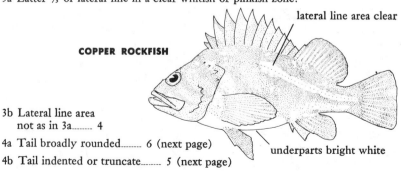

COPPER ROCKFISH

lateral line area clear

underparts bright white

3b Lateral line area not as in 3a........ 4

4a Tail broadly rounded........ 6 (next page)

4b Tail indented or truncate........ 5 (next page)

5a Oblique bars on sides, back
   strongly mottled; head spines
   strong, at least 5 pairs
   present:

CALICO ROCKFISH

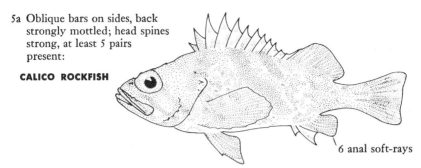

6 anal soft-rays

5b Body color uniform dark gray on back, silvery below; head spines weak, usually
   no more than 4 pairs present:

**SILVERGRAY
ROCKFISH**

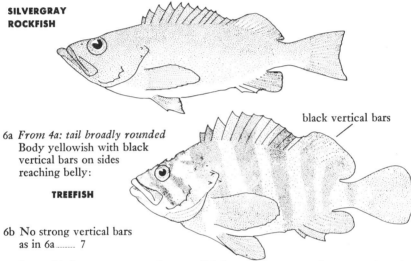

black vertical bars

6a *From 4a: tail broadly rounded*
   Body yellowish with black
   vertical bars on sides
   reaching belly:

   TREEFISH

6b No strong vertical bars
   as in 6a........ 7

7a Interorbital space convex, flat, or slightly concave; space between preocular
   spine bases much wider than space between tips of nasal spines; no yellow band
   reaching to caudal fin, or large diagonal spots above lateral line... 10 (next page)

7b Interorbital space strongly concave; space between preocular spine bases usually
   narrower than or about equal to distance between tips of nasal spines; yellow
   longitudinal stripe on back or diagonal spots above lateral line present........ 8

8a Continuous yellow stripe extending
   from membranes of 3rd and 4th
   dorsal spines to tail; 7 anal
   soft-rays (rarely 6 or 8);
   usually 10 (occ. 9 or 11)
   unbranched pectoral rays:

CHINA ROCKFISH

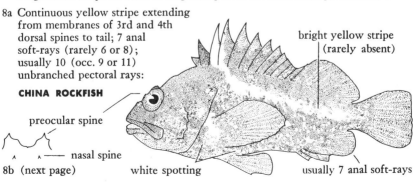

bright yellow stripe
(rarely absent)

preocular spine

nasal spine

8b (next page)   white spotting   usually 7 anal soft-rays

ROCKFISHES, Family Scorpaenidae (continued)

BLACK-AND-YELLOW ROCKFISH, *Sebastes chrysomelas.* · Natividad Is., Baja California (LACM 32062), to Eureka. Length to 15.25 in. Intertidal to 120 ft. Body black with yellow blotches and spotting. Common in kelp beds and rocky areas. D XIII,12–14; A III,6–7; Pect. 17–18; LLp 35–40; GRt 26–30.

GOPHER ROCKFISH, *Sebastes carnatus.* San Roque, Baja California, to Eureka. Length to 15.6 in. Subtidal to 180 ft. Olive-brown with flesh colored or whitish spotting and blotches. Common. D XIII,12–14; A III,5–7; Pect. 16–18; LLp 35–42; GRt 27–30; Vert. 26.

BROWN ROCKFISH, *Sebastes auriculatus.* Hipolito Bay, Baja California (CF&G Cruise 71A5), to S.E. Alaska. Length to 21.5 in. Depth, shallow to 180 ft. Brown with light orange-brown mottling; a dark brown spot on opercle. Common. D XIII, 12–15; A III,5–8; Pect. 15–19; LLp 42–49; GRt 25–30; Vert. 26.

QUILLBACK ROCKFISH, *Sebastes maliger.* Pt. Sur to Gulf of Alaska. Length to 24 in. Depth 75 to 900 ft. Slate-brown with yellow mottling on back and in dorsal fin; orange spotting on undersurface. Uncommon. D XIII,12–14; A III,6–7; Pect. 16–18; LLp 35–48; GRt 29–33.

GRASS ROCKFISH, *Sebastes rastrelliger.* Playa Maria Bay, Baja California, to Yaquina Bay, Oregon. Length to 22 in. Intertidal to 150 ft. Dark green above, mottled with lighter green and brown below. Common in kelp beds. D XIII, 12–14; A III,6; Pect. 18–20; LLp 42–47; GRt 22–25; Vert. 26.

KELP ROCKFISH, *Sebastes atrovirens.* Pt. San Pablo, Baja California (LACM 32082), to Timber Cove, Sonoma Co. Length to 16.75 in. Subtidal to 150 ft. Mottled brown. Common. D XIII,13–14; A III,6–7; Pect. 16–18; LLp 37–44; GRt 28–35; Vert. 26.

8b No continuous yellow stripe as in 8a; 6 diagonal spots between dorsal fin and lateral line; 6 (rarely 5 or 7) anal soft-rays; usually 8 or 9 (occ. 7 or 10) unbranched pectoral rays 9

9a Large spots on back yellow, body blackish: **BLACK-AND-YELLOW ROCKFISH**

9b Large spots on back whitish to flesh-colored, body brown:

    GOPHER ROCKFISH

      (same color pattern as in 9a above)

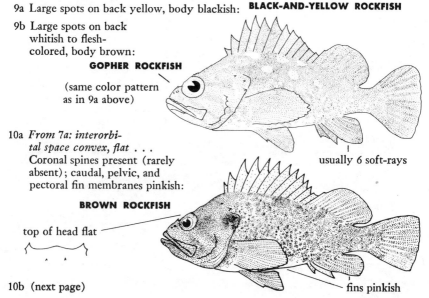

10a *From 7a: interorbital space convex, flat* . . . Coronal spines present (rarely absent); caudal, pelvic, and pectoral fin membranes pinkish:

usually 6 soft-rays

    BROWN ROCKFISH

    top of head flat

10b (next page)   fins pinkish

10b Coronal spines absent; caudal, pelvic, and pectoral fins without pink........ 11

11a Orange-yellow area in fin membranes of 2nd to 6th or 8th dorsal spines extending part way down back; pectoral and pelvic fins blackish:

QUILLBACK ROCKFISH

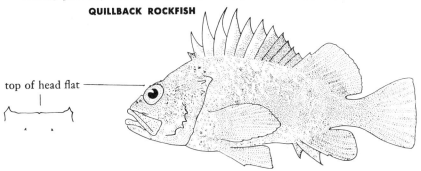

top of head flat

11b No orange-yellow area as above; pectoral and pelvic fins not blackish........ 12

12a Gill rakers 22–25, short and blunt (see drawing) on 1st gill arch (in juveniles up to about 7 inches TL the rakers are short only on upper limb); no scales on mandibles:

GRASS ROCKFISH

gill rakers short and blunt on 1st arch

12b Gill rakers 28–35, long and slender in both juveniles and adults; mandibles usually without scales but occasionally with scales: KELP ROCKFISH (see 13a)

13a *From 2a: mandibles with scales, rough to touch*
Tail rounded; head spines strong, at least 5 pairs present:

KELP ROCKFISH

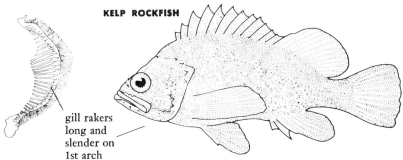

gill rakers long and slender on 1st arch

13b Tail indented or deeply forked; head spines weak or obsolete, usually with 4 pairs or less........ 14

14a Body shades of olive, yellow-brown, or bronze; 57–70 scale rows below lateral line (YELLOWTAIL ROCKFISH occ. has 55 or 56) .... 16 (page 97)

14b Body shades of black or blue; 50-56 scale rows below lateral line................ 15 (next page)

ROCKFISHES, Family Scorpaenidae (continued)

BLACK ROCKFISH, *Sebastes melanops*. Paradise Cove to Amchitka Isl., Alaska. Length to 23.75 in. Depth, surface to 300 ft. Black with gray mottling on sides. Common. D XIII,13–16; A III,7–9; Pect. 18–20; LLp 46–53; GRt 33–39; Vert. 26.

BLUE ROCKFISH, *Sebastes mystinus*. Pt. Santo Tomas, Baja California, to Bering Sea(?). Length to 21 in. Depth, surface to 300 ft. Dark blue with light blue mottling; young reddish to 2.5 in. Common. D XIII,15–17; A III,8–10; Pect. 16–18; LLp 44–56; GRt 33–38; Vert. 26.

SQUARESPOT ROCKFISH, *Sebastes hopkinsi*. Guadalupe Isl. to Farallon Isls. Length to 11.25 in. Depth 60 to 600 ft. Yellow-brown with dark brown blotches. Uncommon. D XIII,14–17; A III,6–7; Pect. 16–18; LLp 49–58; GRt 35–41.

SPECKLED ROCKFISH, *Sebastes ovalis*. Off Cape Colnett, Baja California, to San Francisco. Length to 22 in. Depth 100 to 1200 ft. Tan with dark spots. Common. D XIII,13–16; A III,7–8; Pect. 17–19; LLp 45–55; GR 8–9 + 22–24 = 30–33 (max. GRt 34).

WIDOW ROCKFISH, *Sebastes entomelas*. Todos Santos Bay, Baja California, to Kodiak Isl. Length to 21 in. Depth, near surface (young) to 1050 ft. Brassy brown on sides often with a reddish flush on belly. Common. D XIII,14–16; A III,8; Pect. 17–19; LLp 52–57; GRt 34–47; Vert. 26.

YELLOWTAIL ROCKFISH, *Sebastes flavidus*. San Diego to Kodiak Isl. Length to 26 in. Surface to 900 ft. Brown to dark gray, light areas under dorsal fin. Common. D XIII,14–16; A III,7–9; Pect. 17–19; LLp 49–60; GR 9–12 + 23–27 = 33–39; Vert. 26.

OLIVE ROCKFISH, *Sebastes serranoides*. San Benito Isls., Baja California, to Redding Rock, Del Norte Co. Length to 24 in. Surface to 480 ft. Olive-brown with light areas under dorsal fin. Common. D XII–XIII,15–17; A III,8–10; Pect. 17–18; LLp 50–56; GRt 29–36; Vert. 26.

15a Spinous dorsal membranes blackish with solid black spotting; anal fin rounded; maxillary extends to under rear of orbit:

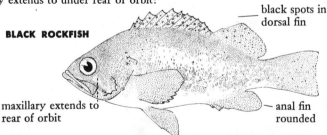

BLACK ROCKFISH

black spots in dorsal fin

maxillary extends to rear of orbit

anal fin rounded

15b Spinous dorsal fin membranes blackish but without spotting; posterior margin of anal fin indented or straight; maxillary does not extend to rear of orbit:

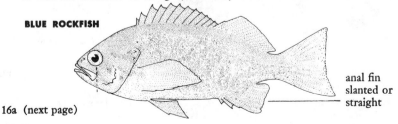

BLUE ROCKFISH

anal fin slanted or straight

16a (next page)

16a *From 14a: body shades of olive, yellow-brown, or bronze*
Tip of 2nd anal spine extends beyond tip of 3rd anal spine; body with angular dark blotches on and above lateral line:

SQUARESPOT ROCKFISH

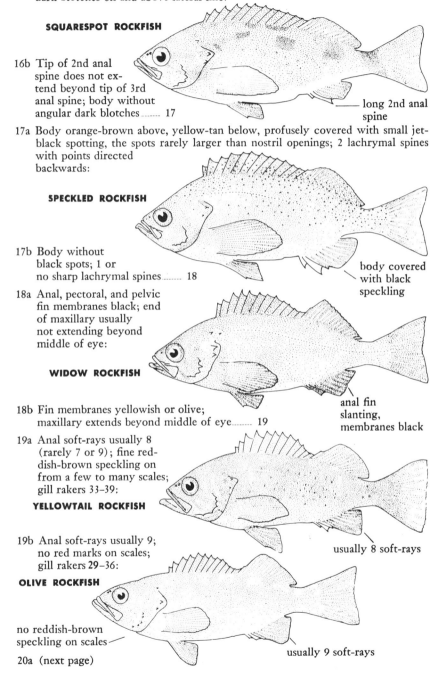

16b Tip of 2nd anal spine does not extend beyond tip of 3rd anal spine; body without angular dark blotches 17

— long 2nd anal spine

17a Body orange-brown above, yellow-tan below, profusely covered with small jet-black spotting, the spots rarely larger than nostril openings; 2 lachrymal spines with points directed backwards:

SPECKLED ROCKFISH

17b Body without black spots; 1 or no sharp lachrymal spines 18

body covered with black speckling

18a Anal, pectoral, and pelvic fin membranes black; end of maxillary usually not extending beyond middle of eye:

WIDOW ROCKFISH

18b Fin membranes yellowish or olive; maxillary extends beyond middle of eye 19

anal fin slanting, membranes black

19a Anal soft-rays usually 8 (rarely 7 or 9); fine reddish-brown speckling on from a few to many scales; gill rakers 33–39:

YELLOWTAIL ROCKFISH

19b Anal soft-rays usually 9; no red marks on scales; gill rakers 29–36:

OLIVE ROCKFISH

usually 8 soft-rays

no reddish-brown speckling on scales

20a (next page)

usually 9 soft-rays

ROCKFISHES, Family Scorpaenidae (continued)

STARRY ROCKFISH, *Sebastes constellatus*. N of Thetis Bank, Baja California, to San Francisco. Length to 16.75 in. Depth 80 to 900 ft. (See key for color). Common. D XIII,12–14; A III,5–7; Pect. 16–18; LLp 37–46; GR 7–9 + 17–21 = 25–30; Vert. 25–26.

GREENSPOTTED ROCKFISH, *Sebastes chlorostictus*. Cedros Isl., Baja California, to Copalis Head, Washington. Length to 19.75 in. Depth 160 to 660 ft. Common. D XIII,11–15; A III,5–7; Pect. 16–18; LLp 35–43; GR 9–11 + 21–25 = 31–36; Vert. 26–27.

ROSY ROCKFISH, *Sebastes rosaceus*. Turtle Bay, Baja California, to Puget Sound. Length to 12.75 in. Depth 50 to 420 ft. Common. D XIII,11–14; A III,5–7; Pect. 16–18; LLp 36–46; GR 8–11 + 20–24 = 29–34; Vert. 26–27.

ROSETHORN ROCKFISH, *Sebastes helvomaculatus*. 8 mi. W of Pt. Loma to south of Kodiak Isl. Length to about 16 in. Depth 438 to 1500 ft. Uncommon. D XIII,12–14; A III,6–7; Pect. 15–18; LLp 34–45; GR 8–11 + 20–23 = 28–33; Vert. 26.

PINKROSE ROCKFISH, *Sebastes simulator*. Guadalupe Isl. to San Pedro. Length to about 12 in. Depth 325 to 960 ft. Uncommon. D XIII,12–14; A III,5–6; Pect. 16–18; LLp 33–39; GR 8–10 + 20–23 = 28–33; Vert. 26.

20a *From 1a: body color bright red, pink, or red-orange*
Area between dorsal fin and lateral line without whitish blotches; interorbital space convex, flat, or slightly concave on all but the FLAG, REDBANDED, AND CHAMELEON ROCKFISH which have a deeply concave interorbital space........ 30 (page 102)

20b From 3 to 5 white areas (sometimes yellowish or pink) on back; interorbital space moderately to deeply concave 21

21a Body red-orange, profusely covered with small, white spots:

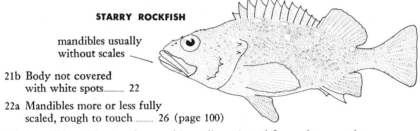

STARRY ROCKFISH

mandibles usually
without scales —

21b Body not covered
with white spots........ 22

22a Mandibles more or less fully
scaled, rough to touch ...... 26 (page 100)

22b Mandibles without scales or with small patches of fine scales, smooth to touch........ 23

23a Body red-orange to pink with sharply defined bright green spots and vermiculations on back and top of head:

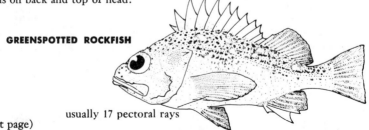

GREENSPOTTED ROCKFISH

usually 17 pectoral rays

23b (next page)

23b No sharply defined bright green spots as in 23a 24

24a White blotches bordered with purplish-red; a purple bar across nape behind
eyes:

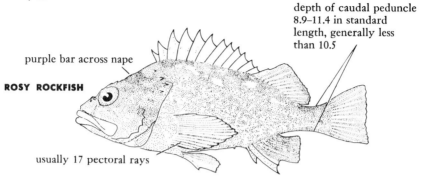

purple bar across nape

ROSY ROCKFISH

depth of caudal peduncle
8.9–11.4 in standard
length, generally less
than 10.5

usually 17 pectoral rays

24b White blotches not bordered by purple-red; no purple bar across nape........ 25

25a Body pinkish-yellow on sides, greenish-yellow on back; pectoral rays usually
16; lachrymal width 1.3–1.9 into interorbital space:

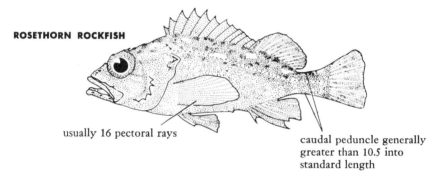

ROSETHORN ROCKFISH

usually 16 pectoral rays

caudal peduncle generally
greater than 10.5 into
standard length

25b Color plain red; pectoral rays usually 17; lachrymal width 1.9–2.5 into interorbital space:

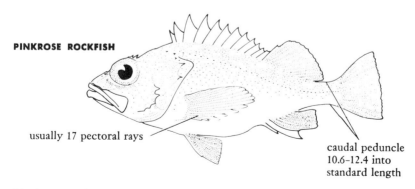

PINKROSE ROCKFISH

usually 17 pectoral rays

caudal peduncle
10.6–12.4 into
standard length

26a (next page)

ROCKFISHES, Family Scorpaenidae (continued)

FRECKLED ROCKFISH, Sebastes lentiginosus. Los Coronados Isls., Baja California, to Santa Catalina Isl. Length to about 9 in. Depth 130 to 550 ft. Uncommon. D XIII,12–13; A III,6–7; Pect. 16–18; LLp 33–41; GR 9–12 + 24–27 = 34–39; Vert. 26.

HONEYCOMB ROCKFISH, Sebastes umbrosus. 51 mi. WSW Pt. San Juanico, Baja California, to Pt. Pinos, Monterey Co. Length to 10.5 in. Depth 90 to 250 ft. Common. D XIII,11–13; A III,5–7; Pect. 15–18; LLp 34–44; GR 9–12 + 23–27 = 33–38.

SWORDSPINE ROCKFISH, Sebastes ensifer. Ranger Bank, Baja California, to San Francisco. Length to 12 in. Depth 250 to 1420 ft. Orange-red, white below often with purplish-red mottling on back. Uncommon. D XIII,12–14; A III,5–7; Pect. 16–18; LLp 34–44; GR 10–12 + 24–28 = 34–40; Vert. 26.

PINK ROCKFISH, Sebastes eos. Sebastian Viscaino Bay, Baja California, to San Francisco (?). Length to 22 in. Depth 250 to 1200 ft. Pink with olive-green vermiculations on upper parts of body, the green spots "fuzzy" on edges, fading in large individuals. Common in deeper waters. D XIII,11–13; A III,6–7; Pect. 17–18; LLp 34–42; GR 8–10 + 18–21 = 26–31.

GREENBLOTCHED ROCKFISH, Sebastes rosenblatti. Ranger Bank, Baja California, to Avila and probably to San Francisco. Length to about 19 in. Depth 200 to 1300 ft. Color similar to PINK ROCKFISH. Common in deeper waters. D XIII,11–13; A III,5–6; Pect. 16–18; LLp 34–42; GR 9–10 + 20–24 = 29–34; Vert. 26.

26a *From 22a: mandibles scaled*
　　Premaxillaries extending forward forming dentigerous knobs; body densely freckled with dark green:

FRECKLED ROCKFISH

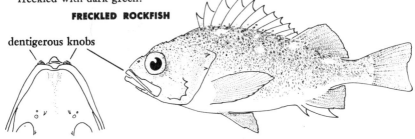

dentigerous knobs

26b No dentigerous knobs as in 26a; body without green freckling........ 27

27a Scales along midbody bordered with black forming a honeycomb appearance:

HONEYCOMB ROCKFISH

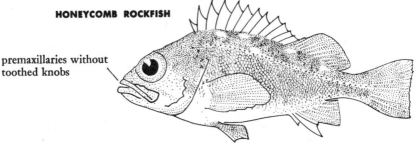

premaxillaries without toothed knobs

27b Scales without dark margins as in 27a........ 28 (next page)

28a Lower jaw slightly projecting, with a symphyseal knob projecting downward and forward; 2nd anal spine usually extends to tips of longest anal soft-rays:

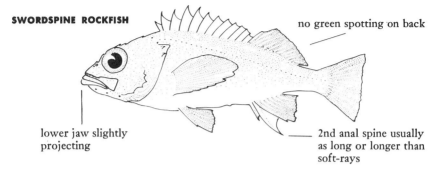

SWORDSPINE ROCKFISH   no green spotting on back

lower jaw slightly
projecting

2nd anal spine usually
as long or longer than
soft-rays

28b Jaws subequal, lower jaw with a symphyseal knob generally round and not much projecting; 2nd anal spine not extending to tips of longest anal soft-rays........ 29

29a First 4 to 7 gill rakers on 1st gill arch rudimentary and spinulated, gill rakers 26–31; usually without spines on lower edge of gill cover:

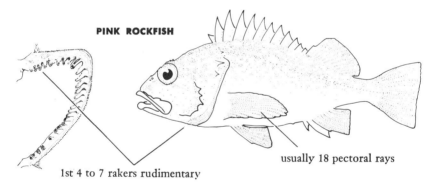

PINK ROCKFISH

usually 18 pectoral rays

1st 4 to 7 rakers rudimentary

29b First 4 to 7 gill rakers on 1st gill arch not rudimentary and spinulated, gill rakers 29–34; usually with spines on lower edge of gill cover:

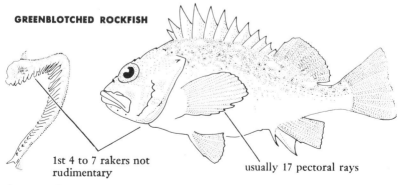

GREENBLOTCHED ROCKFISH

1st 4 to 7 rakers not
rudimentary

usually 17 pectoral rays

30a (next page)

ROCKFISHES, Family Scorpaenidae (continued)

SHORTBELLY ROCKFISH, *Sebastes jordani.* Off Cape Colnett, Baja California (CF&G Cruise 70A7), to La Perouse Bank, British Columbia. Length to 12 in. Near surface (juveniles) to 930 ft., adults usually below 300 ft. Olive-pink dorsally, light pink on sides. Common in predator stomachs. D XIII,13–16; A III,8–11; Pect. 19–22; LLp 52–59; GRt 42–47.

TIGER ROCKFISH, *Sebastes nigrocinctus.* Pt. Buchon to S.E. Alaska. Length to 24 in. Depth 200 to 900 ft. Body red with black vertical bars. Uncommon. D XIII-XIV,13–15; A III,6–7; Pect. 18–20; LLp 41–50; GRt 27–31.

FLAG ROCKFISH, *Sebastes rubrivinctus.* Cape Colnett, Baja California, to Aleutian Isls., but records north of San Francisco may be of REDBANDED ROCKFISH, which recently has been removed from synonymy. Length to 25 in. Depth 100 to 600, deeper records to 1500 ft. may be of REDBANDED. Common. D XIII,12–15; A III,6–7; Pect. 16–18; LLp 39–47; GR 7–8 + 19–22 = 26–30.

REDBANDED ROCKFISH, *Sebastes babcocki.* San Diego to Amchitka Isl., Alaska. Length to 21.75 in. Depth 900 to 1560 ft. Common in deep waters. D XIII,13–15; A III,7; Pect. 19–20; LLp 41–48; GR 8–10 + 21–23 = 29–33.

GREENSTRIPED ROCKFISH, *Sebastes elongatus.* Cedros Isl., Baja California, to 2 mi. S E Green Isl., Montaque Isl., Alaska. Length to 15 in. Depth 200 to 1320 ft. Green stripes join near tail, except pink lateral line persists. Common. D XIII,12–14; A III,6–7; Pect. 16–18; LLp 40–45; GRt. 28–33.

30a *From 20a: no whitish blotches on back*
   Vent about midway between pelvic fin base and anal fin:

SHORTBELLY ROCKFISH

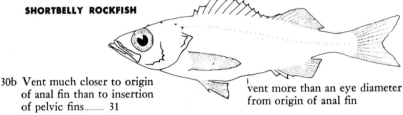

30b Vent much closer to origin
     of anal fin than to insertion
     of pelvic fins_____ 31

vent more than an eye diameter
from origin of anal fin

31a Body without vertical bars, or if bars present those under soft dorsal fin do not extend onto anal fin _____ 34 (next page)

31b Body with 4 to 6 reddish to black bars, the bars (or bar) under soft dorsal fin extending onto anal fin_____ 32

32a Bars black or reddish black, numbering 5 or 6 on body:

TIGER ROCKFISH

black vertical bars

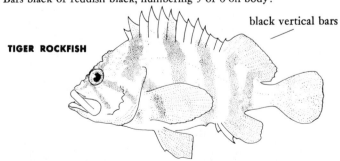

32b Vertical bars red or pink, numbering 4 on body_____ 33 (next page)

33a Mandibles without scales or with an occasional patch; lachrymal width into interorbital space 1.0–1.3:

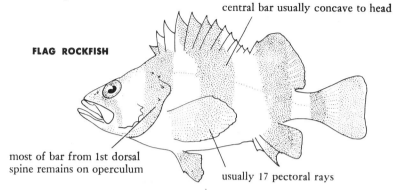

central bar usually concave to head

FLAG ROCKFISH

most of bar from 1st dorsal spine remains on operculum

usually 17 pectoral rays

33b Mandibles with scales (in fish over 4 inches TL); lachrymal width into interorbital space 1.7–2.2:

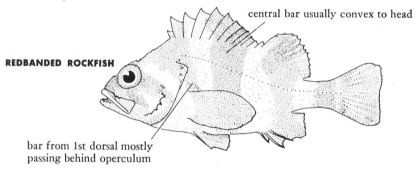

central bar usually convex to head

REDBANDED ROCKFISH

bar from 1st dorsal mostly passing behind operculum

34a *From 31a: body without bars extending onto anal fin*
Body pink with 4 dark green horizontal stripes; interorbital space into head length 7.0–8.1:

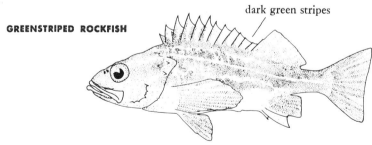

dark green stripes

GREENSTRIPED ROCKFISH

34b Body without green horizontal stripes as above; interorbital space into head length less than 7.0 times (rarely YELLOWEYE ROCKFISH measures 7.0)........ 35

35a Head spines visible with at least 5 pairs present........ 37 (next page)

35b Head spines weak, hard to locate with 3 or less pairs present........ 36 (next page)

ROCKFISHES, Family Scorpaenidae (continued)

BOCACCIO, *Sebastes paucispinis.* Pt. Blanca, Baja California, to Kruzof Isl. and Kodiak Isl., Alaska. Length to 36 in. From surface (young) to 1050 ft. Uniform dusky-red on back, pinkish below; young with dark brown spotting on sides. Common. D XII–XIV,13–15; A III,8–10; Pect. 15–16; LLp 54–70; GR 8–9 + 20–22 = 28–31; Vert. 26.

CHILIPEPPER, *Sebastes goodei.* Magdalena Bay, Baja California, to 40 mi. SW Cape Scott, NW coast of Vancouver Isl., B.C. Length to 22 in. From surface (young) to 1080 ft. Common. D XIII,13–14; A III,8–9; Pect. 16–18; LLp 48–57; GRt 34–39.

BRONZESPOTTED ROCKFISH, *Sebastes gilli.* Ensenada to Monterey. Length to 22 in. Depth 660 to 960 ft. Common in deeper waters of southern California. D XIII,13–14; A III,7–8; Pect. 18–20; LLp 41–45; GRt 26–29.

YELLOWEYE ROCKFISH, *Sebastes ruberrimus.* (Alt. common name, TURKEY-RED ROCKFISH). Ensenada to Gulf of Alaska. Length to 36 in. Depth 150 to 1200 ft. Common. D XIII,13–16; A III,5–8; Pect. 18–20; LLp 39–46; GRt 25–30; Vert. 26.

COWCOD, *Sebastes levis.* Ranger Bank and Guadalupe Isl., Baja California, to Usal, Mendocino Co. Length to 37 in., and wt. to 28.5 lbs. Depth 68 ft. (young) to 1200 ft. Yellowish-red with faint vertical bars in adult, yellow with dark bars in juveniles. Common off southern California. D XIII,12–13; A III,6–7; Pect. 17–18; LLp 45–52; GRt 29–32.

36a Maxillary extends to or beyond rear margin of eye; lateral line in a cream-colored or pinkish-brown zone; anal soft-rays usually 9 (rarely 8 or 10); gill rakers 28–31:

BOCACCIO

maxillary extends to
behind eye   usually 9 soft-rays

36b Maxillary extends to about middle of eye; lateral line in a wide, bright red zone; anal soft-rays 8 (rarely 9); gill rakers 34–39:

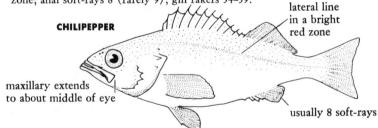

lateral line
in a bright
red zone

CHILIPEPPER

maxillary extends
to about middle of eye

usually 8 soft-rays

37a *From 35a: at least 5 pairs of head spines present*
    Mandibles with scales .... 42 (page 106)

37b Mandibles without scales 38

38a Later ⅔ of lateral line in a clear zone; body reddish-brown to copper; belly white, often turning pink upon exposure to air: COPPER ROCKFISH (see 3a, page 92)

38b Lateral line not in a clear zone as in 38a .... 39 (next page)

39a Dentigerous knobs prominent; body uniform whitish-pink. This species is both with and without scales on mandibles: SPLITNOSE ROCKFISH (see 43a, page 106)

39b Dentigerous knobs lacking; body red-orange......... 40

40a Back with roundish brown spots, and 2 bright clear orange areas under soft dorsal fin; mouth oblique, lower jaw curving upward:

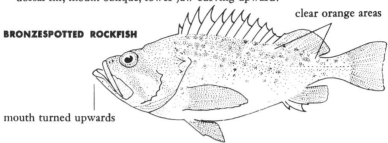

clear orange areas

BRONZESPOTTED ROCKFISH

mouth turned upwards

40b Back without brown spotting and without 2 clear orange areas as above; lower jaw nearly horizontal......... 41

41a Ridges on head serrated, the spines numerous and difficult to differentiate in fish over about 11 inches TL; in fish under 12 inches there are 2 bright white horizontal stripes along sides; eyes bright yellow:

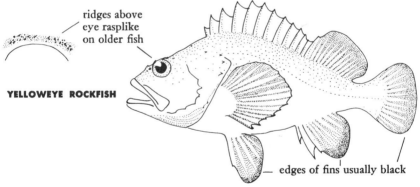

ridges above
eye rasplike
on older fish

YELLOWEYE ROCKFISH

— edges of fins usually black

41b Ridges on head not serrated, with 5 or 6 distinct pairs of head spines; no white horizontal stripes on sides; eyes not bright yellow but may be brownish-yellow:

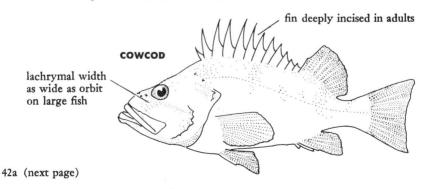

fin deeply incised in adults

COWCOD

lachrymal width
as wide as orbit
on large fish

42a (next page)

ROCKFISHES, Family Scorpaenidae (continued)

SPLITNOSE ROCKFISH, *Sebastes diploproa.* N of San Martin Isl., Baja California, to Prince William Sound, Alaska. Length to 18 in. Depth 700 to 1560 ft. Uniform pink-red. Common. D XIII,11–14; A III,6–8; Pect. 17–19; LLp 33–43; GRt 32–37.

CHAMELEON ROCKFISH, *Sebastes phillipsi.* 17 mi. WSW of Newport Pier (SIO 65–153) to Monterey Bay. Length to 17 in. Depth 570 to 900 ft. Light pink when first caught, turning crimson. Uncommon. D XIII,12–13; A III,6; Pect. 18; LLp 29–33; GR 11–12 + 26–27 = 37–39 (minimum known total 36).

DWARF-RED ROCKFISH, *Sebastes sp.* A new species being described by Robert N. Lea and John E. Fitch. San Clemente Isl. Length to 6.8 in. Deep water form. Body red. Rare. D XIII,14; A III,8; Pect. 17; LLp 30–33; GR 10 + 27–28 = 37–38; Vert. 27.

AURORA ROCKFISH, *Sebastes aurora.* San Diego to 30 mi. SW Amphridite Pt., Vancouver Isl., B.C. Length to 15.5 in. Depth 600 to 1800 ft. Uniform pink-red. Common. D XIII,12–14; A III,5–6; Pect. 16–18; LLp 27–30; GRt. 24–28.

BLACKGILL ROCKFISH, *Sebastes melanostomus.* Cedros Isl., Baja California, to Washington (?). Reported to Bering Sea but Tsuyuki and Westrheim (1970) state the northern limit "lies south of British Columbia". Length to 24 in. Depth 720 to 1800 ft. Mouth cavity and gill membranes mostly black. Common. D XIII,12–15; A III,6–8; Pect. 17–20; LLp 29–33; GRt 27–35; Vert. 27.

42a *From 37a: mandibles with scales*
Dentigerous knobs absent or weak; anterior lachrymal spine, if present, directed backwards (rarely downwards)......... 44 (next page)

42b Dentigerous knobs prominent; anterior lachrymal spine projecting forward (sometimes downward in fish under 4 inches TL)........ 43

43a Anterior lachrymal spine entire; interorbital space slightly concave to flat; no spines on lower rim or orbit:

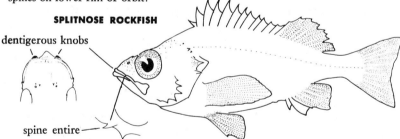

SPLITNOSE ROCKFISH

dentigerous knobs

spine entire

43b Anterior lachrymal spine multifid; top of head strongly concave; from 2 to 4 spines present on lower rim of orbit:

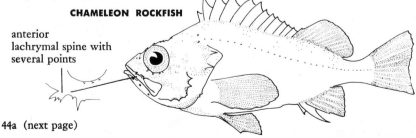

CHAMELEON ROCKFISH

anterior lachrymal spine with several points

44a (next page)

44a *From 42a: dentigerous knobs absent or weak*
   Lateral line pores more than 35........ 49 (next page)

44b Lateral line pores less than 35........ 45

45a Supraocular spines absent;
   gill rakers over 36:

   DWARF-RED ROCKFISH

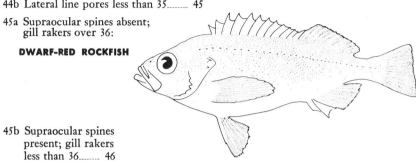

45b Supraocular spines
   present; gill rakers
   less than 36........ 46

46a Anal soft-rays 6 (rarely 5); gill rakers 24-28; orbit width 1.4-1.8 into 2nd anal
   spine:

   AURORA ROCKFISH

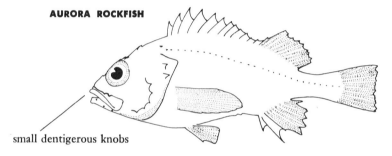

small dentigerous knobs

46b Anal soft-rays 7 or 8 (rarely 6); gill rakers 27-35; orbit width 0.7-1.4 into 2nd
   anal spine........ 47

47a Membranes of gill cover (branchiostegals) jet-black (at least dorsally of the
   pectoral fins); orbit 1.2-1.3 into longest dorsal soft-ray:

   BLACKGILL ROCKFISH

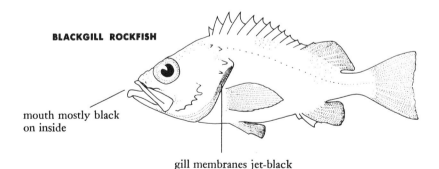

mouth mostly black
on inside

gill membranes jet-black

47b Membranes of branchiostegals not blackened as above; orbit width 1.4-2.0 into
   longest dorsal soft-ray........ 48 (next page)

ROCKFISHES, Family Scorpaenidae (continued)

ROUGHEYE ROCKFISH, Sebastes aleutianus. Monterey to Aleutian Isls. and Japan. Length to 38 in. Depth 600 to 2400 ft. Red-orange, edges of fins often black. Uncommon. D XIII,12–15; A III,6–8; Pect. 17–19; LLp 29–34; GR 9–11 + 20–24 = 30–35; Vert. 27.

SHORTRAKER ROCKFISH, Sebastes borealis. Eureka to S.E. Kamchatka. Length to about 33.5 in. Depths around 1000 ft. Pink-red with vague vertical bars; mouth and gill cavities red with dark blotches. Rare. D XIII–XIV,12–15; A III,6–8; Pect. 17–20; LLp 28–32; GRt 27–31; Vert. 27.

REDSTRIPE ROCKFISH, Sebastes proriger. San Diego to Bering Sea. Length to 20 in. Depth 300 to 900 ft. Uncommon. D XIII,13–15; A III,6–7; Pect. 16–18; GRt 36–43; Vert. 27.

BANK ROCKFISH, Sebastes rufus. Guadalupe Isl. to off Mad River (CF&G Cruise 70S2). Length to 20.1 in. Depth 102 to 810 ft. Dusky on back, light red on body; black in membranes of anal fin; usually with black spots on body and in dorsal fin. Common. D XIII,13–16; A III,8–9; Pect. 17–19; LLp 49–56; GR 10–11 + 23– 26 = 33–37 (known minimum total 32). There is a form of this species that frequents deep water over muddy or sandy bottom without black spotting on body or in fins. Commercial fishermen at Morro Bay and Monterey Bay refer to this as the RED-WIDOW ROCKFISH.

MEXICAN ROCKFISH, Sebastes macdonaldi. Ascuncion Bay, Baja California, to Pt. Sur. Length to 26 in. Depth 660 to 780 ft. Lateral line in a clear red zone, pelvic and anal fins reddish. Common in deeper waters of southern California. D XIII,13–14; A III,7–8; Pect. 18–19; LLp 53–58; GRt 37–38.

PACIFIC OCEAN PERCH, Sebastes alutus. La Jolla to Bering Sea and Japan. Length 20 in. Depth 180 to 2100 ft. Light red with dark area under soft dorsal fin. Common to the north. D XIII,13–17; A III,6–9; Pect. 15–19; LLp 44–53; GRt 30–38; Vert. 27.

48a Ridge below lower rim of eye with 2 to 10 sharp spines; longest anterior gill raker on 1st arch about 5 to 6 times as high as wide:

ROUGHEYE ROCKFISH

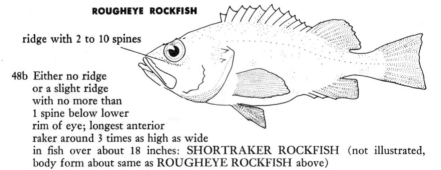

ridge with 2 to 10 spines

48b Either no ridge or a slight ridge with no more than 1 spine below lower rim of eye; longest anterior raker around 3 times as high as wide in fish over about 18 inches: SHORTRAKER ROCKFISH (not illustrated, body form about same as ROUGHEYE ROCKFISH above)

49a *From 44a: lateral line pores more than 35*
At least 3 to 5 vertical or oblique bars or blotches on back, with at least 1 bar extending uninterrupted to below lateral line _____ 57 (page 111)

49b Either none, 1, or 2 faint blotches or bars on back, above the lateral line or interrupted by a clear light red or gray lateral line zone _____ 50 (next page)

50a Supraocular spines present 53

50b Supraocular spines absent 51

51a Pectoral and pelvic fin membranes light red or yellowish, lateral line in a clear gray zone bordered by red stripes:

REDSTRIPE ROCKFISH

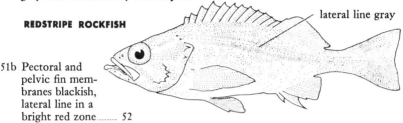

lateral line gray

51b Pectoral and pelvic fin membranes blackish, lateral line in a bright red zone 52

52a Black spots, mostly a little larger than nostril openings, over back and in dorsal fin:

BANK ROCKFISH

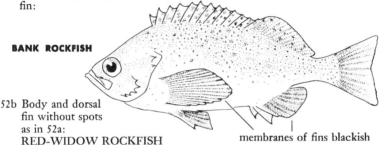

52b Body and dorsal fin without spots as in 52a:
RED-WIDOW ROCKFISH

membranes of fins blackish

53a *From 50a: supraocular spines present*
Membranes of pectoral fins black; upper portion of body uniform blackish-red with a bright red lateral line zone; a flat spine present (rarely absent) below anterior margin of eye:

MEXICAN ROCKFISH

flat spine below eye

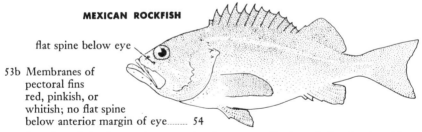

53b Membranes of pectoral fins red, pinkish, or whitish; no flat spine below anterior margin of eye 54

54a Symphyseal knob prominent; anal soft-rays usually 8 or 9 (rarely 6 or 7); a darkened area at base of soft dorsal fin:

dark areas below soft dorsal and on caudal peduncle

PACIFIC OCEAN PERCH

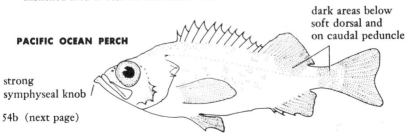

strong symphyseal knob

54b (next page)

ROCKFISHES, Family Scorpaenidae (continued)

YELLOWMOUTH ROCKFISH, *Sebastes reedi*. Crescent City to Sitka, Alaska. Length to about 23 in. Depth 462 to 1200 ft. Uniform red-orange. Rare. D XIII,13–15; A III,7–8; Pect. 18–20; LLp 47–55; GRt 30–36.

CANARY ROCKFISH, *Sebastes pinniger*. Cape Colnett, Baja California, to 17 mi. W Cape San Bartolome, Alaska. Length to 30 in. Surface (juveniles) to 900 ft. Common. D XIII,13–15; A III,7; Pect. 16–18; LLp 39–44; GRt 40–45; Vert. 26.

VERMILION ROCKFISH, *Sebastes miniatus*. San Benito Isls., Baja California, to Vancouver Isl., British Columbia. Length to 30 in. Shallow (juveniles) to 660 ft. Common. D XIII,13–15; A III,6–8; Pect. 16–18; LLp 40–47; GRt 35–43; Vert. 26.

DARKBLOTCHED ROCKFISH, *Sebastes crameri*. 3 mi. SSE Santa Catalina Isl. (LACM 30641) to Bering Sea. Length to 22.5 in. Depth 240 to 1200 ft. Uncommon. D XIII,12–14; A III,6–7; Pect. 18–20; LLp 40–50; GRt 29–34.

STRIPETAIL ROCKFISH, *Sebastes saxicola*. Sebastian Viscaino Bay, Baja California, to S.E. Alaska. Length to 15.3 in. Depth 192 to 1320 ft. Common. D XIII,12–14; A III,5–8; Pect. 15–17; LLp 36–42; GRt 31–35.

54b Symphyseal knob absent or small; anal soft-rays usually 7 (rarely 6 or 8); no darkened area under soft dorsal fin....... 55

55a Anal fin slanting posteriorly (occ. perpendicular) to horizontal axis; pectoral rays 18–20; 57–67 scale rows below lateral line:

YELLOWMOUTH ROCKFISH

inside of mouth with black and yellow —— blotches

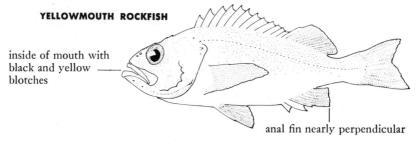

anal fin nearly perpendicular

55b Anal fin slanting anteriorly in fish over 6 inches TL; pectoral rays 16–18; 43–50 scale rows below lateral line 56

56a Underside of mandibles smooth to touch (scales are present but are mostly embedded); lateral line in a clear gray zone; fish up to about 14 inches TL with a black blotch in posterior portion of spinous dorsal fin:

CANARY ROCKFISH

black blotch in fin in fish up to about 14 inches TL

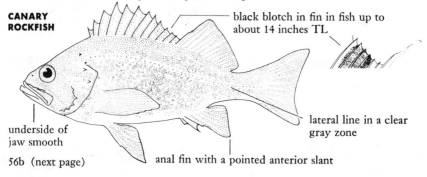

lateral line in a clear gray zone

underside of jaw smooth

56b (next page)

anal fin with a pointed anterior slant

56b Underside of mandibles rough to touch; lateral line not in a clear gray zone; no large black area in spinous dorsal fin:

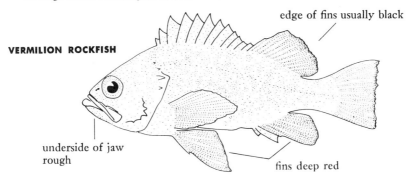

edge of fins usually black

VERMILION ROCKFISH

underside of jaw rough

fins deep red

57a *From 49a: at least 3 to 5 dark bars or blotches on back*
Supraocular spines present; body depth at origin of pelvic fins greater than head length in fish larger than 5 inches TL:

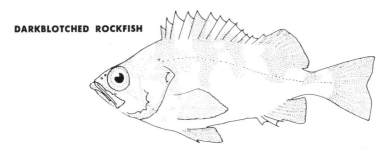

DARKBLOTCHED ROCKFISH

57b Supraocular spines absent; body depth at origin of pelvic fins less (rarely about the same in SHARPCHIN ROCKFISH) than head length........ 58

58a Tail with green stripes in membranes; dorsal soft-rays 12 (occ. 13); unbranched pectoral rays 6 or 7:

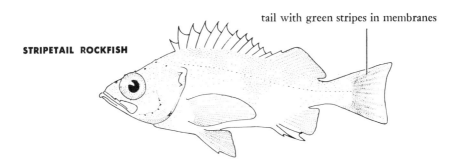

tail with green stripes in membranes

STRIPETAIL ROCKFISH

58b Tail without green stripes (brown stripes present in HALFBANDED ROCK-FISH); dorsal soft-rays 13–15; unbranched pectoral rays 7–9........ 59 (next page)

ROCKFISHES, Family Scorpaenidae (continued)

HALFBANDED ROCKFISH, *Sebastes semicinctus*. Sebastian Viscaino Bay, Baja California, to Pt. Pinos. Length to 10 in. Depth 192 to 1320 ft. Common. D XIII,13; A III,7–8; Pect. 16–18; LLp 42–49; GRt 37–40; Vert. 26.

SHARPCHIN ROCKFISH, *Sebastes zacentrus*. San Diego to Sanak Isl., Alaska. Length to 13 in. Depth 300 to 1050 ft. Uncommon. D XIII,13–15; A III,6–8; Pect. 17–19; LLp 39–45; GRt 31–37 (Calif.), 11–13 + 24–28 = 35–41 (Alaska); Vert. 27–28.

PYGMY ROCKFISH, *Sebastes wilsoni*. Cortez Bank to S.E. Alaska. Length to 8.25 in. Depth 96 to 450 ft. Rare. D XIII,13–14; A III,6–7; Pect. 16–17; LLp 37–44; GRt 38–43 (Phillips, 1957), 10-12 + 30-32 = 40-43 (Follett, 1952).

59a Two strong oblique blackish-red bars in midbody; 2 sharp spines on lower edge of gill cover, the uppermost spine twice the size of the lower:

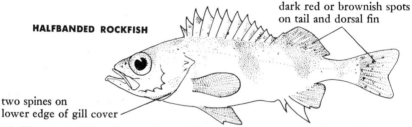

HALFBANDED ROCKFISH

dark red or brownish spots on tail and dorsal fin

two spines on lower edge of gill cover

59b No strong oblique bars as above; either none, 1, or 2 small spines on lower edge of gill cover (if 2 present, the upper is about same size as lower)........ 60

60a Anal soft-rays 7; a dark forked bar from eye to operculum; gill rakers 31–37; symphyseal knob prominent; body depth at origin of pelvics 2.7–3.2 into standard length:

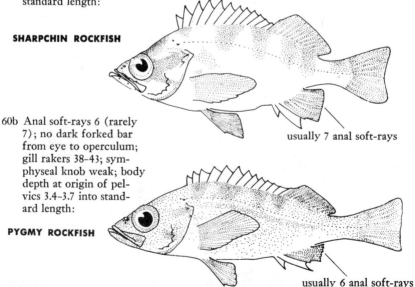

SHARPCHIN ROCKFISH

60b Anal soft-rays 6 (rarely 7); no dark forked bar from eye to operculum; gill rakers 38–43; symphyseal knob weak; body depth at origin of pelvics 3.4–3.7 into standard length:

PYGMY ROCKFISH

usually 7 anal soft-rays

usually 6 anal soft-rays

SEAROBINS, SABLEFISH, and SKILFISH
(Principal sources: Clemens & Wilby, 1961; Phillips, 1966)

LUMPTAIL SEAROBIN, *Prionotus stephanophrys*. Family TRIGLIDAE
Peru to Columbia River, including Gulf of California. Length to 15.5 in. Depth 48 to 360 ft. Purplish-brown above with blackish-brown spots and blotches, underparts white. Uncommon. D X–XI,11–12; A I,10; Pect. 13; Pelvic I,5; branchiostegals 7; LLp 51–52; GR 5 + 15 = 20; Vert. 26.

SPLITNOSE SEAROBIN, *Bellator xenisma*. Family TRIGLIDAE
Columbia north into the Gulf of California; one record north of Gulf of California in the Santa Barbara Channel. Length to 4 in. Depth 198 to 309 ft. Light brown mottled with darker brown and black. One California record. D VII + III,10–11; A I,9; Pect. 11; Pelvic I,5; LLp 35–40; LLs 60–70; GRt 7.

SABLEFISH, *Anoplopoma fimbria*. Family ANOPLOPOMATIDAE
Cedros Isl., Baja California, to Bering Sea and Japan. Length to 3 ft. 4 in. Depth from surface (juveniles) to 5000 ft. Blackish-gray on back and sides, gray to white below. Common. D XVII–XXX + 16-21; A 16-23; Pelvic I,5; LLs (oblique rows) about 190; GRt 18-25; Vert. 61-66.

SKILFISH, *Erilepis zonifer*. Family ANOPLOPOMATIDAE
Moss Landing to S.E. Alaska. Length to 6 ft., and wt. to 200 lbs. Depth, near surface to 1440 ft. Blackish above, whitish below; light blotches on head and anterior portion of body. Rare. D XII–XIV + I–II,15–17; A II–III,11–14; Pect. 16–19; Pelvic I,5; LLp 133; LLs (oblique rows) 122–124; GR 5-6 + 16; Vert. 45–46.

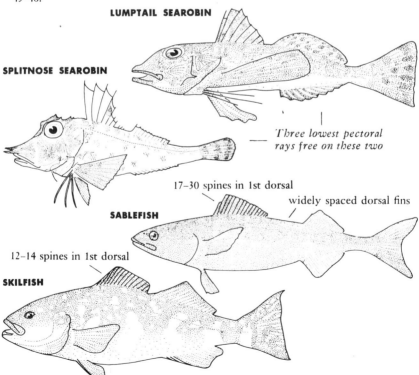

LUMPTAIL SEAROBIN

SPLITNOSE SEAROBIN

Three lowest pectoral rays free on these two

17–30 spines in 1st dorsal

widely spaced dorsal fins

SABLEFISH

12–14 spines in 1st dorsal

SKILFISH

COMBFISHES, Family Zaniolepididae, and
GREENLINGS, Family Hexagrammidae
(Principal sources: Rass, 1962; Quast, 1964, 1965)

SHORTSPINE COMBFISH, *Zaniolepis frenata*. Family ZANIOLEPIDIDAE
Turtle Bay, Baja California (CF&G Cruise 71A5), to southern Oregon. Length
to 10 in. Shallow waters to 1200 ft. Light tan with darker streaks and blotches;
dark oblique bands in dorsal fin. Skin covered with minute rough scales forming
a shagreenlike surface. Uncommon. D XXI,12; A III,15–16; Vert. 41–43.

LONGSPINE COMBFISH, *Zaniolepis latipinnis*. Family ZANIOLEPIDIDAE
San Cristobal Bay, Baja California (CF&G Cruise 71A5), to Vancouver Isl., B.C.
Length to 12 in. Depth 120 to 372 ft. Color and skin texture similar to SHORT-
SPINE COMBFISH but with a wide, black streak from tip of snout to eye, and
dark horizontal bands in dorsal fin. Uncommon. D XXI–XXII,11–12; A III,15–17;
Pect. 14; GR 3 + 8–9 = 11–12; Vert. 40–42.

PAINTED GREENLING, *Oxylebius pictus*. Family HEXAGRAMMIDAE
Pt. San Carlos, Baja California (LACM 32082), to Queen Charlotte Isl., British
Columbia. Length to 10 in., but rarely over 6 in. Intertidal to 160 ft. Brown and
dark red bars and mottling over a grayish-brown body; flaps on head red.
Common. D XV–XVII,14–16; A III–IV,12–13; GR 2–5 + 7–8 = 9–13; Vert. 36–39.

LINGCOD, *Ophiodon elongatus*. Family HEXAGRAMMIDAE
Pt. San Carlos, Baja California, to Kodiak Isl., Alaska. Length to 45 in., and wt.
to 41.5 lbs. in California; reaches 105 lbs. in British Columbia. Ranges in depth by
age: post larvae to 3 in. are pelagic nearshore and offshore; juveniles in shallow
bays and on sand and mud bottoms from beach area to several hundred feet;
adults range from surface to 1400 ft. Color varies from gray-brown to green and
bluish, with darker spotting and mottling on upper parts. Common. D XXV–
XXVIII,19–24; A III,21–24 (spines often embedded and not visible); LLp 154–
180; GR 5–8 + 16–19 = 21–26; Vert. 56–58.

KEY TO THE COMBFISHES, Family Zaniolepididae,
AND GREENLINGS, Family Hexagrammidae:
1a Second dorsal spine not elongated; 1st dorsal soft-ray slightly anterior to or
above origin of anal fin........ 3 (Family Hexagrammidae, next page)

1b Second dorsal spine elongated; 1st dorsal soft-ray above midportion of anal
fin........ 2 (Family Zaniolepididae)

2a Cirrus present on orbit over eye; 2nd dorsal spine shorter than head:

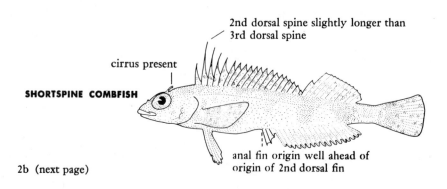

2nd dorsal spine slightly longer than
3rd dorsal spine

cirrus present

SHORTSPINE COMBFISH

anal fin origin well ahead of
origin of 2nd dorsal fin

2b (next page)

2b No cirrus on orbit over eye; 2nd dorsal spine longer than head:

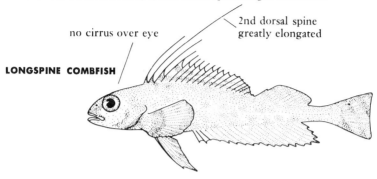

no cirrus over eye

2nd dorsal spine greatly elongated

LONGSPINE COMBFISH

3a *From 1a: 2nd dorsal spine not elongated*
Anal soft-rays 12–13; 3 or 4 anal spines:

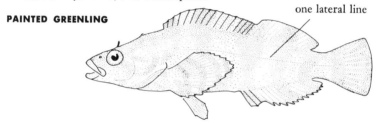

PAINTED GREENLING

one lateral line

3b Anal soft-rays 21 or more; 0–2 anal spines visible (some anal spines may be buried in flesh and not visible) 4

4a One lateral line; head without scales; mouth large with both large canine and smaller sharppointed teeth:

LINGCOD

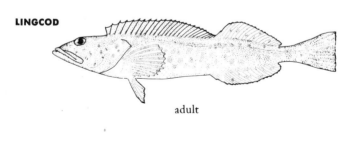

adult

juvenile form

4b (next page)

GREENLINGS, Family Hexagrammidae (continued)

ATKA-MACKEREL, *Pleurogrammus monopterygius.* Monterey to Bering Sea and Sea of Japan. Length to about 19 in. Depth 15 to 400 ft. Upper parts dark to light olive with broad, dark vertical bars on sides. Rare. D XXI,25 (total dorsal fin elements range from 46–50); A 24–28; Pect. 24–26; LLp 139–166; GR 6–7 + 16–19 = 22–26; Vert. 59–61.

WHITESPOTTED GREENLING, *Hexagrammos stelleri.* Puget Sound, Washington, to Japan. This species has been erroneously reported from northern California. A description is given to enable proper identification in case it may be present in California. Length to about 19 in. Shallow areas, mostly subtidal. Light brown to greenish, often tinged with reddish; conspicuous white spots on body. D XX–XXV,18–24; A 22–25; Pect. 18–20; Vert. 51–55.

KELP GREENLING, *Hexagrammos decagrammus.* La Jolla (SIO 59–33) to Aleutian Isls., Alaska. Length to 21 in. Intertidal to 150 ft. Common in kelp bed areas, often taken in deeper water over sand. Female gray-brown with bright golden to light brown spots on body and head; male dark gray with bright blue spots on head and sides; inside of mouth yellowish in both sexes. Common. XX–XXIII,22–26; A O–I,21–25; Pect. 18–20; midlateral scales 112; GR 3–5 + 9–14 = 13–18; Vert. 54–56.

ROCK GREENLING, *Hexagrammos superciliosus.** Pt. Conception (UCLA W 62–133) to at least the Bering Sea. Length to 24 in. Intertidal and shallow rocky areas. Reddish-brown with darker mottling and often with large, bright red blotches on sides; inside of mouth bluish. Common north of San Francisco. D XX–XXIII,20–24; A O–I,21–24; Pect. 19–21; GR 4–5 + 9–11 = 13–16; Vert. 53–55.

4b Five lateral lines; scales present on head; mouth small with numerous small teeth of about same size........ 5

5a Dorsal fin not notched; caudal fin deeply forked:

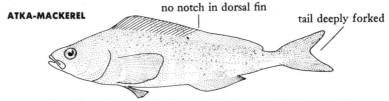

ATKA-MACKEREL   no notch in dorsal fin   tail deeply forked

5b Dorsal fin with a deep notch about midbody; caudal fin rounded or only slightly indented........ 6

6a Fourth lateral line does not extend beyond origin of anal fin; palatines without teeth:

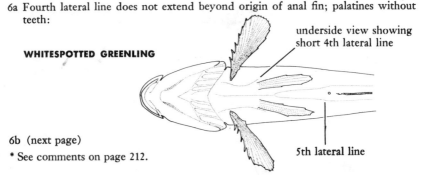

WHITESPOTTED GREENLING   underside view showing short 4th lateral line

5th lateral line

6b (next page)

* See comments on page 212.

6b Fourth lateral line extends well beyond origin of anal fin; palatine teeth present......... 7

7a Two pairs of cirri present on head, one on edge of orbit, the other midway toward dorsal fin (the latter are occasionally absent); flap near edge of orbit no more than ¾ diameter of eye; caudal fin slightly indented; operculum usually completely scaled; inside of mouth yellowish:

KELP GREENLING

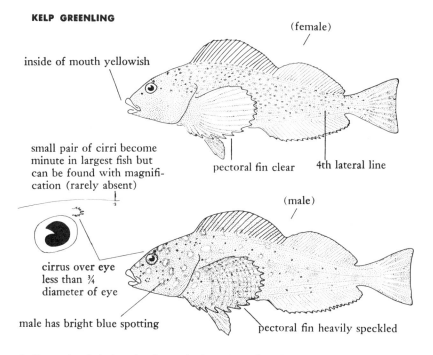

(female)

inside of mouth yellowish

small pair of cirri become minute in largest fish but can be found with magnification (rarely absent)

pectoral fin clear   4th lateral line

(male)

cirrus over eye less than ¾ diameter of eye

male has bright blue spotting

pectoral fin heavily speckled

7b One pair of cirri on head, attached to edge of orbit, and usually longer than ¾ diameter of eye; caudal fin rounded; operculum not completely scaled, the area over suborbital stay naked; inside of mouth bluish:

ROCK GREENLING

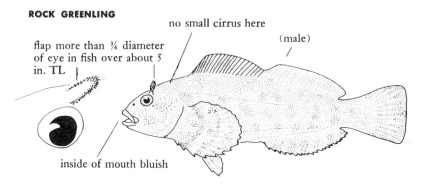

no small cirrus here

(male)

flap more than ¾ diameter of eye in fish over about 5 in. TL

inside of mouth bluish

SCULPINS, Family Cottidae *
(Principal sources: Bolin, 1944, 1950; Clemens and Wilby, 1961)

GRUNT SCULPIN, *Rhamphocottus richardsonii*.* San Nicolas Isl., along mainland from Santa Monica Bay to Bering Sea. Length to 3.3 in. Intertidal to 540 ft. Yellowish with brown streaks; fins reddish and orange. Uncommon. D VII–VIII + 12–14; A 6–8; Pelvic I,3–4; LLp around 25.

ROSYLIP SCULPIN, *Ascelichthys rhodorus*. Moss Beach, San Mateo Co. (CAS 20237), to Sitka, Alaska. Length to 5.9 in. Intertidal and subtidal areas. Dark olive-brown on back, lighter below with bright red on lips and margin of spinous dorsal fin. Uncommon. D VIII–X,17–20; A 13–16; Pect. 16–18; Pelvic absent; LLp 34–38 on body + 1–2 on tail; GR 0–3 + 3–5 = 4–8; Vert. 35–36.

MANACLED SCULPIN, *Synchirus gilli*. San Miguel Isl. (SIO 64–637) to Sitka, Alaska. Length to 2.7 in. Shallow water of bays, tidepools, kelp canopy. Yellowish to reddish-brown. Uncommon. D VIII–X,19–21; A 18–21; Pect. 21–24; Pelvic I,3; LLs 38–42.

CABEZON, *Scorpaenichthys marmoratus*. Pt. Abreojos, Baja California, to Sitka, Alaska. Length to 39 in. Intertidal to 250 ft. Reddish to greenish with intense dark and light mottling. Common. D VIII–XII,15–18; A 11–14; Pect. 14–16; Pelvic I,4–5; LLp 71–88 on body + 4–8 on tail; GR 3–6 + 12–16 = 16–22; Vert. 35–36.

LONGFIN SCULPIN, *Jordania zonope*. Diablo Canyon, San Luis Obispo Co. (LACM 31859), to Ucluelet, Barkley Sound, Vancouver Isl., B.C. Length to 5.12 in. Intertidal to 126 ft. Uncommon. D XVII–XVIII,15–17; A 22–24; Pect. 14; Pelvic I,4–5; LLs 48–50 on body + 2–3 on tail.

THORNBACK SCULPIN, *Paricelinus hopliticus*. NW of Cortez Bank (UCLA W 49–416) to Queen Charlotte Sound, British Columbia. Length to 7.65 in. Surface (juveniles) to 600 ft., mostly in moderate depths. Rare. D XII–XIII,19; A 23; Pect. 15; Pelvic I,5; LLs 43 on body + 1–2 on tail.

KEY TO THE SCULPINS, Family Cottidae:

1a Lowermost pectoral rays free, not connected by membranes; snout greatly elongated, about 2 times length of maxillary:

GRUNT SCULPIN

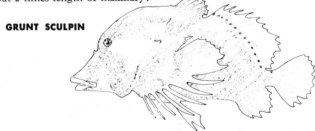

1b Lowermost pectoral rays connected by membranes; snout about equal to or shorter than maxillary⸺ 2

2a Pelvic fins absent:

ROSYLIP SCULPIN

2b Pelvic fins present⸺ 3 (next page)

pelvic fins absent

* See comments on page 213.

3a Pectoral fins united to each other across belly:

MANACLED SCULPIN

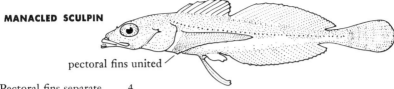

pectoral fins united

3b Pectoral fins separate 4

4a Pelvic fins with 1 spine (usually embedded and not visible) and 2-4 soft-rays (if 4, both pelvics have 4, never one with 5 soft-rays) 7

4b Pelvic fins with 1 spine (embedded) and 5 soft-rays (rarely one of the pelvic fins may have 4 soft-rays, the other 5, but never both with 4 soft-rays) 5

5a Body without scales; anal soft-rays 11-14; a large broad-based cirrus extends along midline of snout:

CABEZON

cirrus on midline — of snout

5b Body scaled; anal soft-rays 22-24; no cirrus on midline of snout 6

6a No enlarged spinous scales along dorsal fin base; dorsal spines 17-18:

17-18 dorsal spines

LONGFIN SCULPIN

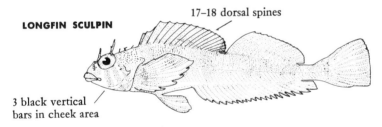

3 black vertical bars in cheek area

6b A row of enlarged spinous scales along dorsal fin base; dorsal spines 12-13:

12-13 spines

THORNBACK SCULPIN

spinous scales below dorsal fin

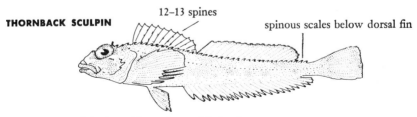

7a *From 4a: pelvic fins with 1 spine and 2-4 soft-rays*
Body subcircular or depressed; dorsal soft-rays 8-23; no granulation of small papillae on body ...... 9 (page 121)

7b Body markedly compressed throughout; dorsal soft-rays 20-30; body almost entirely covered by small papillae giving skin surface a granular texture ...... 8 (next page)

SCULPINS, Family Cottidae (continued)

SAILFIN SCULPIN, *Nautichthys oculofasciatus.* San Miguel Isl. (SIO 54-191) to eastern Kamchatka. Length to 6.8 in. Intertidal to 360 ft. Yellowish-brown to gray; black bars on back, fins, and through eye. Uncommon. D VIII–IX,27–30; A 18–20; Pect. 13–14; Pelvic I,3; LLs 41–45 on body + 1–2 on tail; GR 1 + 7 = 8; Vert. 41.

SILVERSPOTTED SCULPIN, *Blepsias cirrhosus.* San Simeon (UCLA W 56-251) to Aomori, Japan. Length to 7.5 in. Intertidal to 120 ft. Brownish to greenish above, reddish to white below; a row of bright silver spots above pectoral fin. Uncommon. D VI–IX + 20–25; A 18–21; Pect. 11–12; Pelvic I,3; LLs 43–57 on body + 1–3 on tail.

BROWN IRISH LORD, *Hemilepidotus spinosus.* Santa Barbara Isl.; Ventura on mainland (UCLA W 65-26) to Puffin Bay, Alaska. Length to 10 in. Intertidal to 252 ft. Light to dark brown with dark mottling. Uncommon. D XI,18–20; A 14–16; Pect. 14–16; Pelvic I,4; LLs 57–66 on body + 3–6 on tail; GR 0–2 + 5–8 = 5–10; Vert. 35–37.

RED IRISH LORD, *Hemilepidotus hemilepidotus.* South end of Monterey Bay to Sea of Okhotsk. Length to 20 in., but rarely over 12 in. Intertidal to 156 ft. Reddish on back, whitish below. Common. D X–XIII,17–20; A 13–16; Pect. 15–17; Pelvic I,4; LLs 59–69 on body + 2–5 on tail.

STAGHORN SCULPIN, *Leptocottus armatus.* San Quintin Bay, Baja California, to Chignik, Alaska. Length to 12 in. Intertidal to 300 ft. Greenish-brown or gray above, white to yellow below. Common. D VI–VIII,15–20; A 14–20; Pect. 17–20; Pelvic I,4; LLp 37–42 on body + 1–3 on tail; GR 1–3 + 8–12 = 10–13; Vert. 35–38.

BUFFALO SCULPIN, *Enophrys bison.* Monterey to Kodiak Isl., Alaska. Length to 14.6 in. Shallow rocky areas. Dark gray, green or brown above; purplish bony plates on head and along lateral line. Common. D VII–IX + 9–13; A 8–10; Pect. 16–18; Pelvic I,3; LLs 29–33 on body + 0–2 on tail; GR 0–1 + 4–6 = 5–7; Vert. 29–31.

8a Gill membranes joined to isthmus; pelvic fins extend more than ½ distance to anal fin:

SAILFIN SCULPIN

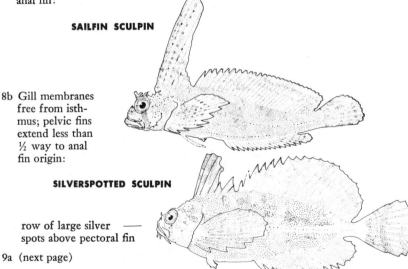

8b Gill membranes free from isthmus; pelvic fins extend less than ½ way to anal fin origin:

SILVERSPOTTED SCULPIN

row of large silver —— spots above pectoral fin

9a (next page)

9a *From 7a: body subcircular or depressed*
Dorsal fins separated or contiguous (barely attached by a membrane); scales below lateral line absent, represented by minute prickles, or restricted to the area covered by pectoral fins........ 11

9b Dorsal fin continuous; large scales in oblique rows below lateral line forming a well defined band extending to about caudal fin base........ 10

10a Seven or 8 rows of scales under dorsal fin; gill membranes completely joined to isthmus or with a free fold narrower than pupil diameter:

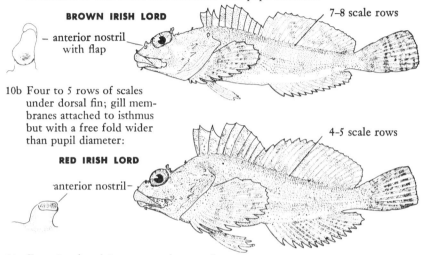

BROWN IRISH LORD

– anterior nostril with flap

7–8 scale rows

10b Four to 5 rows of scales under dorsal fin; gill membranes attached to isthmus but with a free fold wider than pupil diameter:

RED IRISH LORD

anterior nostril–

4-5 scale rows

11a *From 9a: dorsal fins separated or nearly so*
Gill membranes free from isthmus or at least forming a distinct free fold across it........ 14 (next page)

11b Gill membranes completely joined to isthmus........ 12

12a Lateral line scales not evident; dorsal soft-rays 15–20; anal soft-rays 14–20:

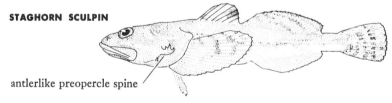

STAGHORN SCULPIN

antlerlike preopercle spine

12b Lateral line scales as conspicuous, heavy bony plates; dorsal soft-rays 8–13; anal soft-rays 6-10........ 13

13a Eight to 10 anal soft-rays; 9–13 dorsal soft-rays; orbit 1.4-2.4 into maxillary:

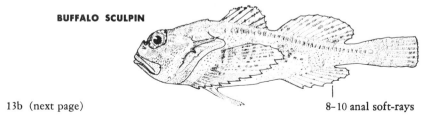

BUFFALO SCULPIN

13b (next page)

8-10 anal soft-rays

SCULPINS, Family Cottidae (continued)

BULL SCULPIN, *Enophrys taurina.* San Nicolas Isl., Santa Catalina Isl. (LACM 902) to off San Francisco (UCLA W 59–73). Length to 6.5 in. Depth 36 to 840 ft. Dark gray to brown above, whitish below. Uncommon. D VI–VIII,8–10; A 6–7; Pect. 16–18; Pelvic I,3; LLs 24–29 on body + 0–3 on tail.

YELLOWCHIN SCULPIN, *Icelinus quadriseriatus.* Cape San Lucas, Baja California, to Russian River (CAS 13997). Length to 3.3 in. Depth 20 to 330 ft. Dark brown to gray above, pale below, with yellow under anterior part of body. Uncommon. D VII–X + 12–16; A 10–15; Pect. 15–17; Pelvic I,2; LLs 34-37 on body + 1 on tail; GR 0 + 3–6 = 3–6; Vert. 33–35.

FRINGED SCULPIN, *Icelinus fimbriatus.* 1.4 mi. SE of Santa Catalina Isl. (LACM 22454), on mainland from Manhattan Beach (UCLA W 57–198) to Monterey Bay. Length to 7.75 in. Moderate depths, from 198 to 870 ft. Dark gray above paler below. Rare. D X + 15–16; A 12–13; Pect. 16–18; Pelvic I,2; LLs 36–37 on body + 1 on tail.

FROGMOUTH SCULPIN, *Icelinus oculatus.* San Diego to Redondo Isl., British Columbia. Length to 7.3 in. Deep water, from 558 to 644 ft. Dark brown above, whitish below. Rare. D X + 16–17; A 13–14; Pect. 17; Pelvic I,2; LLs 37–39 on body + 1 on tail.

DUSKY SCULPIN, *Icelinus burchami.* 5 mi. W of North Mile Marker, La Jolla (SIO H 50-245A), to Behm Canal, Alaska. Length to 5.1 in. Deep water, from 800 to 1430 ft. Dark brown above, grayish below. Rare. D IX–X + 16–18; A 12–14; Pect. 16–19; Pelvic I,2; LLs 35–38 on body + 1 on tail.

13b Six to 7 anal soft-rays; 8–10 dorsal soft-rays; orbit 1.1–1.3 into maxillary:

BULL SCULPIN

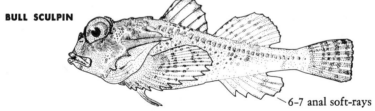

6-7 anal soft-rays

14a *From 11a: gill membranes free from isthmus*
Area between dorsal fins and lateral line entirely without scales or with minute prickly scales........ 32 (page 129)

14b Area between dorsal fins and lateral line with well developed scales in oblique or longitudinal bands, or covering entire area 15

15a Pelvic fins with 1 spine and 3 soft-rays (rarely SMOOTHHEAD and PADDED SCULPINS may have 2 soft-rays); dorsal band more than 2 scales in width, or immediately above lateral line and far removed from dorsal fin .... 22 (page 125)

15b Pelvic fins with 1 spine and 2 soft-rays; dorsal scale band 2 scales in width, extending a little below dorsal fins and well above lateral line........ 16

16a Dorsal band of scales not extending beyond end of second dorsal fin 19

16b Dorsal scale band extends onto dorsal surface of caudal peduncle....... 17

17a Dorsal scale band interrupted for a short space under end of second dorsal fin; pelvic fins extend more than ⅓ of distance to anal origin:

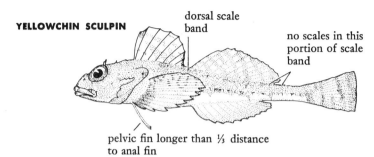

YELLOWCHIN SCULPIN

dorsal scale band

no scales in this portion of scale band

pelvic fin longer than ⅓ distance to anal fin

17b Dorsal scale band continuous; pelvic fins not extending to ⅓ of distance to anal fin origin 18

18a A fringe of cirri along posterior end of maxillary; cirrus at base of nasal spine with expanded and fringed tip:

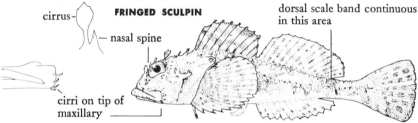

cirrus

FRINGED SCULPIN

dorsal scale band continuous in this area

nasal spine

cirri on tip of maxillary

18b A single cirrus near posterior end of maxillary; cirrus at base of nasal spine long, slender, simple:

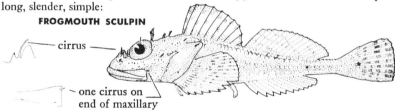

FROGMOUTH SCULPIN

cirrus

one cirrus on end of maxillary

19a *From 16a: dorsal band of scales not extending beyond second dorsal*
Pelvic fins short, extending less than ¼ of distance to anal fin origin; and origin under 3rd to 4th dorsal soft-ray; no scales behind pectoral axilla:

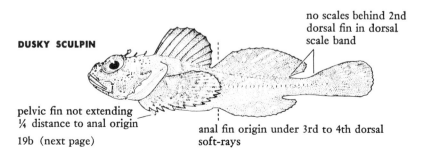

no scales behind 2nd dorsal fin in dorsal scale band

DUSKY SCULPIN

pelvic fin not extending ¼ distance to anal origin

anal fin origin under 3rd to 4th dorsal soft-rays

19b (next page)

SCULPINS, Family Cottidae (continued)

THREADFIN SCULPIN, *Icelinus filamentosus*. Cortez Bank (UCLA W 54-392) to N. British Columbia. Length to 10.62 in. Depth 60 to 1224 ft. Brown to green above, tan below; jet-black cirri on head. Uncommon. D IX–XI + 15–18; A 13–15; Pect. 16–18; Pelvic I,2; LLs 36–39 on body + 1–2 on tail; GR rudimentary knobs; Vert. 35–37.

SPOTFIN SCULPIN, *Icelinus tenuis*. San Benito Isls., Baja California (LACM 21653) to Queen Charlotte Isls., B.C. Length to 5.5 in. Depth 108 to 1224 ft. Light brown above with orangish blotches, cream below. Uncommon. D IX–XI + 16–19; A 13–17; Pect. 15–17; Pelvic I,2; LLs 38–42 on body + 1 on tail; Vert. 38.

PITHEAD SCULPIN, *Icelinus cavifrons*. Santa Maria Bay, Baja California, to Monterey Bay, including Guadalupe Isl. Length to 3.5 in. Depth 36 to 300 ft. Light brown with dark mottling on sides. Uncommon. D IX-X + 12–15; A 11–13; Pect. 14-16; Pelvic I,2; LLp 36–38 on body + 1 on tail; Vert. 35–36.

ROUGHBACK SCULPIN, *Chitonotus pugetensis*. Santa Maria Bay, Baja California, to Ucluelet, British Columbia, including Guadalupe Isl. Length to 9 in. Intertidal to 456 ft. Brown to green above, white below; red areas behind pectoral fin and on back at base of soft dorsal fin. Uncommon. D X–XI + 14–17; A 14–17; Pect. 16–18; Pelvic I,3; LLs 36–39 on body + 1 on tail; GR 0-2 + 6-9 = 6-10; Vert. 35–36.

SNUBNOSE SCULPIN, *Orthonopias triacis*. San Geronimo Isl., Baja California (SIO H 52-158), to Monterey. Length to 4 in. Intertidal to 100 ft. Reddish-brown with dark and light mottling over entire body, second dorsal without spotting. Common. D VIII–IX + 16–18; A 11–13; Pect. 13–15; Pelvic I,3; LLs 36–38 on body + 1 on tail; GR 1 + 5 = 6; Vert. 35.

19b Pelvic fins moderate, extending more than ¼ distance to anal fin origin; anal origin under 1st to 2nd dorsal soft-ray; a few small scales behind pectoral axilla 20

20a No distinct spines at upper posterior angle of orbit; dorsal scale band extending to end of 2nd dorsal; a long cirrus at base of nasal spine:

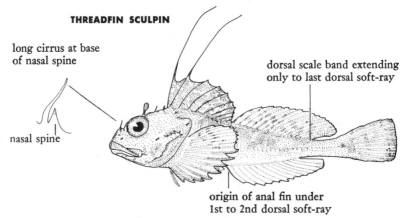

THREADFIN SCULPIN

long cirrus at base of nasal spine

nasal spine

dorsal scale band extending only to last dorsal soft-ray

origin of anal fin under 1st to 2nd dorsal soft-ray

20b Two distinct spines at upper posterior angle of orbit; dorsal scale band not extending to base of last dorsal soft-ray; no cirrus at base of nasal spine............ 21 (next page)

21a Dorsal soft-rays 16-19; anal soft-rays 13-17; top of head gently concave; body
   slender: **SPOTFIN SCULPIN**

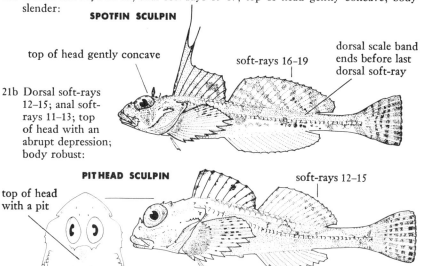

top of head gently concave

soft-rays 16-19

dorsal scale band ends before last dorsal soft-ray

21b Dorsal soft-rays 12-15; anal soft-rays 11-13; top of head with an abrupt depression; body robust:

PITHEAD SCULPIN

soft-rays 12-15

top of head with a pit

22a *From 15a: pelvic soft-rays 3*. First dorsal spine much longer than 2nd; 1st dorsal fin deeply notched between 3rd and 4th spines; upper preopercular spine antlerlike:

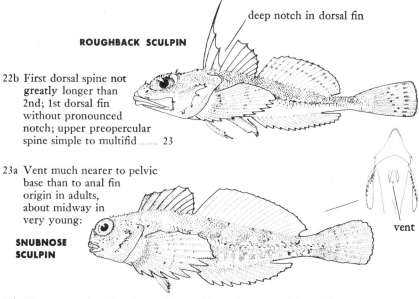

deep notch in dorsal fin

ROUGHBACK SCULPIN

22b First dorsal spine not greatly longer than 2nd; 1st dorsal fin without pronounced notch; upper preopercular spine simple to multifid 23

23a Vent much nearer to pelvic base than to anal fin origin in adults, about midway in very young:

SNUBNOSE SCULPIN

vent

23b Vent not noticeably advanced in position, close to anal fin origin 24

24a Dorsal origin about over tip of opercular flap, and far behind upper end of gill opening; body slender, distance from dorsal to pelvics more than 6 times into standard length; no teeth on palatines ...... 30 (page 128)

24b (next page)

SCULPINS, Family Cottidae (continued)

CORALLINE SCULPIN, *Artedius corallinus*. San Martin Isl., Baja California (LACM 1989), to Orcas Isls., Washington (UCLA W 63–246). Length to 5.5 in. Intertidal to 70 ft. Dark gray to brown above; purplish-red mottling on head and back. Common. D IX + 15–16; A 12–13; Pect. 15–16; Pelvic I,3; LLs 34–35 on body + 1 on tail.

SMOOTHHEAD SCULPIN, *Artedius lateralis*. Sulfur Pt., San Quintin, Baja California SU 15255), to Bering Isl., Commander Isls., USSR. Length to 5.25 in. Intertidal to 25 ft. Brown to greenish above, tan to greenish below. Common. D VIII–X + 15–17; A 12–14; Pect. 15–16; Pelvic I,3; LLs 35–36 on body + 1–2 on tail; GR 1–2 + 6–9 = 8–11; Vert. 32–34.

PADDED SCULPIN, *Artedius fenestralis*. Diablo Cove, San Luis Obispo Co. (LACM 31700), to Unalaska Isl., Alaska. Length to 5.5 in. Intertidal to 180 ft. Light colored, varying from yellowish to greenish; dark bars along sides and black spots in spinous dorsal. Uncommon. D VIII–IX + 16–18; A 12–14; Pect. 15–16; Pelvic I,3; LLs 36–37 on body + 1–2 on tail; GR 1 + 4–5 = 5–6; Vert. 34–35.

BONYHEAD SCULPIN, *Artedius notospilotus*. Pt. San Telmo, Baja California (UCLA W 49–373), to Puget Sound, Washington. Length to 10 in. Intertidal to 150 ft. Dark green to gray above with lighter mottling on sides. Uncommon. D IX + 14–16; A 11–13; Pect. 15–17; Pelvic I,3 (rarely I,2); LLs 35–37 on body + 1–2 on tail; GR 2 + 8–10 = 10–12; Vert. 33–34.

ROUGHCHEEK SCULPIN, *Artedius creaseri*. Pt. San Pablo, Baja California (LACM 32082), to Pescadero Pt., Monterey Co., including Guadalupe Isl. Length to 3 in. Intertidal to 90 ft. Olive-green to light brown; dark bars on back. Uncommon. D X–XI + 12–14; A 9–10; Pect. 15–17; Pelvic I,3; LLs 33 on body + 1 on tail.

24b Dorsal origin over or anterior to upper end of gill opening; body heavy, distance from dorsal to pelvics less than 5 times into standard length; teeth present on palatines........ 25

25a Scales present on head........ 27 (next page)

25b No scales on head........ 26

26a Dorsal scale band with 39–49 oblique rows of scales and 10–18 scales in longest row; a few small scales just behind opercular flap between pectoral base and lateral line:

CORALLINE SCULPIN

26b Dorsal scale band with 18–29 oblique rows of scales and 3–11 scales in longest row; no scales behind opercular flap:

SMOOTHHEAD SCULPIN

27a (next page)

27a *From 25a: scales present on head*
Cirrus present on upper anterior margin of orbit; dorsal scale band more or less merging with head scales........ 29

27b No preorbital cirrus; dorsal scale band originating about under base of 3rd dorsal spine, separated from head scales by a naked area or preceded by scales so minute and scattered that they do not obscure the definite origin of the band........ 28

28a Dorsal scale bands continued on dorsal surface of caudal peduncle where they form a dense patch of scales; scales extending under entire orbit; anal soft-rays 12–14:

PADDED SCULPIN   dense patch of scales

scales under orbit —

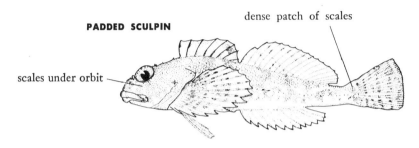

28b Dorsal scale band extending to end of 2nd dorsal fin, sometimes continued on dorsal surface of caudal peduncle by a few widely scattered scales that never form a dense patch; scales extending only under posterior part of orbit; anal soft-rays 11–13:

BONYHEAD SCULPIN

no scales under anterior part of orbit —

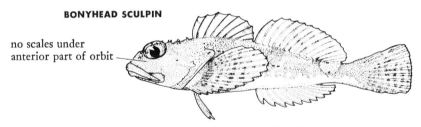

29a *From 27a: cirrus present on upper anterior margin of orbit*
Second dorsal with 12–14 soft-rays; anal soft-rays 9–10; scales extending under entire orbit, present on snout:

ROUGHCHEEK SCULPIN

cirrus

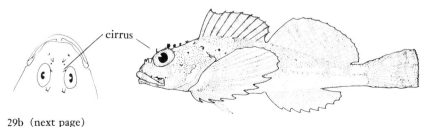

29b (next page)

SCULPINS, Family Cottidae (continued)

SCALYHEAD SCULPIN, *Artedius harringtoni*. San Miguel Isl. (SIO 54-191) to Kodiak Isl., Alaska. Length to 4 in. Intertidal to 70 ft. Brown to olive above, mottled white and tan below; dark bars on back and conspicuous white hexagon patterns in anal fin. Uncommon. D IX–X + 16-18; A 10-14; Pect. 13-15; Pelvic I,3; LLs 35-38 on body + 1-2 on tail; Vert. 34.

SMOOTHGUM SCULPIN, *Radulinus vinculus*. Between Santa Cruz and Anacapa Isls. (UCLA W 50-111) to Diablo Cove, San Luis Obispo Co. (LACM 31739). Length to 2.5 in. Taken from 70 to 90 ft. Brown with three dark brown cross bars on sides. Rare. D X + 17; A 18; Pect. 17; LLs 35.

DARTER SCULPIN, *Radulinus boleoides*. Santa Catalina Isl. to Langara Isl., British Colum. Length to 5.5 in. Moderate depths, from 240 to 480 ft. Olive-gray to gray above, white below; dark cross bars on sides. Rare. D X–XI + 20–22; A 21–23; Pect. 18–20; Pelvic I,3; LLs 39–40.

SLIM SCULPIN, *Radulinus asprellus*. Los Coronados Isls., Baja California, to Kodiak Isl., Alaska. Length to 6 in. Moderate depths, from 156 to 930 ft. Light brown to gray above, lighter below. Uncommon. D VIII–XI + 20–23; A 22–25; Pect. 17–20; Pelvic I,3; LLs 38–41; GR 0–1 + 7–8 = 7–9; Vert. 38–39.

FLABBY SCULPIN, *Zesticelus profundorum*. Northern Baja California to Petropavlosk, Kamchatka. Length to 2 in. Deep water, from 294 to 6490 ft. Rare. D V–VII + 10–13; A 8–11; Pect. 19–21; Pelvic I,2–3; LLs 14–17.

SADDLEBACK SCULPIN, *Oligocottus rimensis*. Dutch Harbor, San Nicolas Isl. (UCLA W 49-65), to British Columbia. Length to 2.56 in. Intertidal. Heavily mottled, greenish to reddish above, light tan to greenish below. Common. D VIII–X + 16–19; A 13–15; Pect. 13–15; Pelvic I,3; LLp 35–40 on body + 0–1 on tail; GR 1 + 4–5 = 5–6; Vert. 35–37.

29b Second dorsal with 16-18 soft-rays; anal soft-rays 10-14; scales extending only under posterior part of orbit if at all, absent from snout:

SCALYHEAD SCULPIN

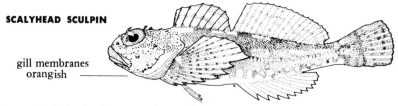

gill membranes
orangish

30a *From 24a: body slender; no teeth on palatines*
Dorsal soft-rays 17; anal soft-rays 18; cirri present on each side slightly below lateral line about on vertical of origin of 2nd dorsal fin; no teeth on vomer:

SMOOTHGUM SCULPIN

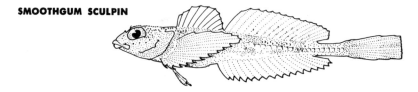

30b Dorsal soft-rays 20-23; anal soft-rays 21-25; no cirri below lateral line as in 30a; teeth present on vomer........ 31 (next page)

31a Snout longer than eye diameter; nasal spines short, triangular:

DARTER SCULPIN

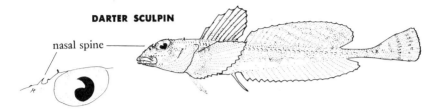

nasal spine

31b Snout equal to or shorter than eye; nasal spines long, needlelike:

SLIM SCULPIN

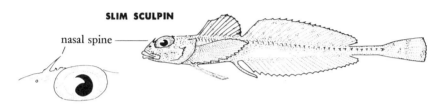

nasal spine

32a *From 14a: back without scales or with minute prickly scales*
   Dorsal spines 5–7; dorsal soft-rays 10–13; 14–17 pores in lateral line:

14-17 lateral line pores

FLABBY SCULPIN

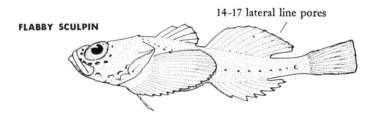

32b Dorsal spines 7–10; dorsal soft-rays 13–20; 33–43 pores in lateral line........ 33

33a Vent located in middle 3rd of distance between pelvic fin base and anal fin
   origin .... 37 (page 131)

33b Vent immediately in advance of anal fin origin 34

34a Preopercular spine simple; body covered with minute prickly scales:

SADDLEBACK SCULPIN

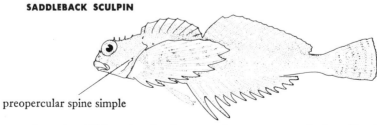

preopercular spine simple

34b Preopercular spine bifid to 4 pointed, except in very young; body without
   visible scales .... 35 (next page)

SCULPINS, Family Cottidae (continued)

TIDEPOOL SCULPIN, *Oligocottus maculosus*. Between White Pt. and Portuguese Bend, Los Angeles Co. (LACM 21250), to Sea of Okhotsk. Length to 3.5 in. Intertidal and shallow rocky areas. Color ranges from greenish to red above, whitish below. Common. D VIII–IX + 15–18; A 11–14; Pect. 13–15; Pelvic I,3; LLp 34–39 on body + 1–2 on tail; GR 0–1 + 4–5 = 5–6; Vert. 33–34.

FLUFFY SCULPIN, *Oligocottus snyderi*. 2 miles S of Rio Socorro, Baja California (UCLA W 46-3), to Samsing Cove, Sitka, Alaska. Length to 3.25 in. Intertidal to subtidal. Bright green to reddish-brown and light pink. Common. D VII–IX + 17–20; A 12–15; Pect. 13–15; Pelvic I,3; LLp 36–39 on body + 1–2 on tail; Vert. 34–37.

ROSY SCULPIN, *Oligocottus rubellio*. San Martin Isl., Baja California (SIO H 52–218), to Fort Bragg. Length to 3.12 in. Intertidal to subtidal. Reddish-brown to red and purplish with white spotting. Common. D VII–IX + 13–17; A 10–14; Pect. 13–15; Pelvic I,3; LLp 34–38 on body + 1–2 on tail; GR 1 + 4–6 = 5–7; Vert. 32–35.

LAVENDER SCULPIN, *Leiocottus hirundo*. Pt. Banda, Baja California, to Gaviota Pier (UCLA W 61-71) and Santa Rosa Island (UCLA W 50-100). Length to 10 in. Intertidal to 120 ft. Olive-green with blue shading mottled with red. Uncommon. D IX + 17; A 15–16; Pect. 17–18; Pelvic I,3; LLp 38 on body + 1–2 on tail.

WOOLY SCULPIN, *Clinocottus analis*. Ascuncion Pt., Baja California, to 2 miles S of Cape Mendocino (CAS 20074), including Guadalupe Isl. (LACM 22048). Length to 7 in., but rarely over 5 in. Intertidal to 60 ft. Color variable ranging from reddish to green with heavy mottling. Common. D VIII–X + 15–18; A 12–15; Pect. 14–17; Pelvic I,3; LLp 35–36 on body + 1 on tail; GR 0–1 + 5–6 = 6–7; Vert. 31–35.

35a No cirri on nasal spines, none on body above lateral line:

TIDEPOOL SCULPIN

nasal spine without —— a cirrus

35b A well developed cirrus on nasal spine, tufts of cirri along base of dorsal fins........ 36

36a No cirri on maxillary or suborbital stay; preopercular spine usually bifid in adults:

FLUFFY SCULPIN

cirrus present on nasal spine

preopercular spine bifid

36b (next page)

36b One to 4 cirri on end of maxillary, small tuft of cirri on suborbital stay; preopercular spine usually trifid in adults:

ROSY SCULPIN

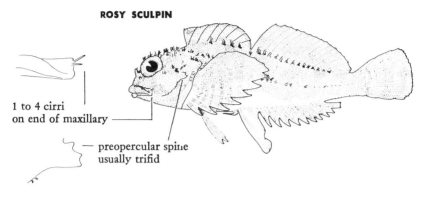

1 to 4 cirri
on end of maxillary

preopercular spine
usually trifid

37a *From 33a: vent midway between pelvic and anal fins*
Anterior end of 1st dorsal fin strongly elevated, first dorsal spine about twice
as long as 3rd spine; no postorbital cirrus and none on base of opercular flap:

LAVENDER SCULPIN

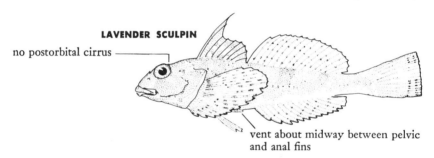

no postorbital cirrus

vent about midway between pelvic
and anal fins

37b Anterior end of 1st dorsal fin not elevated, 1st dorsal spine about equal to, or
shorter than 3rd spine; a large postorbital cirrus, 1 or more cirri on base of
opercular flap........ 38

38a Preopercular spine with 2-3 points; cirri and minute scales present between
dorsal fins and lateral line:

WOOLY SCULPIN

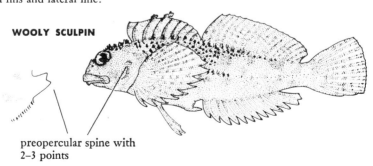

preopercular spine with
2-3 points

38b Preopercular spine simple; neither cirri nor scales present between dorsal fins
and lateral line........ 39 (next page)

SCULPINS, Family Cottidae (continued)

SHARPNOSE SCULPIN, *Clinocottus acuticeps*. Big Sur River (CAS 13613) to Attu Isl., Alaska. Length to 2.5 in. Intertidal and sandy beach areas (occasionally venturing into freshwater). Brownish-green above, white to tan below. Uncommon. D VII–IX + 14-16; A 10-13; Pect. 13-15; Pelvic I,3; LLp 33–36 on body + 1–2 on tail; Vert. 31-33.

CALICO SCULPIN, *Clinocottus embryum*. Pt. Banda, Baja California (SIO H 51–21), to Bering Sea. Length to 2.75 in. Intertidal and shallow rocky areas. Mottled, with olive-green to deep red or pink above, gray or greenish below. Common. D VIII–X + 14-17; A 9–12; Pect. 12-15; Pelvic I,3; LLp 34–38 on body + 1–2 on tail.

MOSSHEAD SCULPIN, *Clinocottus globiceps*. Gaviota (UCLA W 48–34) to Chagafka Cove, Kodiak Isl., Alaska. Length to 7.5 in. Intertidal and shallow rocky areas. Reddish-brown to olive on back, tan below with heavy mottling on sides. Common. D IX–X + 13-17; A 10-12; Pect. 13-14; Pelvic I,3; LLp 34–37 on body + 1–2 on tail; GR 1 + 5 = 6; Vert. 32-34.

BALD SCULPIN, *Clinocottus recalvus*. Pt. Rompiente, Baja California (LACM 32054), to Mill Beach near Brookings, Oregon (LACM 8958). Length to 5.12 in. Intertidal. Light to dark brown, with lighter reddish and white mottling. Common. D VIII–IX + 14-17; A 10-13; Pect. 13-15; Pelvic I,3; LLp 33–37 on body + 1–2 on tail; GR 1 + 4-7 = 5–8; Vert. 32-33.

39a One or 2 cirri on end of maxillary; inner pelvic ray strongly attached to belly by membrane:

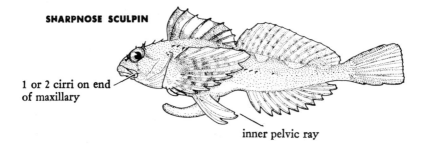

SHARPNOSE SCULPIN

1 or 2 cirri on end of maxillary

inner pelvic ray

39b No cirri on maxillary; inner pelvic ray not attached to belly by membrane......... 40 (next page)

40a Head moderately pointed and angular, definitely not hemispherical; upper lip
terminal; small fleshy tubercle in median line of groove which limits upper lip
dorsally; no cirri behind opercular flap between pectoral base and lateral line:

CALICO SCULPIN

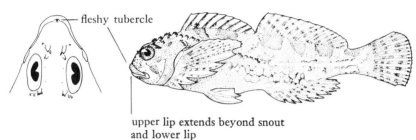

fleshy tubercle

upper lip extends beyond snout
and lower lip

40b Head very bluntly rounded, hemispherical; upper lip inferior except in young
specimens; no fleshy tubercle in groove which limits upper lip dorsally; patch
of cirri behind opercular flap between pectoral base and lateral line_____ 41

41a Cirri in anterior half of interorbital space in specimens over 35 mm standard
length:

MOSSHEAD SCULPIN

cirri present in anterior
half of interorbital space

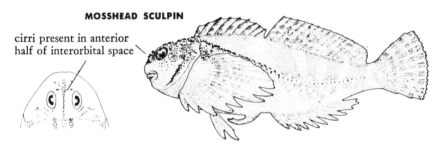

41b No cirri in anterior half of interorbital space:

BALD SCULPIN

no cirri present in anterior
half of interorbital space

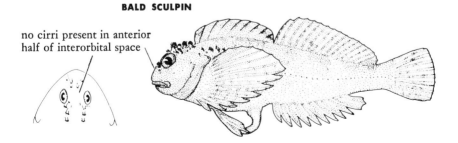

POACHERS, Family Agonidae *1
(Principal sources: Bolin,*2 Clemens & Wilby, 1961; Fitch, 1966)

ROCKHEAD, *Bothragonus swanii*. Lion Rock, San Luis Obispo Co., to Kodiak Isl., Alaska. Length to 3.4 in. Intertidal to 60 ft. Brown, with orange and red mottling. Rare. D III–IV + 4–5; A 4–5; Pect. 12; Pelvic I,2; LLp 32.

TUBENOSE POACHER, *Pallasina barbata*. Bodega Bay to Kamchatka and Japan. Length to 5.3 in. Intertidal to 180 ft. Body gray to brown above, paler below. Uncommon. D VI–IX + 6–9; A 10–14; Pect. 10–13; Pelvic I,2; LLp 45-46; Vert. 47.

KELP POACHER, *Agonomalus sp.*3 Central California, and possibly into Pacific Northwest. Length to 3.4 in. Shallow rocky reef areas. Body mottled with black, white, orange, red, and brown; orange-red flap on snout (see color plate on page 233 in Herald, 1972). Rare. D VIII + 6; A 11; Pect. 12; Pelvic I,2.

WARTY POACHER, *Occella verrucosa*. 4.5 mi. W of Pt. Montara (UCLA W 59-135) to Shelikof, Alaska. Length to 8 in. Depth 66 to 900 ft. Dark gray above, paler below; male with orange and yellow in pelvic region. Common. D VII–IX + 7–9; A 7–12; Pect. 15; Pelvic I,2; LLp 36-38; GR 1–2 + 8–12 = 10–14; Vert. 35–37.

PRICKLEBREAST POACHER, *Stellerina xyosterna*. San Carlos Bay, Baja California (SIO H 52-214), to Strait of Juan de Fuca, British Columbia (has not been reported from southern California). Length to 6.5 in. Depth 15 to 246 ft. Light olive-brown above, paler below; spotting on dorsal surface. Uncommon. D VI–VIII + 5–7; A 8–9; Pect. 17–19; Pelvic I,2; GR 1–3 + 14–16 = 16–18; Vert. 34–37.

STURGEON POACHER, *Agonus acipenserinus*. Eureka to Bering Sea. Length to 12 in. Depth 60 to 180 ft. Body brown above, yellowish to orange below; cirri under chin yellow. One California record. D VIII–X + 7–9; A 6–9; Pelvic I,2; LLp 37-40. (Eureka specimen from CF&G| sample)

BEARDLESS SPEARNOSE, *Ganoideus vulsus*. Pt. Reyes. Length to 4.1 in. Deep water. Brown above, paler below. One collection. D IX + 7; A 9; Pect. 14; Pelvic I,2.

NORTHERN SPEARNOSE, *Agonopsis emmelane*. Pt. Loma to S.E. Alaska. Length to 8 in. Depth 60 to 534 ft. Brown above, white below. Uncommon. D VIII–XI + 7–8; A 10–12; Pect. 14; Pelvic I,2; LLp 38-42.

SOUTHERN SPEARNOSE, *Agonopsis sterletus*. Pt. San Hipolito, Baja California, to San Simeon Pt. (UCLA W 66-67). Length to 5.7 in. Deep water. Brown above, white below. Uncommon. D VIII + 8; A 9; Pect. 12.

KEY TO THE POACHERS, Family Agonidae:

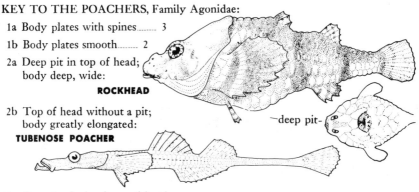

1a Body plates with spines........ 3

1b Body plates smooth........ 2

2a Deep pit in top of head; body deep, wide:

      ROCKHEAD

2b Top of head without a pit; body greatly elongated:

TUBENOSE POACHER

—deep pit-

3a *From 1a: body plates with spines*
    Gill membranes attached to isthmus........ 6 (next page)

3b (next page)   * See comments on page 213.

3b Gill membranes free from isthmus, or if joined, with a free fold across isthmus greater than eye diameter in width........ 4

4a Large flap on snout: **KELP POACHER**

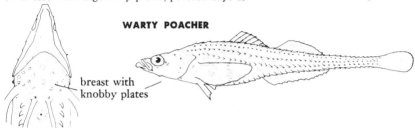

flap on snout

4b No flap on snout........ 5

5a Breast with large bony plates; pectoral rays 15:

WARTY POACHER

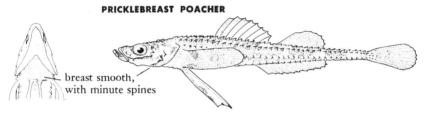

breast with
knobby plates

5b Breast covered with an even felt of minute spines; pectoral rays 17–19:

PRICKLEBREAST POACHER

breast smooth,
with minute spines

6a *From 3a: gill membranes attached to isthmus*
Rostral plate at tip of snout with 1 or 3 upright spines........ 10 (next page)

6b Rostral plate at tip of snout with 2 forward projecting spines........ 7

7a Dense clusters of cirri or small barbels under snout and at corners of mouth; snout long, about 2 times greater than eye diameter:

STURGEON POACHER

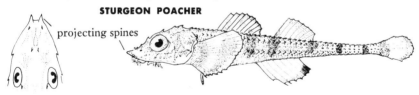

projecting spines

7b No dense clusters of cirri as above; snout length about same as eye diameter.... 8

8a Pectoral rays 14; vomer without teeth: BEARDLESS SPEARNOSE (not illustrated, body form as in 9a below)

8b Pectoral rays 12–14; vomer with teeth........ 9

9a Pelvic fins dark brown with white tips; cirri present below rostral spines:

NORTHERN SPEARNOSE

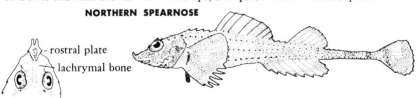

rostral plate
lachrymal bone

9b Pelvic fins white; no cirri below rostral spines: SOUTHERN SPEARNOSE (not illustrated, same body form as in 9a above)

10a (next page)

136   GUIDE TO THE COASTAL MARINE

POACHERS, Family Agonidae (continued)

PYGMY POACHER, *Odontopyxis trispinosa.* Cedros Isl., Baja California, to S.E. Alaska. Length to 3.4 in. Depth 30 to 1208 ft. Body uniform olive-brown. Common. D III–VI + 5–7; A 5–7; Pect. 13–15; Pelvic I,2; LLp 35–38; GR 0 + 7 = 7; Vert. 38–42.

BLACKFIN STARNOSE, *Bathyagonus nigripinnis.* Eureka * to Commander Isls., USSR. Length to 8 in. Depth 300 to 4092 ft. Uniform brown; fins entirely black. Rare. D VI–VIII + 6–7; A 7–9; Pect. 15–16; Pelvic I,2; LLp 40–44; Vert. 45.

SPINYCHEEK STARNOSE, *Asterotheca infraspinata.* Eureka to Bering Sea. Length to 4.75 in. Depth 60 to 600 ft. Light olive-green to brown above, white below. Uncommon. D V–VIII + 5–8; A 5–8; Pect. 15–16; Pelvic I,2; LLp 37–39; Vert. 41.

BIGEYE STARNOSE, *Asterotheca pentacantha.* 5 mi. NE of Cortez Bank light (CAS 24776) to Chirikof Isl., Alaska (BCPM 6559). Length to 9.29 in. Depth 360 to 660 ft. Olive-brown above, paler below. Uncommon. D V–VIII + 5–7; A 6–8; Pect. 14–16; Pelvic I,2; LLp 39–42; Vert. 40–45.

FLAGFIN POACHER, *Xeneretmus ritteri.* Upper Gulf of California (isolated population), and from Cedros Isl., Baja California, to Malibu. Length to 6.25 in. Depth 600 to 1200 ft. Uncommon. D V–VII + 6–7; A 6–7; Pect. 16–17; LLp 41.

BLUESPOTTED POACHER, *Xeneretmus triacanthus.* Rio Rosario, Baja California, to Kuatna Inlet, British Columbia, and possibly to Peter the Great Bay, USSR. Length to 7 in. Depth 240 to 1200 ft. Olive-brown; blue spots on and near head. Common. D V–VI + 6–7; A 6–7; Pect. 13; Pelvic I,2; GR 1 + 8–13 = 9–14; Vert. 41–42.

BLACKEDGE POACHER, *Xeneretmus latifrons.* Ensenada to Burrard Inlet, British Columbia. Length to 7.5 in. Depth 300 to 1224 ft. Light brown above, paler below. Uncommon. D VI–VII + 6–8; A 6–9; Pect. 14–15; LLp 39–41; GR 0 + 10–11; Vert. 39–42.

SMOOTHEYE POACHER, *Xeneretmus leiops.* Santa Catalina Isl. to Strait of Juan de Fuca, British Columbia. Length to 9 in. Depth 468 to 1308 ft. Dusky-olive above, whitish below. Rare. D VI + 7; A 7; Pect. 14; LLp 43.

10a From *6a: 1 to 3 upright spines on rostral plate*
    Top of head with a pit:

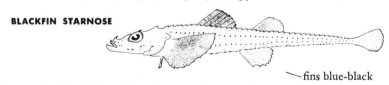

PYGMY POACHER

shallow pit

10b Top of head without a pit........ 11

11a One upright spine on rostral plate........ 14 (next page)

11b Three upright spines on rostral plate........ 12

12a All fins blue-black; lower jaw projecting beyond upper:

BLACKFIN STARNOSE

fins blue-black

12b Fins not blue-black; jaws subequal........ 13 (next page)

* See comments on page 213.

13a Anterior tip of lachrymal with sharp, fine forward projecting spines; body
plates (dorsal series) 35–39: **SPINYCHEEK STARNOSE**

spines on end
of lachrymal

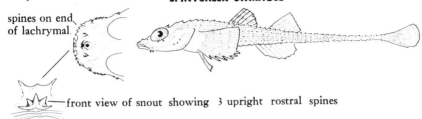

front view of snout showing 3 upright rostral spines

13b Lachrymal without forward projecting spines; body plates (dorsal series)
41–44:

BIGEYE STARNOSE

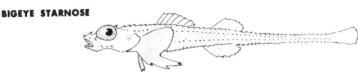

14a *From 11a: one upright spine on rostral plate*
Pectoral rays 16–17; black band on base of rays of both dorsal fins:

FLAGFIN POACHER   black bands

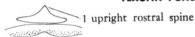 1 upright rostral spine

14b Pectoral rays 13–15; no black band on dorsal fin bases as above........ 15

15a Pectoral rays 13; 1st dorsal fin clear (some fine speckling may be present);
bright blue spots on head and on body near head:

BLUESPOTTED POACHER   dorsal fins clear

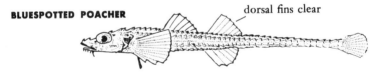

15b Pectoral rays 14–15 ; margin of 1st dorsal black; no bright blue spots as
above 16

16a Spinous scales present on eyeball; 1st dorsal fin with an even black margin:

BLACKEDGE POACHER

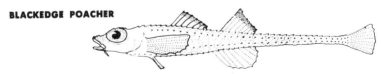

16b No spinous scales on eyeball; margin of 1st dorsal with an enlarged black
blotch anteriorly and often with a narrower black margin posteriorly:

SMOOTHEYE POACHER   black blotch

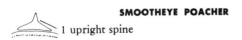 1 upright spine

SNAILFISHES, Family Liparididae *

(Principal sources: Burke, 1930; Hubbs & Schultz, 1934; Clemens & Wilby, 1961)

BLACKTAIL SNAILFISH, *Careproctus melanurus*. Off San Diego to northern British Columbia. Length to 10.25 in. Depth 294 to 5256 ft. Whitish to pink with black caudal fin and dusky on belly. Uncommon. D 54-58; A 47-50; Pect. 30-31; scales absent; LL absent; pyloric caecae 20-27.

SHOWY SNAILFISH, *Liparis pulchellus*. Monterey Bay (CAS 16021) to Peter the Great Bay, USSR. Length to 10 in. Intertidal to 600 ft. Uniform light to dark brown above, paler below; occasionally with wavy lines on sides. Uncommon. D 47-53; A 39-42; Pect. 36-37; scales absent; LL absent; GR $0 + 6$-9; pyloric caecae 32; Vert. 51-53.

SLIPSKIN SNAILFISH, *Liparis fucensis*. North of San Simeon Pt. (UCLA W 63-256) to S.E. Alaska. Length to 7 in. Subtidal to 1272 ft. Olive-brown to dark brown with faint mottling; light oblique bar in caudal fin. Uncommon. D 33-35; A 27-29; Pect. 37-43; scales absent; LL absent; GR $0 + 8$-9; Vert. 39-41.

RINGTAIL SNAILFISH, *Liparis rutteri*. Duxbury Reef (CAS 13707) to Bering Sea. Length to 6.62 in. Intertidal to 240 ft. Uniform black to brown; white band across base of caudal fin; occasionally with faint streaks on sides. Uncommon. D 30-32; A 23-27; Pect. 30-33; scales absent; LL absent; pyloric caecae 23-31.

TIDEPOOL SNAILFISH, *Liparis florae*. 1 mi. south of lighthouse, Pt. Conception (UCLA W 62-135), to Bering Sea. Length to 7.2 in. Intertidal. Uniform brown to olive-brown and purplish. Common. D 31-33; A 25-27; Pect. 29-33; scales absent; LL absent; GR 0-$1 + 3$-$4 = 3$-4; Vert. 39-40.

SLIMY SNAILFISH, *Liparis mucosus*. Playa Maria Bay, Baja California (SIO H 52-168), to Vancouver Isl., B.C. Length to 2.87 in. Intertidal to 50 ft. Uniform gray to brown, often with wavy lines on body. Uncommon. D 28-32; A 22-25; Pect. 27-32.

KEY TO THE SNAILFISHES, Family Liparididae

1a Posterior margin of pelvic disc under gill cavity; disc length less than eye diameter:

BLACKTAIL SNAILFISH

pelvic disc under gill cavity   latter portion of anal and
                                        dorsal fins and caudal fin
                                        black

1b Posterior margin of disc under pectoral fin, behind gill cavity; disc length greater than eye diameter........ 2

2a Dorsal and anal fins connected to caudal fin for more than 4/5 of length of caudal fin:

SHOWY SNAILFISH

2b (next page)

* Includes 6 of the 19 California members of this family.

2b Dorsal and anal fins free from caudal fin or connected for not more than 1/5 its length........ 3

3a Gill slit extending down in front of 12th to 16th pectoral ray:

SLIPSKIN SNAILFISH

3b Gill slit extending down not more than 6 pectoral rays.. 4

4a Whitish band across base of caudal fin extending onto posterior tips of dorsal and anal fins; gill slit above pectoral fin:

whitish band

RINGTAIL SNAILFISH

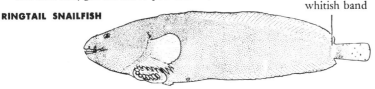

4b No whitish band across caudal fin base; gill slit extending downward in front of from 1 to 6 pectoral rays, usually in front of more than 3 rays...... 5

5a Pelvic disc small, 2.1–2.4 into head; dorsal with a high anterior lobe; vent nearer disc than anal fin; eye 8–9 into head; body deepest at origin of anal fin:

TIDEPOOL SNAILFISH   dorsal lobe pointed, appearing separate from rest of fin

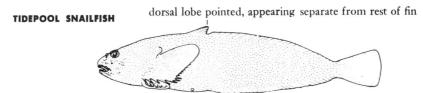

5b Pelvic disc large, 1.7–1.8 into head; dorsal lobe low and broadly rounded; vent nearer anal fin than disc; eye 5–7 into head; body deepest below origin of dorsal fin:

SLIMY SNAILFISH

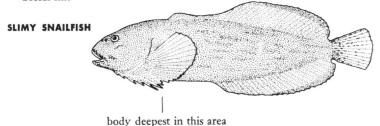

body deepest in this area

SEA BASSES, Family Serranidae

(Principal sources: Barnhart, 1936; Walford, 1937; Roedel, 1953; Rosenblatt &
Zahuranec, 1967; Whitehead & Wheeler, 1967; C. L. Smith, 1971)

STRIPED BASS, *Roccus saxatilis*.* 25 mi. S of California-Mexico border to Barkley
Snd., British Columbia. Length to about 4 ft., and wt. to 90 lbs. in California;
to 6 ft. and 125 lbs. in Atlantic. Bays and along beaches. Silver, with black stripes.
Common north of Monterey. D IX + I–II,12; A III,9–11; Pect. 16–17; LLs 57–
67; GR 8–11 + 14–17 = 22–28; Vert. 25.

GIANT SEA BASS, *Stereolepis gigas*. Gulf of California to Humboldt Bay, including Guadalupe Isl. Length to 7 ft., and wt. to 557 lbs. Depth 18 to 100 ft. Dark
gray, with black spots on sides; juvenile bright red, with black spots. Common
from Channel Isls. south. D XI + I–II,9–10; A III,8–9; GR 2 + 7–8 = 9–10;
Vert. 25–26.

BROOMTAIL GROUPER, *Mycteroperca xenarcha*. Paita, Peru, to San Francisco Bay,
including Galapagos Isls. and Gulf of California. Weight to 97 lbs. Depth, surface to 70 ft. Uniform gray, but sometimes mottled with brown and gray-green.
Rare. D XI,15–16; A III,10–12; Pect. 16–18; GR 9–12 + 18–23 = 27–35; Vert. 24.

GULF GROUPER, *Mycteroperca jordani*. Mazatlan, Mexico, to La Jolla, including
Gulf of California. Recorded weight to 117.5 lbs., reported to 200 lbs. Brown
above, gray below. Rare. D XI,15–17; A III,10–11; Pect. 16–17; GRt 16–21 (10–11
on lower limb).

SPLITTAIL BASS, *Hemanthias peruanus*. Chile to Redondo Beach, including Gulf
of California. Length to 13.8 in. Shallow to 348 ft. Red-orange with darker
speckling. Rare. D X,14; A III,8; Pect. 18; LLs 56–58; GR 23 on lower limb.

SPOTTED CABRILLA, *Epinephelus analogus*. Peru to San Pedro, including Galapagos
Isls. and Gulf of California. Weight to 20 lbs. Depth, surface to 60 ft. Reddish-
brown with dark brown spots over body. Rare. D X,16–18; A III,8; Pect. 19–20;
GR 8–10 + 15–18 = 23–28; Vert. 24.

SNOWY GROUPER, *Epinephelus niveatus*. Warm waters of Atlantic and eastern
Pacific, from Panama to 5 mi. WNW of Los Coronados Isls. Length to about
4 ft. Depth, surface to 1224 ft. Reddish-brown with white spotting. Rare. D X–
XI,14–15; A III,8– 9; Pect. 17–19; GRt 22–27.

KEY TO THE SEA BASSES, Family Serranidae:

1a Operculum with 3 spines.............. 3 (next page)

1b Operculum with 2 spines.............. 2

2a Body with 6–9 black horizontal stripes; more soft-rays than spines in dorsal fin:

STRIPED BASS

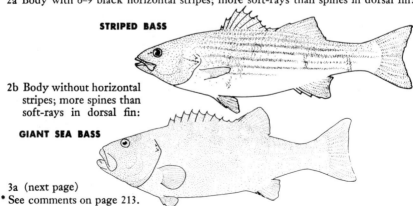

2b Body without horizontal
stripes; more spines than
soft-rays in dorsal fin:

GIANT SEA BASS

3a (next page)
* See comments on page 213.

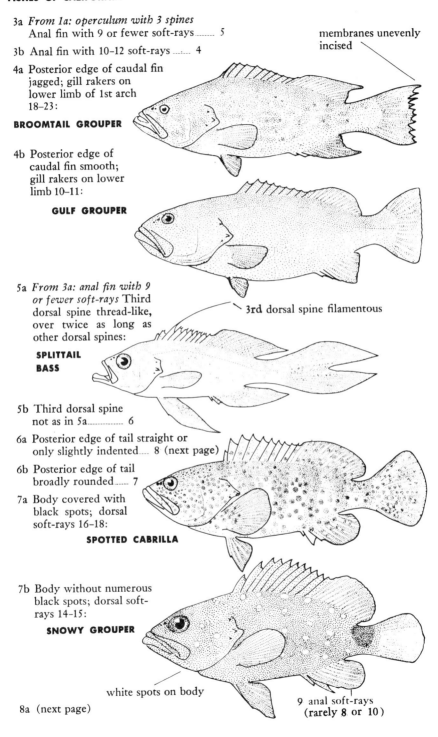

3a *From 1a: operculum with 3 spines*
   Anal fin with 9 or fewer soft-rays 5

membranes unevenly
incised

3b Anal fin with 10–12 soft-rays ....:.... 4

4a Posterior edge of caudal fin
   jagged; gill rakers on
   lower limb of 1st arch
   18–23:

BROOMTAIL GROUPER

4b Posterior edge of
   caudal fin smooth;
   gill rakers on lower
   limb 10–11:

   GULF GROUPER

5a *From 3a: anal fin with 9
   or fewer soft-rays* Third
   dorsal spine thread-like,
   over twice as long as
   other dorsal spines:

   **SPLITTAIL
   BASS**

3rd dorsal spine filamentous

5b Third dorsal spine
   not as in 5a 6

6a Posterior edge of tail straight or
   only slightly indented .... 8 (next page)

6b Posterior edge of tail
   broadly rounded 7

7a Body covered with
   black spots; dorsal
   soft-rays 16–18:

   SPOTTED CABRILLA

7b Body without numerous
   black spots; dorsal soft-
   rays 14–15:

   SNOWY GROUPER

white spots on body

9 anal soft-rays
(rarely **8** or **10**)

8a (next page)

SEA BASSES, Family Serranidae (continued)

KELP BASS, *Paralabrax clathratus*. Magdalena Bay, Baja California, to Columbia River, including Guadalupe Isl. Length to 28.4 in., and wt. to 14.5 lbs. Depth, surface to 150 ft. Olive or brown; whitish angular blotches and spotting on back. Common. D X–XI,12–14; A III,7–8; LLp 68–75; LLs 90–100; GR 11–13 + 20–24 = 32–36; Vert. 24.

SPOTTED SAND BASS, *Paralabrax maculatofasciatus*. Mazatlan, Mexico, to Monterey, including Gulf of California (recorded from San Francisco in late 1800's). Length to 22 in. Shallow to 200 ft. Olive-brown; round black spots on body and fins. Common. D X,13–14; A III,6–8; LLp 66–80; LLs 92–120; GR 6 + 13; Vert. 24.

BARRED SAND BASS, *Paralabrax nebulifer*. Magdalena Bay, Baja California, to Santa Cruz, California, including Guadalupe Isl. Length to 25.6 in. Shallow to 600 ft. Dark gray to greenish; faint crossbars on sides, bars fading after caught. D X,13–15; A III,7; LLp 72–86; LLs 110–120; GR 8–9 + 14–18 = 22–27; Vert. 24.

8a *From 6a: posterior edge of tail straight*
   Third dorsal spine about same length as 4th to 5th dorsal spines:

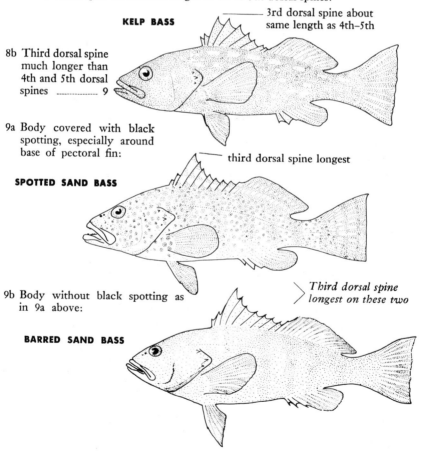

KELP BASS

——— 3rd dorsal spine about same length as 4th–5th

8b Third dorsal spine much longer than 4th and 5th dorsal spines 9

9a Body covered with black spotting, especially around base of pectoral fin:

— third dorsal spine longest

SPOTTED SAND BASS

9b Body without black spotting as in 9a above:

Third dorsal spine longest on these two

BARRED SAND BASS

CATALUFA, CARDINALFISH, and OCEAN WHITEFISH

POPEYE CATALUFA, *Pseudopriacanthus serrula*. Family PRIACANTHIDAE
Peru to Malibu, including Galapagos Isls. and Gulf of California. Length to 9.5
in. Depth 84 to 198 ft. Uniform crimson-red. Rare. D X,11; A III,10-11; LLp
36; LLs 37; GR on lower limb about 16.

GUADALUPE CARDINALFISH, *Apogon guadalupensis*. Family APOGONIDAE
Gulf of California to San Clemente Isl., including Guadalupe Isl. Length to
about 5 in. Depth 30 to 60 ft. Bluish-gray above, red-orange below. Rare. D V
+ I,10; A II,8; LLs 26.

OCEAN WHITEFISH, *Caulolatilus princeps*. Family BRANCHIOSTEGIDAE
Peru to Vancouver Isl., British Columbia, including Galapagos Isls. and Gulf of
California. Length to 40 in. Surface to 300 ft. Yellowish-brown above, paler
below; yellow edging on fins; pores on sides white. Common in southern California, rare north of Monterey. D VIII-IX,23-26; A I-II,23-25; Pect. 19; LLs
116-134; GR 6-10; + 12-15; Vert. 27.

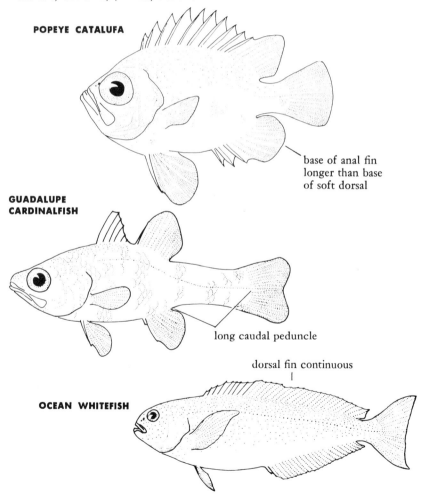

POPEYE CATALUFA

base of anal fin
longer than base
of soft dorsal

GUADALUPE
CARDINALFISH

long caudal peduncle

dorsal fin continuous

OCEAN WHITEFISH

REMORAS, Family Echeneididae

(Principal sources: Follett & Dempster, 1960; Strasburg, 1964; Lachner, 1966)

SLENDER SUCKERFISH, *Phtheirichthys lineatus*. Worldwide in warm seas, north to southern California on our coast. Free living or on sharks. Length to 30 in. Body blackish with 2 white lateral bands; all fins with white margins. Rare. D laminae 9–11, soft-rays 30–40; A 29–38; Pect. 17–21; GR $1 + 10$–11; Vert. 40.

SHARKSUCKER, *Echeneis naucrates*. Worldwide in warm seas; in eastern Pacific north to southern California. Usually found on sharks, but also on variety of hosts such as sea turtles, ships. Length to 38 in. Dark gray to brown; black stripe in midbody bordered by white. Rare. D laminae 20–28; soft-rays 31–42; A 30–38; Pect. 21–24; GR 11–16 on lower limb; Vert. 30.

WHALESUCKER, *Remilegia australis*. Scattered spots throughout warmer seas; in eastern Pacific from Chile to Vancouver Isl., B.C. Attached to marine mammals. Length to 30 in. Variable in color, from uniform light gray to blue, violet, brown, and nearly black; usually with white edging on fins. Rare. D laminae 24–28, soft-rays 20–27; A 20–26; Pect. 21–24; GR 1–$3 + 13$–$19 = 14$–21; Vert. 27.

WHITE SUCKERFISH, *Remorina albescens*. Indo-Pacific oceanic area; in eastern Pacific from Chile to San Francisco. Length to 12 in. Uniform grayish-brown. Rare. D laminae 12–14, soft-rays 17–22; A 16–26; Pect. 16–21; Vert. 26.

HARDFIN MARLINSUCKER, *Rhombochirus osteochir*. Worldwide in warm seas, in eastern Pacific from Peru to Santa Catalina Isl. Free living and attached to swordfish, marlins, sailfish, wahoo. Length to 13.6 in. Uniform brown. Rare. D laminae 16–20, soft-rays 20–27; A 20–26; Pect. 20–24; Vert. 27.

GRAY MARLINSUCKER, *Remora brachyptera*. Found in most warm seas; in eastern Pacific from Chile to La Jolla (SIO H 47-173). Free living and on swordfish and billfishes. Length to 12 in. Light brown to gray above, darker below. Rare. D laminae 14–17, soft-rays 27–34; A 25–30; Pect. 23–27; Vert. 27.

REMORA, *Remora remora*. In all warm seas; in eastern Pacific from Chile to San Francisco, including the Gulf of California. Free living and attached to sharks, sea turtles, ships. Length to 34 in. Uniform black or dark brown. Uncommon. D laminae 16–20, soft-rays 21–27; A 21–25; Pect. 26–30; GR 4–$6 + 25$–$28 = 29$–34; Vert. 27.

KEY TO THE REMORAS, Family Echeneididae:

1a Disc laminae * 9–11:

SLENDER SUCKERFISH

1b Disc laminae 12 or more........ 2

2a Sides with a longitudinal black stripe in midbody bordered with white; anal soft-rays 30–38:

SHARKSUCKER

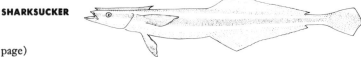

2b (next page)

* The disc is a modified 1st dorsal fin, the spines appearing as rough cross structures referred to as laminae.

2b Sides without a black stripe bordered with white; anal soft-rays less than 28.... 3

3a Disc laminae 24-28:   disc length about ½ of body length

    WHALESUCKER

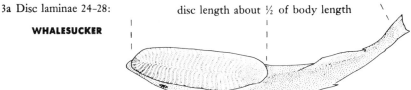

3b Disc laminae 20 or less........ 4

4a Disc width into disc length about 1.5 times (less than 1.6); disc laminae 12-14:

    WHITE SUCKERFISH

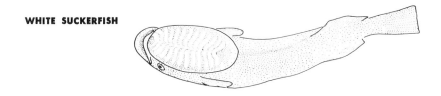

4b Disc width into disc length at least 2 times; disc laminae 14-20.................. 5

5a Disc extending posteriorly well beyond end of depressed pectoral fin:

    HARDFIN MARLINSUCKER

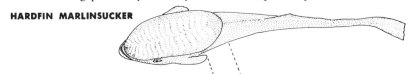

         disc extends well beyond tip of pectoral fin

5b Disc not extending posteriorly as far as tip of depressed pectoral fin.............. 6

6a Disc laminae 14-17; dorsal soft-rays 27-34 (rarely under 28); total gill rakers on 1st arch less than 21:

    GRAY MARLINSUCKER

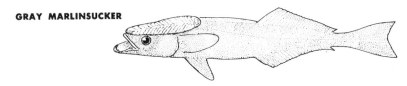

6b Disc laminae 16-20; dorsal soft-rays 21-27; total gill rakers on 1st arch 29-34:

    REMORA

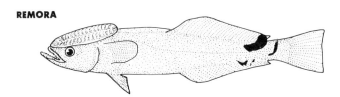

JACKS, Family Carangidae
(Principal sources: Meek & Hildebrand, 1923-1928; Walford, 1937; Lane, 1962)

JACK MACKEREL, *Trachurus symmetricus*. Reported from Galapagos Isls., Revillagigedo Isls. and Acapulco, Mexico, but known range from Magdalena Bay, Baja California, to S.E. Alaska. Length to 32 in. Depth, surface to 150 ft. Metallic blue to olive-green above, silvery below. Common. D VIII + I,28-38; A II + I, 22-33; LLs 87-111, the latter 40-55 as enlarged shields; GR 7-15 + 25-42 = 32-57; Vert. 23-25.

MEXICAN SCAD, *Decapterus hypodus*. Galapagos Isls. to Pacific Grove, including Guadalupe Isl. Length to 18.25 in. Depth, surface to 78 ft. Dark to light green above, yellowish below. Uncommon. D VII-VIII + I,29-33 + 1 finlet; A II + I, 25-29 + 1 finlet; LL enlarged shields over 30; Vert. 24.

PILOTFISH, *Naucrates ductor*. All warm seas; in eastern Pacific from Galapagos Isls. to Mussel Pt., Monterey Co. (CAS 15483). Length to 24 in. Epipelagic. Black to dark brown above, with six crossbars. Uncommon. D III-VI + I,24-29 A I-II + I,15-18; GR 5-8 + 12-19 = 18-26; Vert. 25.

YELLOWTAIL, *Seriola dorsalis*. Chile to southern Washington, including Gulf of California. Length to 5 ft., wt. to 80 lbs. Depth, surface to 80 ft. Olive-brown to brown above, with yellow stripe along side; fins yellowish. Common. D IV-VII + I,31-39; A O-II + I,19-23; GR 7-8 + 18-22 = 26-30; Vert. 25.

PACIFIC AMBERJACK, *Seriola colburni*. Peru to Barn Kelp off Oceanside (LACM 30621), including Galapagos Isls. and Gulf of California. Weight to 180 lbs. Pelagic, inshore. Bronze to reddish-brown above, yellowish to reddish below; fins blackish except pelvic. Rare. D V-VII + I,28-32; A II + I,18-21; Pect. 21; LLs 167; GR 6-9 + 16-19 = 22-28; Vert. 24.

LEATHERJACKET, *Oligoplites saurus*. Atlantic and Pacific oceans; in eastern Pacific from Peru to southern California, including Galapagos Isls. Length to 12 in. Inshore, shallow areas. Greenish-yellow above, silvery below; fins yellow. Rare. D IV-V + I,19-21; A II + I,19-21; GR 6-7 + 20-21 = 27; Vert. 26.

KEY TO THE JACKS, Family Carangidae:

1a Pectoral fin long, extending beyond base of 1st anal soft-ray .... 10 (page 149)

1b Pectoral fin not extending beyond base of 1st anal soft-ray 2

2a Lateral line without bony shields, dorsal spines shorter than dorsal soft-rays 5

2b Lateral line with shields; dorsal spines equal to or longer than dorsal soft-rays 3

3a Dorsal soft-rays 18–24; anal soft-rays 15–21: (juvenile *Caranx*) .... 13 (page 149)

3b Dorsal soft-rays 28 or more; anal soft-rays 22 or more _____ 4

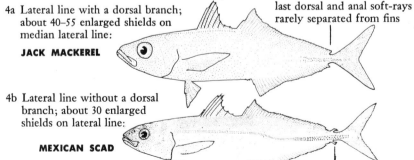

4a Lateral line with a dorsal branch; about 40–55 enlarged shields on median lateral line:

JACK MACKEREL

last dorsal and anal soft-rays rarely separated from fins

4b Lateral line without a dorsal branch; about 30 enlarged shields on lateral line:

MEXICAN SCAD

5a (next page)

isolated finlets behind dorsal and anal fins

5a *From 2a: lateral line without bony shields* Body with 5-6 dark vertical bars, the bars extending to bases of dorsal and anal fins:

PILOTFISH

5b Body without vertical bars or with narrow bars which do not extend to fin bases 6

6a First anal soft-ray even with 1st to 4th dorsal soft-rays; less than 25 soft-rays in dorsal fin; pelvic fins shorter than pectoral fins 8

6b First anal soft-ray even with about the 9th to 12th dorsal soft-rays; more than 27 soft-rays in dorsal fin; pelvic fins equal to or longer than pectoral fins 7

7a Body gray above with yellow stripe in midbody; head longer than body depth at origin of dorsal fin; longest dorsal soft-ray about ½ length of head:

YELLOWTAIL

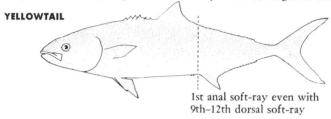

1st anal soft-ray even with
9th–12th dorsal soft-ray

7b Body reddish-bronze without yellow stripe in midbody; head shorter than body depth at origin of dorsal fin; longest dorsal soft-ray about ⅔ length of head in fish over 8 inches total length:

PACIFIC AMBERJACK

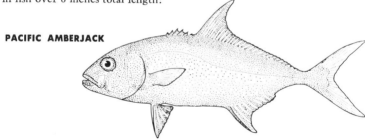

8a *From 6a: 1st anal soft-ray under 1st to 4th dorsal soft-ray*
Nose pointed, the lower jaw projecting; head length into body depth at origin of anal fin less than 1½ times; scales totally embedded, skin leathery:

LEATHERJACKET

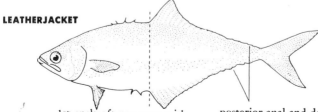

8b (next page)   1st anal soft-ray even with   posterior anal and dorsal soft-
              1st to 4th dorsal soft-rays   rays forming a saw-toothed edge

JACKS, Family Carangidae (continued)

GAFFTOPSAIL POMPANO, *Trachinotus rhodopus*. Peru to Zuma Beach, including Galapagos Isls. and Gulf of California. Length to 24 in. Shallow inshore areas. Body silvery; faint yellow bars on sides; fins yellow to reddish. One California record. D V–VI + I,19–21; A II + I,17–21; GR 8–10 + 13–16 = 22–26; Vert 24.

PALOMA POMPANO, *Trachinotus paitensis*. Peru to Redondo Beach, including Galapagos Isls. and Gulf of California. Length to 20 in. Shallow inshore areas. Bluish above, silver below. One California record. D VI–VIII,20–27; A II+I (occasionally III),20–24; Pect. 17–18; GR 5–7 + 9–12 = 15–18; Vert. 24.

PACIFIC MOONFISH, *Vomer declivifrons*. Peru to Long Beach. Length to 10 in. Inshore, pelagic. Bluish above, sides silvery; often with a black spot on upper angle of operculum. One California record. D VIII + I,21–22; A II + I,17–19; LL shields nearly obsolete; GR 8 + 28–32; Vert. 24.

COTTONMOUTH JACK, *Uraspis secunda*. In all tropical seas; in eastern Pacific from Costa Rica to Santa Catalina Isl. Length to 15 in. Usually around offshore islands and banks. Blackish with pale bars; inside of mouth and tongue bright white. One California record. D V–VI + I,27–30; A II + I,21–22; Pect. I,22; LL with 32–38 keeled shields; GR 6 + 16 = 22.

PACIFIC BUMPER, *Chloroscombrus orqueta*. Peru to San Pedro, including Gulf of California. Length to 12 in. Shallow inshore areas. Dark blue above, silvery below; black spot on operculum. Rare. D VII–VIII + I,26–30; A II + I,25–30; LL shields nearly obsolete, less than 20; GR 30–35 on lower limb; Vert. 24.

GREEN JACK, *Caranx caballus*. Cape Aguja, Peru, to north of Santa Cruz Isl. (LACM 9946), including Galapagos Isls. and Gulf of California. Length to 15 in. Shallow inshore areas. Bluish-gray above, silvery below. Uncommon. D VIII + I,21–24; A II + I,17–21; LL shields 38–52; GR 14–16 + 25–31; Vert. 25.

CREVALLE JACK, *Caranx hippos*. Worldwide in tropical seas; in eastern Pacific north to San Diego harbor.* Length to 30 in. Shallow inshore areas. Bluish above, silver below; juveniles with dark bars on sides. Rare. D VII–VIII + I,18–23; A II+I,15–18; Pect. I,18–21; LL shields 25–42; GR 15–19 on lower limb; Vert. 24.

8b Nose blunt, the jaws subequal with lower jaw sometimes slightly projecting, body deep, depth at origin of anal fin more than 1½ times head length; scales slightly embedded, visible⸺ 9

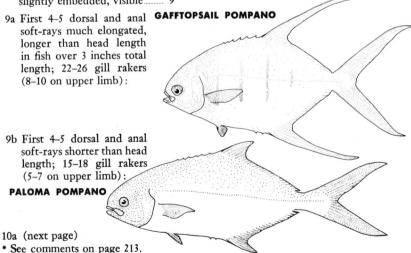

9a First 4–5 dorsal and anal **GAFFTOPSAIL POMPANO** soft-rays much elongated, longer than head length in fish over 3 inches total length; 22–26 gill rakers (8–10 on upper limb):

9b First 4–5 dorsal and anal soft-rays shorter than head length; 15–18 gill rakers (5–7 on upper limb):

PALOMA POMPANO

10a (next page)
* See comments on page 213.

10a *From 1a*: *pectoral fins extend beyond base of 1st anal soft-ray*
Head nearly vertical with a prominent hump over eye:

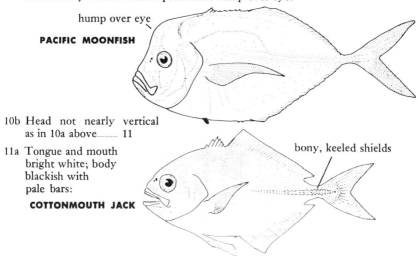

hump over eye

PACIFIC MOONFISH

10b Head not nearly vertical
as in 10a above......... 11

11a Tongue and mouth
bright white; body
blackish with
pale bars:

COTTONMOUTH JACK

bony, keeled shields

11b Tongue and mouth not bright white; body greenish to blue above, silver
below....... 12

12a Dorsal soft-rays 26-30; anal soft-rays 25-30; ventral contour of body greater
than dorsal contour:

PACIFIC BUMPER

shields small, difficult
to see

12b Dorsal soft-rays 18-24;
anal soft-rays 15-21;
dorsal contour of body
greater than ventral con-
tour....... 13

ventral body contour
strongly curved

13a *From 12b and 3a*
Gill rakers 25-31 on
lower limb; breast with
scales:

GREEN JACK

13b Gill rakers on lower limb
15-19; breast without scales
except for a small patch at
base of pelvic fins: **CREVALLE JACK**

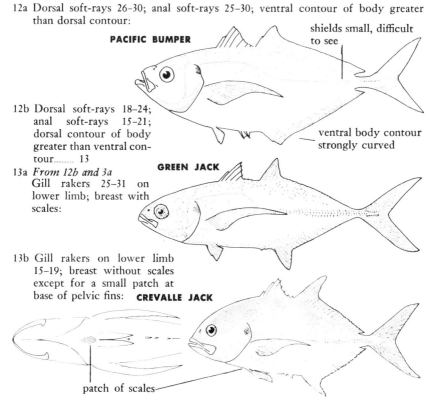

patch of scales

ROOSTERFISH, DOLPHINFISH, POMFRETS *, and FANFISH

ROOSTERFISH, *Nematistius pectoralis*. Family NEMATISTIIDAE
Peru to San Clemente Isl., including Galapagos Isls. and Gulf of California.
Weight to 78 lbs. Shallow inshore areas, young sometimes found in tidepools.
Dusky with yellowish tinges on back, silvery below, with two dark diagonal
stripes along back and sides; outermost parts of dorsal spines black, middle of
spines yellow; the base of dorsal fin dusky. Common in Mexico and Central
America, one California record. D VIII + I,26-28; A I–III,15–17; Pect. 16; Pelvic
I,5 appearing as I,6 but the last soft-ray divided in flesh and appearing as two;
LLs 119–130; GR 6-7 + 10–13 = 16-20; Vert. 24.

DOLPHINFISH, *Coryphaena hippurus*. Family CORYPHAENIDAE
Worldwide in warmer seas; in eastern Pacific from Chile to Grays Harbor,
Washington, including Galapagos Isls. and Gulf of California. Length recorded
to 6 ft., and weight to 45 lbs., but reported to 90 lbs. Epipelagic. Color variable
and changing rapidly; blue to green above, sides yellowish with dark blue and
green spots white below. Uncommon. D 54-65; A 24-30; Pect. 19-20; LLs 211–
301; GR 4-7 + 11–12 = 15–16 (GRt 19–26 including rudiments); Vert. 30-31.

BIGSCALE POMFRET, *Taractichthys steindachneri*.* Family BRAMIDAE
In warmer waters of Indo-Pacific; north to Santa Monica on our coast. Length
to 3 ft. Pelagic, but found in deeper waters. Uniform blackish. Rare. D 33-37; A
26–28; Pect. 20-22; midlateral scales 34-38; GR 2-3 + 7-9 = 9-11; Vert. 44-46.

PACIFIC POMFRET, *Brama japonica*.* Family BRAMIDAE
Throughout northern temperate Pacific Ocean to Bering Sea and Sea of Japan.
Length to 20 in. in California, world maximum size to 24 in. Epipelagic. Uni-
form dusky. Uncommon. D III–V,30-35; A O–III,25–29; Pect. 21–23; midlateral
scales 65–75; GRt 16–21; Vert. 39–41. (Mead, 1972, gives total fin ray elements
D 33-36 and A 27-30).

FANFISH, *Pteraclis aesticola*.* Family BRAMIDAE
In northern and southeastern Pacific Ocean; north to Santa Rosa Creek, San
Luis Obispo Co. on our coast. Length to 24 in. Usually in deep water. Body
silver; fins jet-black. Rare. D elements 46-55; A elements 40-43; Pect. 15-20; LL
55–56; GR 1-2 + 7 (not incl. rudiments); Vert. 45.

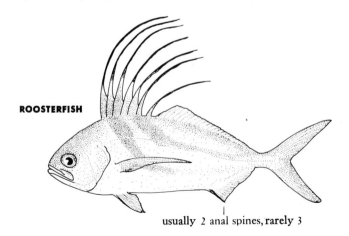

ROOSTERFISH

usually 2 anal spines, rarely 3

---

* See comments on page 213.

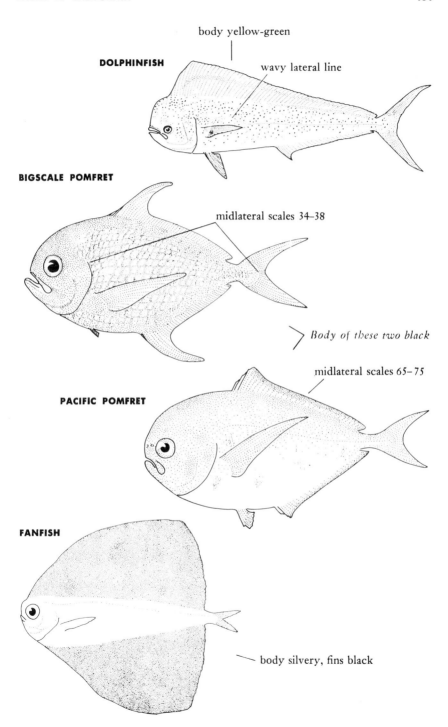

DOLPHINFISH

body yellow-green

wavy lateral line

BIGSCALE POMFRET

midlateral scales 34–38

Body of these two black

PACIFIC POMFRET

midlateral scales 65–75

FANFISH

body silvery, fins black

MOJARRAS, SALEMA, SARGO, PORGY, GOATFISH, and SPADEFISH

PACIFIC FLAGFIN MOJARRA, *Eucinostomus sp.**   Family GERREIDAE
Callao, Peru, to Anaheim Bay. Length to 8.2 in. Shallow inshore areas. Greenish on back, silver below; dorsal fin tricolored, black on tip, silver in middle, and dusky along base. One California record. D IX,10; A III,7–8; GR 5 + 8; Vert. 24.

SILVER MOJARRA, *Eucinostomus argenteus.*   Family GERREIDAE
Seymour Isl., Peru, to San Diego Bay. Length to about 8 in. Shallow inshore areas and bays. Greenish above, silver below; dorsal fin uniformly dusky. One California record. D IX,9–10; A II–III,7–8; Pect. 13; LLs 42; GR 4-7 + 7–8 = 12–15; Vert. 24.

SALEMA, *Xenistius californiensis.*   Family PRISTIPOMATIDAE
Peru to Monterey Bay, including Gulf of California. Length to 10 in. Depth 4 to 35 ft. Blue to greenish above, silvery below; 6–8 orange-brown horizontal stripes on sides. Common in southern California and Mexico, rare north of Santa Barbara. D IX–XI + I–II,11–14; A III,9–12; LLs 52; GR 11–13 + 15–24; Vert. 26.

SARGO, *Anisotremus davidsonii.*   Family PRISTIPOMATIDAE
Gulf of California (isolated population), and from Magdalena Bay, Baja California, to Santa Cruz, California. Length recorded to 17.4 in., reported to 23 in. Depth, surface to 130 ft. Gray above, sides and belly silver; dark vertical bar in pectoral area. Common in southern California, rare north of Pt. Conception. D XI–XII,14–16; A III,9–11; LLs 60–62; GR 9–12 + 13–16 = 22–27; Vert. 26.

PACIFIC PORGY, *Calamus brachysomus.*   Family SPARIDAE
150 mi. S of Lima, Peru, to Oceanside, including Galapagos Isls. and Gulf of California. Length about 2 ft., and wt. to 5 lbs. Depth, surface to 225 ft. Reddish and greenish on back and sides; dusky bars and mottling on body and fins. Rare. D XII–XIII,11–13; A II–III,9–11; Pect. 13–16; LLs 48; GR 4-6 + 5-6 = 10–11; Vert. 24.

MEXICAN GOATFISH, *Mulloidichthys dentatus.*   Family MULLIDAE
Northern Peru to Long Beach. Length to 12.2 in. Shallow inshore areas. Bright pink or rose; with a dark red lateral stripe. Rare. D VII + I,8; A I–II,6; LLs 37.

PACIFIC SPADEFISH, *Chaetodipterus zonatus.*   Family EPHIPPIDAE
Northern Peru to San Diego, including Gulf of California. Length to 25.5 in. Shallow inshore areas. Dusky on back, whitish below; 6 black vertical bars. Rare. D VIII + I,18–23; A II–III,16–20; Pect. 16; LLp 48–50; LLs 70–90; GR 5-6 + 9–10 = 15–16; Vert. 24.

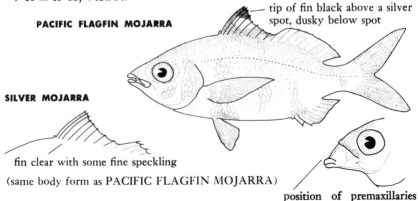

PACIFIC FLAGFIN MOJARRA

— tip of fin black above a silver spot, dusky below spot

SILVER MOJARRA

fin clear with some fine speckling

(same body form as PACIFIC FLAGFIN MOJARRA)

position of premaxillaries when pulled downward

* See comments on page 214.

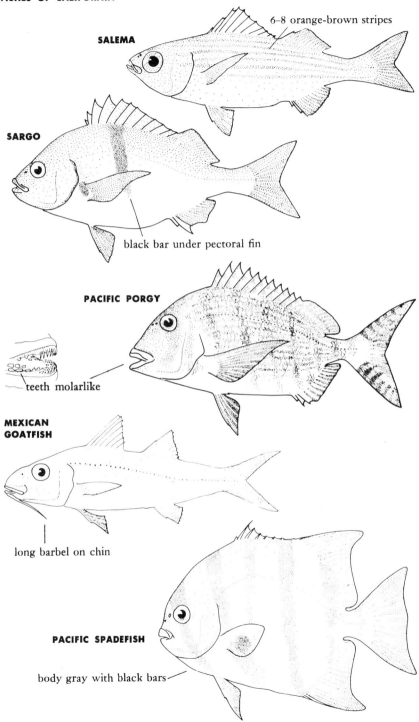

SALEMA

6–8 orange-brown stripes

SARGO

black bar under pectoral fin

PACIFIC PORGY

teeth molarlike

MEXICAN GOATFISH

long barbel on chin

PACIFIC SPADEFISH

body gray with black bars

CROAKERS, Family Sciaenidae
(Principal sources: Roedel, 1953; McPhail, 1958; Walker, 1961)

QUEENFISH, *Seriphus politus.* West of Uncle Sam Bank, Baja California, to Yaquina Bay, Oregon. Length to 12 in. Depth, surface to 180 ft. Bluish on back, silvery below; fins yellowish. Common in southern California, rare north of Monterey. D VII–IX + I,18–21; A II,21–23; LLs 65; GR 7–10 + 15–17; Vert. 25.

WHITE SEABASS, *Cynoscion nobilis.* Gulf of California (isolated population), Magdalena Bay, Baja California, to Juneau, Alaska. Length to 5 ft., recorded wt. 83 lbs., reported to 90 lbs. Depth, surface to 400 ft. Bluish to gray above with dark speckling, silvery below; young have several dark vertical bars. Common. D IX–X + I,19–23; A I–II,8–10; LLp 70–80; LLs 88; GR 5 + 11–13 = 16–18; Vert. 25.

ORANGEMOUTH CORVINA, *Cynoscion xanthulus.* Acapulco, Mexico, into the Gulf of California; introduced into Salton Sea. Length to 3 ft. Shallow inshore areas. Bluish above, silver below; tail yellow; inside of mouth bright yellow-orange. D VIII–IX + I,19–21; A I–II,8–9; LLp 66; LLs 86; GR 3–4 + 9–10 = 12–14; Vert. 22.

SHORTFIN CORVINA, *Cynoscion parvipinnis.* Mazatlan, Mexico, to near Santa Barbara Isls., including Gulf of California. Length to 20 in. Shallow inshore areas. Bright blue-gray above, silvery below. Uncommon, none seen since 1930's along coastline. D IX–X + I,20–24; A II,9–11; LLp 75; GR 2–4 + 7–8 = 9–11; Vert. 23.

YELLOWFIN CROAKER, *Umbrina roncador.* Gulf of California to Pt. Conception (reported to San Francisco in late 1800's). Length to 18 in. Surf area to 150 ft. Back irridescent blue to gray, sides silver overlaid with dark wavy lines; fins yellowish. Common in southern California. D X–XI + I,25–30; A II,6–7; **Pect.** I,16–18; LLs 54–58; GR 7–9 + 10–14; Vert. 24–25.

KEY TO THE CROAKERS, Family Sciaenidae:

1a Snout projecting beyond mouth; lower jaw usually shorter than upper............ 5
(next page)

1b Snout not projecting beyond mouth; lower jaw extends beyond upper............ 2

2a Wide space (more than eye diameter) between dorsal fins; anal soft-rays 21–23:

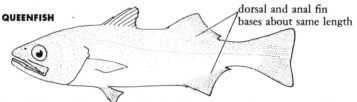

QUEENFISH — dorsal and anal fin bases about same length

2b Dorsal fins contiguous or slightly joined by membrane; anal soft-rays 11 or less........ 3

3a No large canine teeth in middle of upper jaw, teeth all about same size:

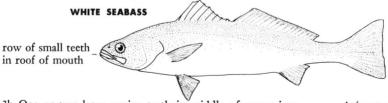

WHITE SEABASS

row of small teeth in roof of mouth

3b One or two large canine teeth in middle of upper jaw................ 4 (next page)

4a Tail pointed; pectoral fin even with or extending beyond tip of pelvic fin when depressed;

ORANGEMOUTH CORVINA

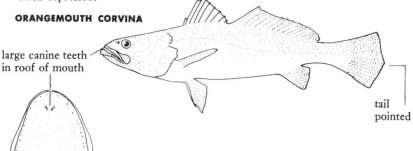

large canine teeth in roof of mouth

tail pointed

4b Tail slightly indented (middle rays shortest); pectoral fin short, not extending to tip of pelvic fin when depressed:

SHORTFIN CORVINA

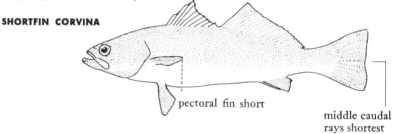

pectoral fin short

middle caudal rays shortest

5a *From 1a: snout projecting*
Lower jaw without a single barbel (the WHITE CROAKER may have a cluster of minute barbels on chin, but the longest is shorter than width of lower lip)........ 7

5b Lower jaw with a single barbel, the barbel longer than width of center of lower lip........ 6

6a Anal fin with two spines; pectoral fins yellowish; preopercle with bony teeth or spines on posterior margin:

YELLOWFIN CROAKER

body with dark wavy, oblique lines on sides

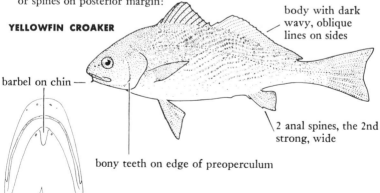

barbel on chin —

2 anal spines, the 2nd strong, wide

bony teeth on edge of preoperculum

6b (next page)

CROAKERS, Family Sciaenidae (continued)

CALIFORNIA CORBINA, *Menticirrhus undulatus*. Gulf of California to Pt. Conception. Recorded to 28 in., and 7 lbs., reported to 30 in. and 8.5 lbs. Surf area to 45 ft. Uniform gray with incandescent reflections; wavy diagonal lines on sides. Common. D X–XI + I–II,23–27; A I–II,7–9; Pect. I,17–19; LLs 60; GR 5–8 + 4–10; Vert. 25.

WHITE CROAKER, *Genyonemus lineatus*. Magdalena Bay, Baja California, to Vancouver Isl., B.C. Length to 15.4 in. Depth, surface to 330 ft. Incandescent brownish to yellowish on back, silver below; fins yellow to white. Common. D XII–XV + I,18–25; A II,10–12; Pect. I,17; LLs 52–54; GR 9–12 + 17–21 = 27–33; Vert. 26.

BAIRDIELLA, *Bairdiella icistia*. Pacific coast of Mexico to Almejas Bay, Baja California (SIO 64-829), including the Gulf of California; introduced into the Salton Sea. Length to 12 in. Shallow inshore areas. Grayish on back, silver below. Common in Salton Sea. D X–XII,24–28; A II,7–8; LLp 52; LLs 51–62; GR 6–8 + 17 = 23–25; Vert. 25.

SPOTFIN CROAKER, *Roncador stearnsii*. Mazatlan, Mexico, to Pt. Conception, including Gulf of California. Length to 27 in. Surf area to 50 ft. Silvery-gray above, white below; dark wavy lines on sides. Common. D IX–X + I,21–25; A II,7–9; LLs 60; GR 10–14 + 15–19; Vert. 25.

BLACK CROAKER, *Cheilotrema saturnum*. Magdalena Bay, Baja California (SIO 62-114), to Pt. Conception. Length to 15 in. Depth, surface to 150 ft. Blackish with coppery reflections on back, silver below; pelvic fins black. Common. D IX–XI + I–II,25–28; A II,6–9; LLs 55–60; GR 6–9 + 8–14; Vert. 24-25.

6b Anal fin with one weak spine; pectoral fins black; no bony teeth on posterior edge of preopercle (edge is serrated but not bony):

CALIFORNIA CORBINA

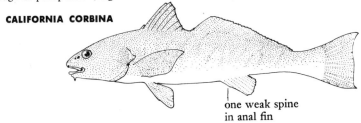

one weak spine
in anal fin

7a *From 5a: lower jaw without a large, single barbel*
Dorsal fin with 12–16 spines; anal soft-rays 10–12; lower jaw often with a cluster of minute barbels:

WHITE CROAKER

minute barbels often
present in center of chin

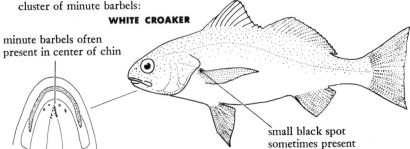

small black spot
sometimes present

7b (next page)

7b Dorsal fin with 12 or less spines; anal soft-rays 6-9; no chin barbels................. 8

8a Second anal spine extends past tip of last soft-ray when fin is depressed against body:

BAIRDIELLA

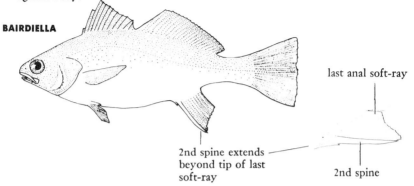

last anal soft-ray

2nd spine extends beyond tip of last soft-ray

2nd spine

8b Second anal spine does not reach tip of last soft-ray when fin is depressed.... 9

9a Black area at base of pectoral fin; edge of preoperculum with bony teeth; length of pectoral fin into head less than 1.2 times:

SPOTFIN CROAKER

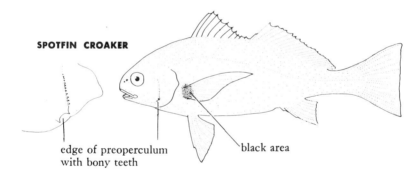

edge of preoperculum with bony teeth

black area

9b No black spot at base of pectoral fin; edge of preoperculum without bony teeth; pectoral fin into head 1.4 to 1.6 times:

BLACK CROAKER

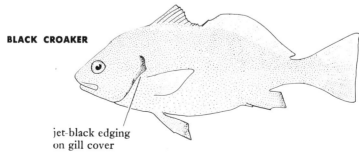

jet-black edging on gill cover

OPALEYE, HALFMOON, ZEBRAPERCH, BUTTERFLYFISHES, and ARMORHEAD
(Principal sources: Hubbs & Rechnitzer, 1958; Follett et al, 1960;
Follett & Dempster, 1963)

OPALEYE, *Girella nigricans.* Family GIRELLIDAE
Cape San Lucas, Baja California, to San Francisco. Length to 25.38 in. and wt.
to 13.46 lbs. Intertidal to 95 ft. Dark olive-green; usually with 2 light spots at
base of dorsal fin; eye brilliant opal blue-green. Common. D XII–XIV,12–15;
A III,10–13; LLs 50; GR 11–14 + 16–21 = 28–34; Vert. 27.

ZEBRAPERCH, *Hermosilla azurea.* Family KYPHOSIDAE
Gulf of California to Monterey. Length to 17.4 in. Intertidal to 25 ft. Dusky-
brown to black above, whitish below; dark bars on sides; bright blue spot on
operculum. Uncommon. D XI,11; A III,10; LLs 55; GR 6–7 + 11–14; Vert. 25.

HALFMOON, *Medialuna californiensis.* Family SCORPIDIDAE
Gulf of California to Klamath River, including Guadalupe Isl. Length to 19 in.,
and wt. to 4 lbs. 12 oz. Depth, surface to 130 ft. Dark blue above, light blue
below. Common. D IX–X,22–27; A III,17–21; LLs 58; GR 6–8 + 14–17; Vert. 25.

SCYTHEMARKED BUTTERFLYFISH, *Chaetodon falcifer.* Family CHAETODONTIDAE
Galapagos Isls. to Santa Catalina Isl., including Guadalupe Isl. Length to about
6 in. Depth, surface to 300 ft. Body purplish-gray and yellowish on back, belly
yellow. Rare. D XIII,20–21; A III,14–16; Pect. 14–15; LLp 42–46; GR 5 + 11 =
16; Vert. 24.

THREEBANDED BUTTERFLYFISH, *Chaetodon humeralis.* Family CHAETODONTIDAE
Peru to San Diego, including Galapagos Isls. Length to 10 in. Shallow inshore
areas. Brownish-yellow; 3 dark vertical bands. One provisional record for California. D XI–XIII,18–20; A III,14–17; LLs 30–40; GR obsolete; Vert. 24.

PELAGIC ARMORHEAD, *Pentaceros richardsoni.* Family PENTACEROTIDAE
In all oceans; in eastern Pacific north to Columbia River and over to Japan.
Length to 15 in., reported to 21 in. Depth, surface to 1320 ft. Bluish-brown
above, pale below; reddish on head; orange on anal and pelvic spines. Rare.
D XIII–XIV,8–10; A IV,7–9; Pect. 17–19; LLp 64–78; GR 6–8 + 17–18; Vert. 25.

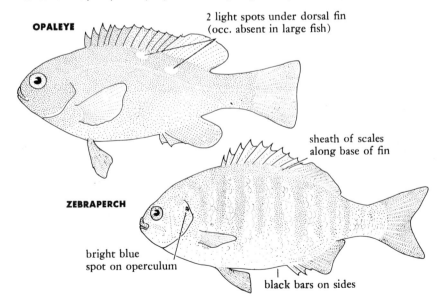

OPALEYE

2 light spots under dorsal fin
(occ. absent in large fish)

sheath of scales
along base of fin

ZEBRAPERCH

bright blue
spot on operculum

black bars on sides

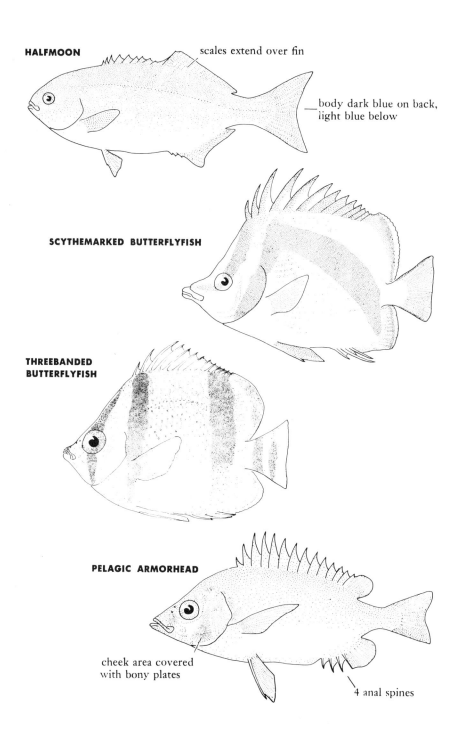

HALFMOON — scales extend over fin

body dark blue on back, light blue below

SCYTHEMARKED BUTTERFLYFISH

THREEBANDED BUTTERFLYFISH

PELAGIC ARMORHEAD

cheek area covered with bony plates

4 anal spines

SURFPERCHES, Family Embiotocidae*
(Principal sources: Tarp, 1952; Clemens & Wilby, 1961)

RUBBERLIP SURFPERCH, _Rhacochilus toxotes_. Thurloe Head, Baja California (LACM 32069), to Russian Gulch State Beach, Mendocino Co., including Guadalupe Isl. Length to 18.5 in. Depth, surface to 150 ft. Brown with brassy overtones, tan below. Common. D IX–XI,20–25; A III,27–30; Pect. 21–24; LLs 69–76 + 6–9 on tail; GR 8–9 + 17–19 = 26–28; Vert. 35–38.

BLACK SURFPERCH, _Embiotoca jacksoni_. Pt. Abreojos, Baja California, to Fort Bragg, including Guadalupe Isl. Length to 15.35 inches. Surface to 130 ft. Black or brown to reddish; yellowish on belly; dark vertical bars on sides. Common. D IX–XI,18–22; A III,23–27; Pect. 20–22; LLs 52–59 + 6–10 on tail; GR 7–10 + 13–14 = 20–23; Vert. 32–36.

BARRED SURFPERCH, _Amphistichus argenteus_. Playa Maria Bay, Baja California, to Bodega Bay. Length to 17 in., and wt. to 4.5 lbs. Depth, surface to 240 ft. Olive-green to yellow-green on back, silvery below; vertical bars on sides. Common. D IX–XII,21–27; A III–IV,24–29; Pect. 25–28; LLs 59–67 + 5–7 on tail; GR 5–7 + 11–14 = 17–21; Vert. 29–33.

CALICO SURFPERCH, _Amphistichus koelzi_. 0.5 mi. north of Arroyo San Isidro, Baja California (SIO 62–740), to Shi Shi Beach, Washington. Length to 12 in. Depth, surface to 30 ft. Silvery; olive-green mottling and bars on sides. Common. D IX–XI,24–28; A III,25–32; Pect. 25–29; LLs 61–68 + 4–6 on tail; GR 6–8 + 14–18 = 21–26; Vert. 32–35.

REDTAIL SURFPERCH, _Amphistichus rhodoterus_. Monterey Bay to Vancouver Isl., B.C. Length to 16 in. Depth, surface to 24 ft. Body silver; olive-green mottling and bars on sides; tail pink to deep purple. Common. D VIII–X,25–29; A III, 26–32; Pect. 27–28; LLs 60–70 + 4–6 on tail; GR 6–8 + 10–14; Vert. 30–33.

KEY TO THE SURFPERCHES, Family Embiotocidae:

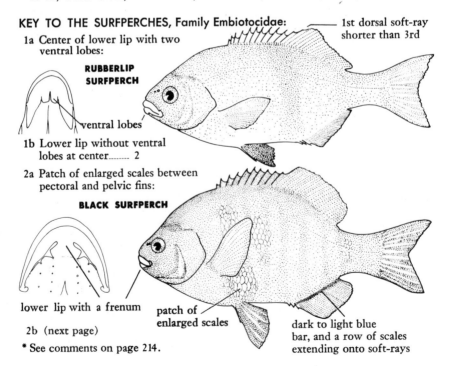

1a Center of lower lip with two ventral lobes:

RUBBERLIP SURFPERCH

ventral lobes

1st dorsal soft-ray shorter than 3rd

1b Lower lip without ventral lobes at center_____ 2

2a Patch of enlarged scales between pectoral and pelvic fins:

BLACK SURFPERCH

lower lip with a frenum

2b (next page)

patch of enlarged scales

dark to light blue bar, and a row of scales extending onto soft-rays

* See comments on page 214.

2b No patch of enlarged scales as in 2a......... 3

3a Base of anal fin without a row of scales extending over soft-rays; either none or no more than 3 yellow to olive-yellow vertical bars on sides.... 6 (next page)

3b Base of anal fin with a row of scales extending over base of soft-rays; 6 or more solid or somewhat broken yellowish or light olive vertical bars on sides............ 4

4a Upper jaw slightly extending beyond lower; no red in caudal fins; dorsal spines always shorter than longest dorsal soft-ray; lower lip always with a frenum:

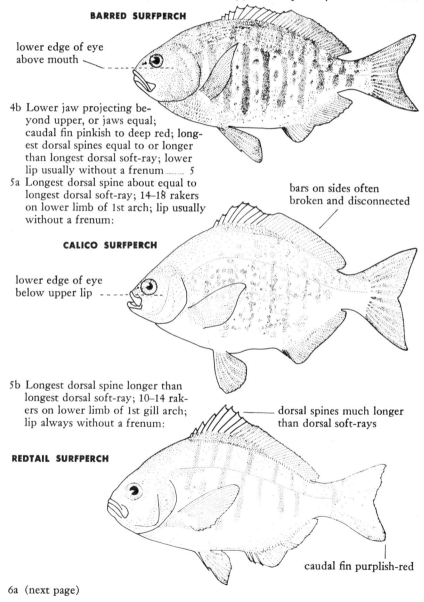

BARRED SURFPERCH

lower edge of eye
above mouth

4b Lower jaw projecting beyond upper, or jaws equal;
caudal fin pinkish to deep red; longest dorsal spines equal to or longer
than longest dorsal soft-ray; lower
lip usually without a frenum....... 5

5a Longest dorsal spine about equal to
longest dorsal soft-ray; 14–18 rakers
on lower limb of 1st arch; lip usually
without a frenum:

bars on sides often
broken and disconnected

CALICO SURFPERCH

lower edge of eye
below upper lip ------

5b Longest dorsal spine longer than
longest dorsal soft-ray; 10–14 rakers on lower limb of 1st gill arch;
lip always without a frenum:

—— dorsal spines much longer
than dorsal soft-rays

REDTAIL SURFPERCH

caudal fin purplish-red

6a (next page)

SURFPERCHES, Family Embiotocidae (continued)

SPOTFIN SURFPERCH, *Hyperprosopon anale.* Blanca Bay, Baja California, to Seal Rock, Oregon. Length to 6 in. Depth, surface to 210 ft. Body silver with dusky on back; large black spots in dorsal and anal fins. Uncommon. D VII–IX,20–25; A III,21–26; Pect. 23–27; LLs 57–66 + 4–6 on tail; GR 7–9 + 17–21; Vert. 32–35.

WALLEYE SURFPERCH, *Hyperprosopon argenteum.* Pt. San Rosarito, Baja California (SIO H 52–162), to Vancouver Isl., B.C., including Guadalupe Isl. Length to 12 in. Depth, surface to 60 ft. Body silver with faint duskyness on back; tips of pelvic fins black. Common. D VII–XI,25–29; A III,30–35; Pect. 25–28; LLs 68–73 + 5–7 on tail; GR 7–10 + 20–23 = 28–32; Vert. 33–38.

SILVER SURFPERCH, *Hyperprosopon ellipticum.* Rio San Vicente, Baja California, to Schooner Cove, near Tofino, Vancouver Isl., B.C. Length to 10.5 in. Depth, surface to 360 ft. Silver with duskyness on back, and dusky bars on sides; tail usually pink. Common. D VIII–X,25–29; A III,29–35; Pect. 26–28; LLs 59–67 + 4–6 on tail; GR 7–8 + 15–19; Vert. 32–35.

SHINER SURFPERCH, *Cymatogaster aggregata.* San Quintin Bay, Baja California, to Port Wrangell, Alaska. Length to 7 in., reported to 8 in. Depth, surface to 480 ft. Gray to greenish above, underparts silver. Female with 3 yellow bars on sides interspersed with black. Male in breeding season nearly black, the speckling covering the yellow areas. Common. D VIII–XI,18–23; A III,22–26; Pect. 19–21; LLs 36–43 + 4–6 on tail; GR 9–11 + 19–22 = 28–33; Vert. 34–38.

ISLAND SURFPERCH, *Cymatogaster gracilis.* Found only around Channel Isls. Length to 7.5 in. Surface to 30 ft. Color similar to SHINER but with golden on underparts. Common. D IX–X,19–22; A III,24–26; Pect. 19–21; LLs 38–44 + 4–5 on tail.

6a *From 3a: no row of scales extending onto anal soft-rays*
Lower lip with a frenum .... 11 (Page 164)

6b Lower lip without a frenum 7

7a Conspicuous black spot in spinous dorsal:

SPOTFIN SURFPERCH

lower lip without a frenum

lower jaw extends beyond upper

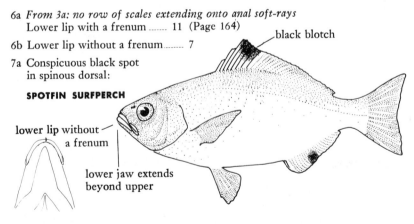

black blotch

7b No black area in spinous dorsal as above 8

8a Total length 3 times or more than greatest body depth; 3 scales between insertion of dorsal fin and lateral line; lateral line with less than 46 scales 10

8b Total length less than 3 times greatest body depth; 5–6 scales between insertion of dorsal fin and lateral line; lateral line with more than 55 scales 9

9a Pelvic fins with black tips; tail white with black edging; 20-23 rakers on lower
   limb of 1st gill arch:

WALLEYE SURFPERCH

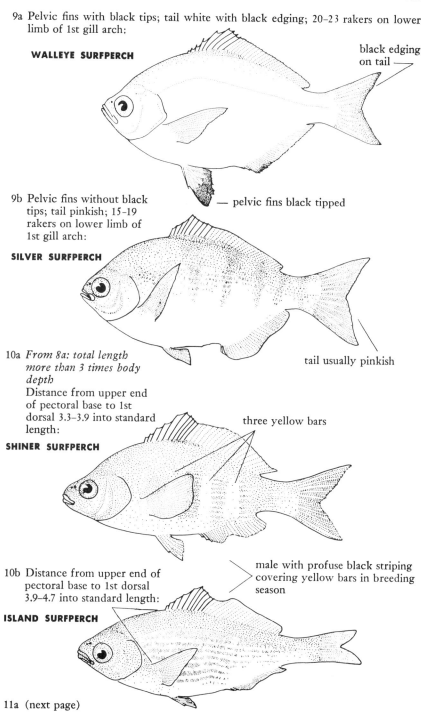

black edging
on tail ⟶

9b Pelvic fins without black
   tips; tail pinkish; 15-19
   rakers on lower limb of
   1st gill arch:

— pelvic fins black tipped

SILVER SURFPERCH

10a *From 8a: total length
   more than 3 times body
   depth*
   Distance from upper end
   of pectoral base to 1st
   dorsal 3.3-3.9 into standard
   length:

tail usually pinkish

three yellow bars

SHINER SURFPERCH

10b Distance from upper end of
   pectoral base to 1st dorsal
   3.9-4.7 into standard length:

male with profuse black striping
covering yellow bars in breeding
season

ISLAND SURFPERCH

11a (next page)

SURFPERCHES, Family Embiotocidae (continued)

PINK SURFPERCH, Zalembius rosaceus. Gulf of California (isolated population), and from San Cristobal Bay, Baja Californa, to Drakes Bay, including Guadalupe Isl. Length to 8 in. Depth 30 to 300 ft. Brownish-pink; 2 chocolate-brown spots under dorsal fin. Uncommon. D IX–XI,16–20; A III,18–22; Pect. 17–19; LLs 47–56 + 4–6 on tail; GR 5–7 + 10–12 = 16–19; Vert. 33–37.

RAINBOW SURFPERCH, Hypsurus caryi. Rio Santo Tomas, Baja California (SIO H 45–221), to Cape Mendocino. Length to 12 in. Surface to 130 ft. Red and blue stripes on sides; pelvic fins bright blue and red-orange. Common. D IX–XI, 20–24; A III,20–24; Pect. 21–23; LLs 63–71 + 0–8 on tail; GR 7–8 + 13–14 = 20–22; Vert. 36–38.

STRIPED SURFPERCH, Embiotoca lateralis. Pt. Cabras, Baja California (SIO H 46–57b), to Port Wrangell, Alaska. Length to 15 in. Depth, surface to 55 ft. Red, blue, and yellow stripes on body; pelvic fins dusky. Common. D X–XII,23–26; A III,29–33; Pect. 21–24; LLs 59–65 + 6–8 on tail; GR 7–10 + 14–17 = 22–27; Vert. 33–35.

KELP SURFPERCH, Brachyistius frenatus. Turtle Bay, Baja California, to Vancouver Isl., B.C., including Guadalupe Isl. Length to 8.5 in. Depth, surface to 100 ft. Golden-brown to reddish above, tan below. Common. D VII–X,13–16; A III–IV, 20–25; Pect. 17–18; LLs 37–44 + 4–6 on tail; GR 7–9 + 17–20 = 24–29; Vert. 32–35.

DWARF SURFPERCH, Micrometrus minimus. Cedros Isl., Baja California (SIO H 53–110), to Bodega Bay. Length to 6.25 in. Tidepools to 30 ft. Silvery with greenish-blue reflections; yellow on sides with dark stripes. Common. D VIII–XI, 12–16; A III,13–23; Pect. 18–22; LLs 37–45 + 3–6 on tail; GR 5–7 + 11–16 = 17–22; Vert. 31–36.

REEF SURFPERCH, Micrometrus aurora. Pt. Baja, Baja California (SIO H 51–401), to Tomales Bay. Length to 7.1 in. Intertidal to 20 ft. Silvery wth blue, green, and black on back; orange on sides; crescent-shaped black marks on scales posterior to pectoral fins. Common. D VII–IX,15–19; A III,17–21; Pect. 17–20; LLs 43–52 + 4–5; GR 5–7 + 13–14 = 18–21; Vert. 34–37.

11a *From 6a page 162: lower lip with a frenum*
Body uniform pinkish with two chocolate-brown spots at base of soft dorsal fin; last anal soft-ray extended, threadlike: **PINK SURFPERCH**   dark spots

11b Body not pink with spots under soft dorsal; last anal soft-ray not extended........ 12

12a Body without blue, red, or yellow stripes.... 14 (next page)

12b Body with blue, red or yellow stripes........ 13   **RAINBOW SURFPERCH**

13a Snout and upper jaw extending beyond lower jaw; anal base shorter than distance from pelvic base to anal fin origin:

13b (next page)

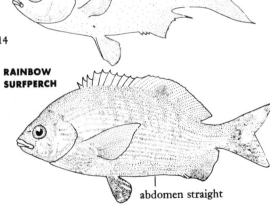

abdomen straight

13b Jaws subequal, terminal; anal base longer than distance from pelvic base to anal fin origin:

STRIPED SURFPERCH

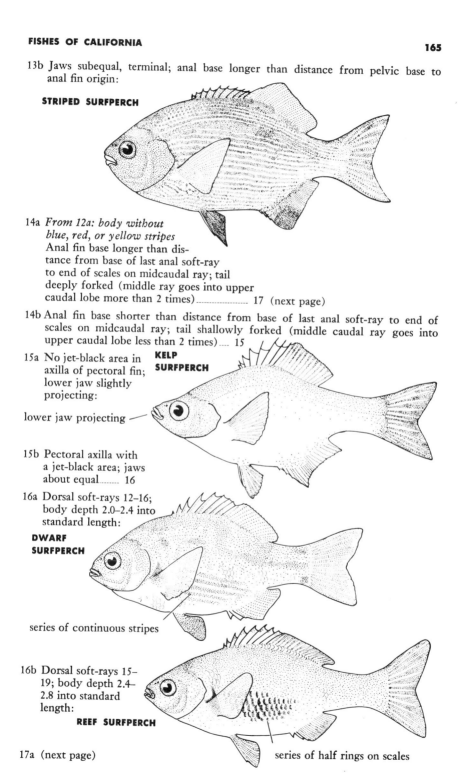

14a *From 12a: body without blue, red, or yellow stripes* Anal fin base longer than distance from base of last anal soft-ray to end of scales on midcaudal ray; tail deeply forked (middle ray goes into upper caudal lobe more than 2 times)_____ 17 (next page)

14b Anal fin base shorter than distance from base of last anal soft-ray to end of scales on midcaudal ray; tail shallowly forked (middle caudal ray goes into upper caudal lobe less than 2 times)____ 15

15a No jet-black area in axilla of pectoral fin; lower jaw slightly projecting: **KELP SURFPERCH**

lower jaw projecting ⟶

15b Pectoral axilla with a jet-black area; jaws about equal_____ 16

16a Dorsal soft-rays 12–16; body depth 2.0–2.4 into standard length:

DWARF SURFPERCH

series of continuous stripes

16b Dorsal soft-rays 15–19; body depth 2.4–2.8 into standard length:

REEF SURFPERCH

series of half rings on scales

17a (next page)

SURFPERCHES, Family Embiotocidae (continued)

PILE SURFPERCH, *Damalichthys vacca*. Guadalupe Isl. (SIO 54-213) to Port Wrangell, Alaska. Length to 17.4 in. Surface to 150 ft. Blackish on back, silvery to dusky on sides; a dark bar in midbody. Common. D IX–XI,21–25; A III,25–31; Pect. 19–22; LLs 56–69 + 5–8 on tail; Vert. 34–39; GR 6–8 + 11–14 = 18–22; Vert. 34–39.

WHITE SURFPERCH, *Phanerodon furcatus*. Pt. Cabras, Baja California, to Vancouver Isl., B.C. Length to 12.4 in. Depth, surface to 140 ft. Silvery with dusky speckling on back; a thin black line at base of soft dorsal fin; pelvic fins white. Common. D IX–XI,20–26; A III,29–34; Pect. 20–21; LLs 56–67 + 5–7 on tail; GR 7–9 + 12–13 = 20–21; Vert. 37–41.

SHARPNOSE SURFPERCH, *Phanerodon atripes*. San Benito Isls., Baja California, to Bodega Bay. Length to 11.5 in. Depth, surface to 750 ft. Silvery with reddish-brown marks on back; pelvic fins dusky, black tipped. Common only in Monterey Bay. D X–XI,22–24; A III,27–30; Pect. 20–22; LLs 63–68 + 5–6 on tail.

17a *From 14a; anal fin base long; tail deeply forked*
    Longest dorsal soft-ray about twice as long (1.6–3.0) as longest dorsal spine; 8–9 scales between 1st dorsal spine and lateral line:

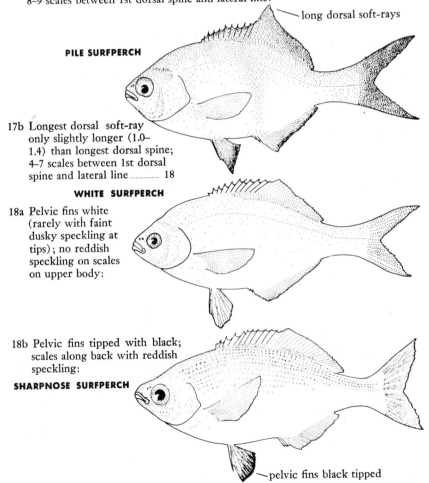

long dorsal soft-rays

PILE SURFPERCH

17b Longest dorsal soft-ray only slightly longer (1.0–1.4) than longest dorsal spine; 4–7 scales between 1st dorsal spine and lateral line............ 18

WHITE SURFPERCH

18a Pelvic fins white (rarely with faint dusky speckling at tips); no reddish speckling on scales on upper body:

18b Pelvic fins tipped with black; scales along back with reddish speckling:

SHARPNOSE SURFPERCH

pelvic fins black tipped

DAMSELFISHES and MULLET
(Principal sources: Limbaugh, 1955; Fitch & Lavenberg, 1971)

GARIBALDI, Hypsypops rubicundus. Family POMACENTRIDAE
Magdalena Bay, Baja California, to Monterey Bay, including Guadalupe Isl.
Length to 14 in. Depth, surface to 95 ft. Adult uniform golden-orange; young
reddish-orange, with bright blue spots. Common in southern California, but rare
north of Pt. Conception. D XI–XIII,15–17; A II,12–15; LLp 21; LLs 30; GR
3 + 12; Vert. 26.

BLACKSMITH, Chromis punctipinnis. Family POMACENTRIDAE
Pt. San Pablo, Baja California (LACM 32082), to Monterey. Length to 12 in.
Depth, surface to 150 ft. Dark blue to black on back, gray-blue on sides; black
spots on posterior half of body. Common in southern California, uncommon
north of Pt. Conception. D XII–XIII,10–13; A II,10–12; LLp 18; LLs 29; Vert. 26.

STRIPED MULLET, Mugil cephalus. Family MUGILIDAE
Found in all warm seas; in eastern Pacific from Galapagos Isls. to Monterey,
including Gulf of California; introduced into Salton Sea. Length to 3 ft., and
wt. to 15 lbs. Depth, surface to 400 ft. Silver, with black stripes. Common in
Salton Sea. D IV–V + I,6–8; A III,7–9; midlateral scales 37–41; Vert. 24.

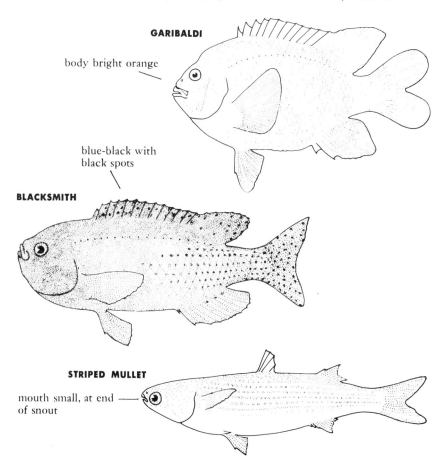

GARIBALDI

body bright orange

blue-black with
black spots

BLACKSMITH

STRIPED MULLET

mouth small, at end
of snout

BARRACUDA, BOBOS, and WRASSES
(Principal sources: Limbaugh, 1955; Fitch & Lavenberg, 1971)

CALIFORNIA BARRACUDA, Sphyraena argentea. Family SPHYRAENIDAE
Cape San Lucas, Baja California, to Kodiak Isl., Alaska. Reported to 5 ft. but recent records are to 4 ft., and wt. to 18 lbs. Depth, surface to 60 ft. Dark brown above with bluish reflections, silvery below. Common south of Morro Bay. D V + I,8-10; A I + II,8-10; LLs 166; Vert. 24.

YELLOW BOBO, Polydactylus opercularis. Family POLYNEMIDAE
Peru to Los Angeles Harbor (UCLA W 54-348), including Gulf of California. Length to 14 in. Shallow inshore areas. Greenish-brown above, yellowish below. Rare. D VIII + I,11-13; A III,12-14; lowermost 8-9 pectoral rays detached from fin and free; LLs 68-75; GR 17 + 20 = 37; Vert. 24.

BLUE BOBO, Polydactylus approximans. Family POLYNEMIDAE
Callao, Peru, to Monterey, including Galapagos Isls. Length to 14 in. Shallow inshore areas. Silvery-blue above, yellowish below. Rare. D VIII + I,12-14; A III,13-15; lowermost 5-6 pectoral rays detached from fin and free; LLs 58-62; GR 11-16 + 16-19 = 28-35; Vert. 24.

CALIFORNIA SHEEPHEAD, Pimelometopon pulchrum. Family LABRIDAE
Northern Gulf of California (isolated population),* and from Cape San Lucas, Baja California, to Monterey, including Guadalupe Isl. Length to 3 ft., and wt. to 36.25 lbs. Depth, surface to 180 ft. Adult female uniform brownish-red to rose; male with black head, red band in middle, and black in posterior portion of body; chin white on both sexes. Common in southern California, uncommon north of Pt. Conception. D XII,10; A III,10-12; LLs 60; Vert. 28.

SENORITA, Oxyjulis californica. Family LABRIDAE
Cedros Isl., Baja California, to Sausalito (recent observations north only to Santa Cruz). Length to 10 in. Depth, surface to 180 ft. Reddish-orange above, yellow below; black area on caudal fin base. Common. D IX-X,13; A III,13; LLs 28; GR 6 + 12-15 = 18-21; Vert. 26-27.

ROCK WRASSE, Halichoeres semicinctus. Family LABRIDAE
Gulf of California to Pt. Conception, including Guadalupe Isl. Length to 12.9 in., reported to 15 in. Depth, surface to 78 ft. Greenish-brown; dusky vertical bars; male with dark blue bar under pectoral fin. Common. D IX,11-12; A III,12; LLs 26; GR 8 + 12 = 20; Vert. 26.

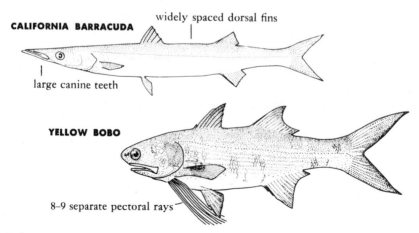

CALIFORNIA BARRACUDA

widely spaced dorsal fins

large canine teeth

YELLOW BOBO

8-9 separate pectoral rays

* See comments on page 214.

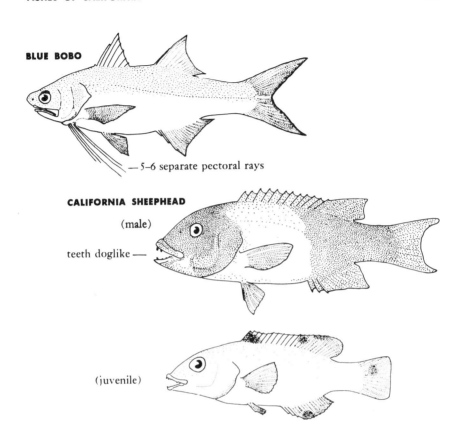

BLUE BOBO

— 5–6 separate pectoral rays

CALIFORNIA SHEEPHEAD

(male)

teeth doglike —

(juvenile)

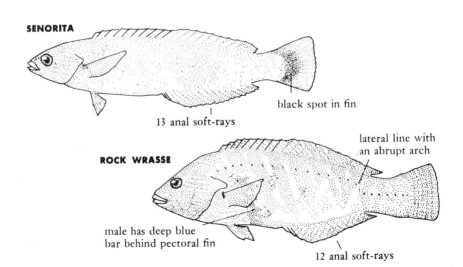

SENORITA

black spot in fin

13 anal soft-rays

lateral line with
an abrupt arch

ROCK WRASSE

male has deep blue
bar behind pectoral fin

12 anal soft-rays

SANDFISH, RONQUILS, STARGAZER, and WOLF-EEL
(Principal sources: Kanazawa, 1952; Clemens & Wilby, 1961)

PACIFIC SANDFISH, *Trichodon trichodon*. Family TRICHODONTIDAE
San Francisco to Bering Sea and Kamchatka. Length to 12 in. Shallow inshore areas. Light brown above, silvery below; dark stripe on and above lateral line. Rare. D XIII–XV + I,18–20; A 28; Pect. 22; scales absent; Vert. 47.

RONQUILS, Genus *Rathbunella*. Family BATHYMASTERIDAE
This genus is being revised at this time with several new species being considered. There are two recognized species; one common, the SMOOTH RONQUIL, *Rathbunella hypoplecta*, and the other rare and little known, the ROUGH RON-QUIL, *Rathbunella alleni*. These species are quite similar and only a description of the SMOOTH RONQUIL is given: Northern Baja California to the Pacific northwest. Length to about 8.5 in. Intertidal to several hundred feet. Dark brown to purplish with lighter areas. D 46 (first 15 soft-rays are unbranched); A 33; Pect. 18; Pelvic I,5; LLp 82.

NORTHERN RONQUIL, *Ronquilus jordani*. Family BATHYMASTERIDAE
Monterey Bay (CAS 36071) to Bering Sea. Length to 7.12 in. Depth 60 to 540 ft. Male is orange above, olive-green below; female is olive-green above, paler below; both sexes have 2 yellow stripes below lateral line. Rare. D 41-48 (first 20-30 soft-rays are unbranched); A 31-34; Pect. 18; LLp about 93; Vert. 49.

SMOOTH STARGAZER, *Kathetostoma averruncus*. Family URANOSCOPIDAE
Peru to Pt. Piedras Blancas, San Luis Obispo Co. Length to 12.25 in. Depth 42 to 1260 ft. Dark gray to black above; light oval and round spots on back and in upper fins. Uncommon. D 13; A 13; scales absent.

WOLF-EEL, *Anarrhichthys ocellatus*. Family ANARHICHADIDAE
Imperial Beach, San Diego Co., to Kodiak Isl., Alaska and Sea of Japan. Length to 6 ft. 8 in. Intertidal to 400 ft. Dark to light gray with darker and lighter mottling and circular patterns over entire body. Common. D (all spines) 218–250; A O-I,180-233; Pect. 19; Pelvic absent; LL absent; scales minute, embedded; GR 3-5 +11-15 = 15-20; Vert. 221-251.

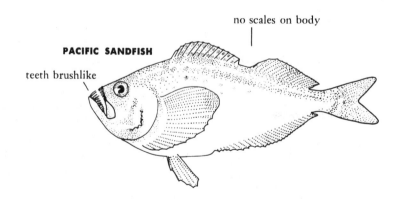

no scales on body

PACIFIC SANDFISH

teeth brushlike

SMOOTH RONQUIL

first 15 soft-rays unbranched

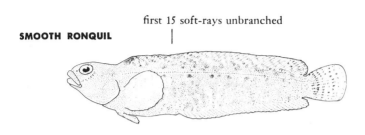

NORTHERN RONQUIL

first 20–30 soft-rays unbranched

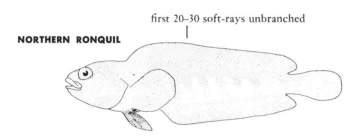

SMOOTH STARGAZER

eyes on top of head

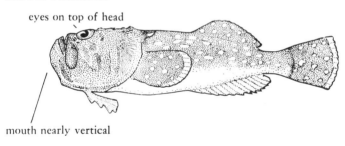

mouth nearly vertical

WOLF-EEL

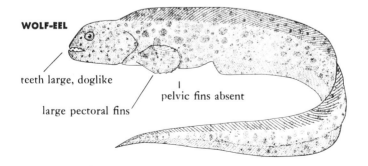

teeth large, doglike

large pectoral fins

pelvic fins absent

COMBTOOTH BLENNIES, Family Blenniidae
(Principal sources: Stephens et al, 1970; John Stephens [1]; Carl L. Hubbs [2])

BAY BLENNY, Hypsoblennius gentilis. Gulf of California (not present at Cape San Lucas) to Monterey. Length to 5.8 in. Intertidal to 80 ft. Brown and green, with reddish spotting; throat reddish. Common, normally found in bays and estuaries. D XI–XIII,16–18; A II,16–19; Pect. 11–12; Pelvic I,3.

ROCKPOOL BLENNY, Hypsoblennius gilberti. Magdalena Bay, Baja California, to Pt. Conception. Length to 5.5 in. Intertidal to 33 ft. Body olivaceus, but varies with color of surroundings. Common. D XII,18–19; A II,19–21; Pect. 13–15; Pelvic I,3; Vert. 37–38.

MUSSEL BLENNY, Hypsoblennius jenkinsi. Puerta Marquis, Mexico (SIO 62-704), to Coal Oil Pt., Santa Barbara Co.,[1] including Gulf of California. Length to 4.4 in. Intertidal to 70 ft. Mottled brown and reddish. Common. D XI–XIII,15–19; A II,15–20; Pect. 12–15; Pelvic I,3.

KEY TO THE BLENNIES, Family Blenniidae:

1a Flap above eye not divided lengthwise into filaments, but is serrated (often deeply) on posterior edge; pectoral rays 11–12:

BAY BLENNY

orbital cirrus

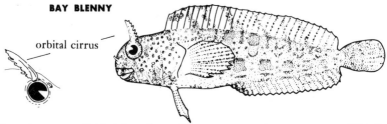

1b Flap above eye divided into long filaments; pectoral rays 13–15 (MUSSEL BLENNIES from the Gulf of California may have 12)........ 2

2a Lateral line extends to above midportion of anal fin; flap over eye divided close to base into 7 or more filaments:

ROCKPOOL BLENNY

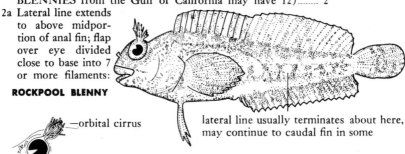

—orbital cirrus

lateral line usually terminates about here, may continue to caudal fin in some

2b Lateral line extends only to about tip of pectoral fin; flap over eye with 7 or less filaments, with the lower ¼ to ½ of the flap undivided:

MUSSEL BLENNY

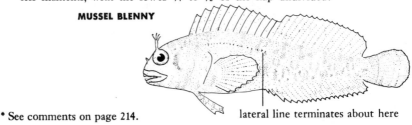

[*] See comments on page 214.   lateral line terminates about here

CLINIDS, Family Clinidae
(Principal sources: Clark Hubbs, 1952, 1953; Rosenblatt & Parr, 1969)

REEF FINSPOT, *Paraclinus integripinnis.* Almejas Bay, Baja California (SIO 62-121), to Santa Cruz Isl. Length to 2.5 in. Intertidal to 50 ft. Body dark brown; mottled with reddish to cream areas; a jet-black ocellus between 22nd to 27th dorsal spines. Common. D XXX–XXXIII; A II,18–21; Pect. 12–14; Pelvic 0–I,3; LLs 34–39; GR 2 + 4 = 6; Vert. 37–39.

ORANGETHROAT PIKEBLENNY, *Chaenopsis alepidota.* Banderas Bay, Mexico (SIO 62-42), to Anacapa Isl.,* including Gulf of California. Length to 6 in. Depth to 35 ft. Light olive-green, with dark blotches on sides; pearly dots on sides and at bases of dorsal and anal fins. Uncommon. D XVIII–XXI,34–38; A II,34–38; Pect. 12–14; Pelvic I,3.

YELLOWFIN FRINGEHEAD, *Neoclinus stephensae.* Pt. San Hipolito (SIO 67-61), to Monterey (CAS 14403). Length to 4 in. Depth 10 to 90 ft. Body dark gray, with purplish bars on sides; blue spots on belly. Uncommon. D XXV–XXVII,15–17; A II, 29–30; Pect. 15; LLs 19–20; GR 6–8 + 12–14 = 18–22.

KEY TO THE CLINIDS, Family Clinidae:

1a Dorsal fin wholly of spines; large ocellus present in posterior portion of dorsal fin:

REEF FINSPOT

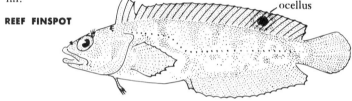

ocellus

1b Dorsal fin with both spines and soft-rays; no ocellus in dorsal fin as above 2

2a More soft-rays than spines in dorsal fin; greatest body depth into total length more than 10 times:
ORANGETHROAT PIKEBLENNY

2b More spines than soft-rays in dorsal fin; greatest body depth into total length less than 8 times 3

3a Maxillary not extending behind eye .... 6(next page)

3b Maxillary extends well behind eye 4

4a Orbital cirri divided from base; no large ocellus in center of membrane between 1st and 2nd dorsal spines; total gill rakers 18-22; head length 4.2-5.3 into standard length:

YELLOWFIN FRINGEHEAD

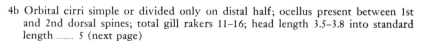

4b Orbital cirri simple or divided only on distal half; ocellus present between 1st and 2nd dorsal spines; total gill rakers 11-16; head length 3.5-3.8 into standard length .... 5 (next page)

* See comments on page 214.

CLINIDS, Family Clinidae (continued)

ONESPOT FRINGEHEAD, *Neoclinus uninotatus*. San Diego Bay to Bodega Bay. Length to 9 in. Depth 10 to 90 ft. Dark brown, with black speckling; one ocellus in dorsal fin. Uncommon. D XXIII–XXVII,14-17; A II,26-31; Pect. 14-16; LLs 17-26; GR 3–5 + 8-11 = 11-16; Vert. 47-48.

SARCASTIC FRINGEHEAD, *Neoclinus blanchardi*. Cedros Isl., Baja California (LACM 32050), to San Francisco. Length to 12 in. Depth 10 to 200 ft. Brown tinged with red; two ocelli in dorsal fin. Uncommon. D XXIII–XXVII,15-18; A II,26-30; Pect. 14-15; LLs 20-27; GR 4-6+ 8 = 12-14; Vert. 46-49.

ISLAND KELPFISH, *Alloclinus holderi*. Pt. San Pablo, Baja California (LACM 32082), to E of Pelican Pt., Santa Cruz Isl. (SIO H 51-241), including Guadalupe Isl. Length 4 in. Depth, surface to 162 ft. Gray, with reddish stripes; about six dark bars on sides; dorsal fin red-orange, with a green spot anteriorly. Common. D XXIV–XXVI,9-11; A II,21-23; Pect. 13-14; Pelvic I,3; LLs 47-54; GR 4 + 9.

DEEPWATER BLENNY, *Cryptotrema corallinum*. San Quintin Bay, Baja California (SIO 62-517), to Santa Cruz Isl. Length to 5 in. Depth 78 to 300 ft., young are probably pelagic. Dusky-olive above, with streaks of red; dark blotches on sides. Uncommon. D XXVI–XXVIII,11-12; A II,24-27; Pect. 13-15; Pelvic I,3; LLs 65-75; GR 4 + 11.

GIANT KELPFISH, *Heterostichus rostratus*. Cape San Lucas, Baja California, to British Columbia, including Guadalupe Isl. Length to 24 in. Depth, surface to 132 ft. Color varies from light brown to green and purplish with lighter mottling. Common. D XXXIII–XXXVIII,11-13; A II,31-35; Pect. 12-14; Pelvic I,3; LLs 73-83; GR 5-7 + 12-13 = 18-20; Vert. 56-58.

STRIPED KELPFISH, *Gibbonsia metzi*. Pt. Rompiente, Baja California (LACM 32054), to Vancouver Isl., B.C. Length to 9.25 in. Depth, surface to 30 ft. Reddish to light brown, usually with darker stripes on sides. Common. D XXXIV–XXXVII,7-10; A II,24-29; Pect. 11-13; Pelvic I,3; scale rows above LL 180-235; LLp 64-71; GR 3-4 + 7-8 = 11; Vert. 50-53.

5a One ocellus in dorsal fin between 1st and 2nd spines, none between 5th to 9th spines; anteriormost orbital cirrus longer than eye and divided at tip:

ONESPOT FRINGEHEAD

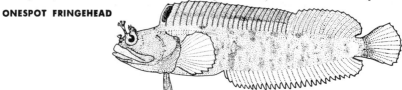

5b Two ocelli in dorsal fin, one between 1st and 2nd spines, the other between 5th to 9th spines; all orbital cirri shorter than eye and undivided:

SARCASTIC FRINGEHEAD
(male)

head of female

maxillary shorter than in male

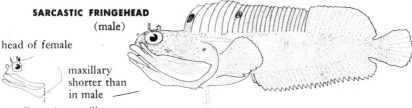

6a *From 3a: maxillary not extending behind eye*
Pectoral fin short, not extending to 1st anal soft-ray; maxillary does not reach middle of eye and goes into head more than 2.5 times; no hooklike projection on anterior surface of pectoral girdle .... 8 (next page)

6b Pectoral fin long, extending beyond 1st anal soft-ray; maxillary extends beyond middle of eye and goes into head less than 2.5 times; hooklike projection on anterior surface of pectoral girdle present 7

7a Lateral line descends to midbody immediately posterior to tip of pectoral fin; anal soft-rays 21–23:

ISLAND KELPFISH   abrupt arch in lateral line

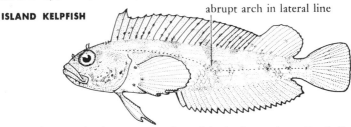

7b Lateral line remains in upper portion of body for at least ⅔ of distance to caudal fin; anal soft-rays 24–27:

DEEPWATER BLENNY   lateral line remains high on side

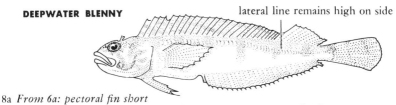

8a *From 6a: pectoral fin short*
Tail forked; more than 30 anal soft-rays; 11 or more dorsal soft-rays:

GIANT KELPFISH

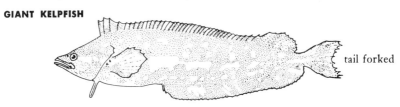

tail forked

8b Tail rounded (in adults); less than 30 anal soft-rays; 10 or less dorsal soft-rays 9

9a Dorsal soft-rays equally spaced, 7–10 in number:

STRIPED KELPFISH   dorsal soft-rays
equally spaced

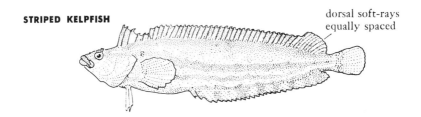

9b Spaces between posterior dorsal soft-rays wider than spacing between anterior soft-rays, the soft-rays totaling 5–8 ... 10 (next page)

CLINIDS, Family Clinidae (continued)

SPOTTED KELPFISH, *Gibbonsia elegans*. Magdalena Bay, Baja California (CAS 13634), to Pt. Piedras Blancas, including Guadalupe Isl. Length to 6.2 in. Depth, surface to 185 ft. Color variable, ranging from green to light brown or reddish. Uncommon. D XXXI–XXXV,5–8; A I–III,21–25; Pect. 11–13; Pelvic I,2–3; scale rows above LL 125–170; LLp 62–71; GR 4–5 + 8–12 = 12–16; Vert. 47–49.

CREVICE KELPFISH, *Gibbonsia montereyensis*. Rio Santo Tomas, Baja California (SIO H 52-158), to British Columbia. Length to 4.44 in. Surface to 25 ft. Reddish to brown or lavender. Common. D XXXIV–XXXVI,5–8; A II,23–28; Pect. 11–13; Pelvic I,3; scale rows above LL 130–175; LLp 61–70; GR 3–5 + 7–9 = 10–13; Vert. 49–51.

SCARLET KELPFISH, *Gibbonsia erythra*. Pt. Banda, Baja California (SIO 59-305), to Santa Cruz Isl. (SIO H 51-244). Length to 6 in. Depth 48 to 120 ft. Red to reddish brown. Uncommon. D XXXIV–XXXVI,6–8; A II,25–27; Pect. 12–13; Pelvic I,3; scale rows above LL 150–180; LLp 63–67; GR 2–4 + 9–10 = 12–14.

10a Scales present on caudal fin:

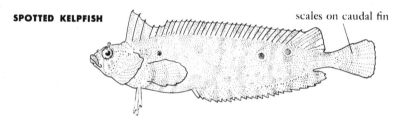

10b No scales on caudal fin........11

11a Posterior portion of caudal peduncle without scales:

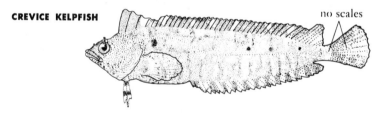

11b Posterior portion of caudal peduncle with scales:

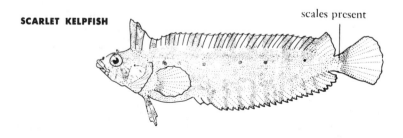

WRYMOUTHS and MONKEYFACE-EEL
(Principal sources: Hubbs, 1927; Clemens & Wilby, 1961)

GIANT WRYMOUTH, *Delolepis gigantea.* Family CRYPTACANTHODIDAE
Humboldt Bay to Bering Sea. Length to 46 in. Depth 20 to 420 ft. Pale brown tinged with yellow and violet, lighter below. Rare. D LXXIII–LXXVII; A II, 43–49, confluent with caudal fin; Pelvic absent; scales present on posterior portion of body, and only on lateral line anteriorly.

DWARF WRYMOUTH, *Lyconectes aleutensis.* Family CRYPTACANTHODIDAE
Eureka to Bering Sea. Length to 12 in. Depth 150 to 1146 ft. Uniform pink or red to gray. Uncommon. D LX–LXIX; A II,45–49, confluent with caudal fin; Pelvic absent; scales absent.

MONKEYFACE-EEL, *Cebidichthys violaceus.* •Family CEBIDICHTHYIDAE
San Quintin Bay, Baja California, to Crescent City. Length to 30 in. Intertidal to 80 ft. Uniform dull black; 2 darker bars below eye. Common. D XXII–XXV, 40–43; A I–II,39–42; Pelvic absent; GR 3–4 + 6–10 = 9–14; Vert. 65–71. (There are two other undescribed species of Cebidicthyidae off southern California and Mexico; one in deep water, the other intertidal. These are being described by Carl L. Hubbs of Scripps Institution of Oceanography, La Jolla.)

body brown

GIANT WRYMOUTH

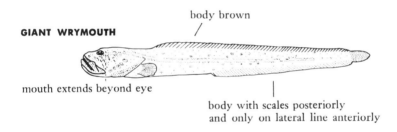

mouth extends beyond eye

body with scales posteriorly
and only on lateral line anteriorly

body pinkish

DWARF WRYMOUTH

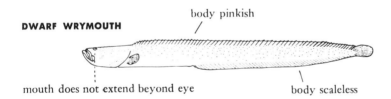

mouth does not extend beyond eye

body scaleless

MONKEYFACE-EEL

one lateral line

humps on head

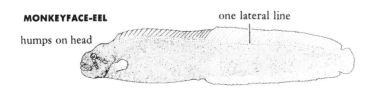

PRICKLEBACKS, Family Stichaeidae
(Principal sources: Schultz, 1936; Makushok, 1958;
Clemens & Wilby, 1961; Peden, 1966a)

HIGH COCKSCOMB, *Anoplarchus purpurescens*. Santa Rosa Isl. (UCLA W 49-11) to Pribilof Isls., Bering Sea. Length to 7.75 in. Intertidal to 100 ft. Black, gray, or purplish, occasionally reddish. Common. D LIV–LX; A I–II,35–41; Pelvic absent; GR 3–5 + 5–10 = 8–14; Vert. 58–64.

SIXSPOT PRICKLEBACK, *Askoldia?* sp.* This undescribed species has been taken only at Diablo Cove, San Luis Obispo Co., at depths around 20 ft. Length to 3.8 in. Reddish-brown; six black ocelli in dorsal fin; edge of caudal fin white. Rare. D LXI–LXIV; A II,39–40; Pelvic 0–I; Vert. 68.

BLACK PRICKLEBACK, *Xiphister atropurpureus*. 1 mi. S of Pt. China, south of Rio Santo Tomas, Baja California (SIO H 50-282), to Kodiak Isl., Alaska. Length to 12 in. Intertidal to 25 ft. Reddish-brown to black; prominent white bar across base of caudal fin. Common. D LXV–LXXIII; A I,49–55; Pect. minute, 11–12; Pelvic absent; GR 2–3 + 6–10 = 8–12; Vert. 73–80.

ROCK PRICKLEBACK, *Xiphister mucosus*. Pt. Arguello Boat Station (UCLA W 56-265) to Port San Juan, Alaska. Length to 23.07 in. Intertidal to 60 ft. Greenish-black to gray or brownish. Common. D LXXI–LXXVIII; A I,46–50; Pect. 12; Pelvic absent; Vert. 73–83.

RIBBON PRICKLEBACK, *Phytichthys chirus*. Southern California to Bering Sea. Length to 8 in. Intertidal to 40 ft. Olive-green to brownish above, yellow to green below; small dark spots along sides. Uncommon. D LXIX–LXXVIII; A II–III,40–50; Pelvic absent; Vert. 75–76.

KEY TO THE PRICKLEBACKS, Family Stichaeidae

1a Pelvic fins present, longer than eye diameter ...... 6 (page 180)

1b Pelvic fins absent, or represented by minute spines less than ½ eye diameter in length 2

2a Gill membranes attached to isthmus:

HIGH COCKSCOMB

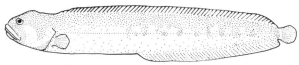

2b Gill membranes free from isthmus .... 3 (next page)

* See comments on page 214.

3a Pectoral fins large, the longest ray going into head less than 2 times; 6 equally spaced ocelli in dorsal fin:

ocelli in dorsal fin

SIXSPOT PRICKLEBACK

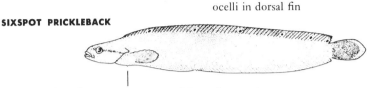

pelvic fins absent, or represented by minute spines

3b Pectoral fins small, going into head more than 2 times; no ocelli in dorsal fin as in 3a above........ 4

4a Origin of dorsal fin about ½ head length (at least 2 eye diameters) behind tip of pectoral fin, and about ½ the distance from snout to origin of anal fin:

white band

BLACK PRICKLEBACK

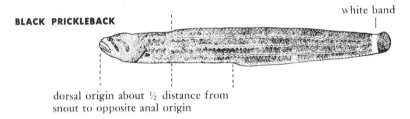

dorsal origin about ½ distance from snout to opposite anal origin

4b Origin of dorsal fin over or slightly posterior to tip of pectoral fin, and about ⅓ the distance from snout to origin of anal fin 5

5a Pectoral fin less than eye diameter; 1 anal spine:

pectoral fin shorter than eye diameter

ROCK PRICKLEBACK

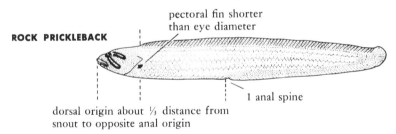

1 anal spine

dorsal origin about ⅓ distance from snout to opposite anal origin

5b Pectoral fin equal to or longer than eye diameter; 2–3 anal spines:

RIBBON PRICKLEBACK

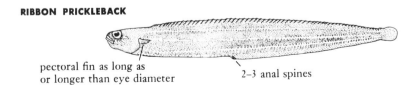

pectoral fin as long as or longer than eye diameter

2–3 anal spines

6a (next page)

PRICKLEBACKS, Family Stichaeidae (continued)

MOSSHEAD WARBONNET, *Chirolophis nugator*. Cuyler Harbor, San Miguel Isl. (SIO 54-191), to Kodiak Isl., Alaska. Length to 5.62 in. Intertidal to 264 ft. Reddish-brown; male has pale bars on sides and 12–13 ocelli in dorsal fin; female has bars in dorsal fin instead of ocelli. Uncommon. D LIII–LV, A I,37–42; Pelvic I,4.

WHITEBARRED PRICKLEBACK, *Poroclinus rothrocki*. San Diego to Bering Sea. Length to 10 in. Depth 150 to 420 ft. Light brown above, white below; 10–12 white vertical bars on sides. Uncommon. D LVII–LXVII; A III,40-44; Pect. 14-15; Pelvic I,3; GR rudimentary.

SNAKE PRICKLEBACK, *Lumpenus sagitta*. Humboldt Bay to Bering Sea and Sea of Japan. Length to 20 in. Shallow bays to 678 ft. Light green dorsally, cream below; numerous dark green to brown streaks on sides. Uncommon. D LXIV–LXXII; A I,45–50; Pect. 15–16; Pelvic I,3–4; Vert. 75–80.

BLUEBARRED PRICKLEBACK, *Plectobranchus evides*. San Diego to central British Columbia. Length to 5.38 in. Depth 276 to 900 ft. Dusky-olive; about 25 bars on sides. Uncommon. D LIV–LVII; A II,34–36; Pect. 15; Pelvic I,3.

CRISSCROSS PRICKLEBACK, *Plagiogrammus hopkinsi*. San Nicolas Isl. (UCLA W 50-185) to Pacific Grove (CAS 21199). Length to 7.75 in. Intertidal to 70 ft. Black to dusky-brown; dark stripe through eye; fins black. Uncommon. D XXXVII–XLI; A II,26–29; Pelvic I,4 (appearing as I,5, the last soft-ray divided close to base); Vert. 43.

MASKED PRICKLEBACK, *Stichaeopsis?* sp.* Pt. Arguello (UCLA W 64-8) to Monterey.* Length to 12.75 in. Intertidal to 70 ft. Body light brown, with darker brown to blackish streaks on upper parts; belly and cheek area cream colored; a dark line through eye to above pectoral fin. Uncommon. D XLVII–LII; A II,32–34; Pect. 15–16; Pelvic I,3.

6a *From 1a: pelvic fins present, longer than eye diameter*
Top of head covered with cirri:

MOSSHEAD WARBONNET

cirri on head–

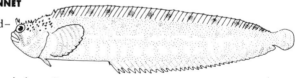

6b Top of head without cirri_____ 7

7a Gill membranes free from isthmus, or at least with a free fold across isthmus_____ 9(next page)

7b Gill membranes attached to isthmus and without a free fold_____ 8

8a Dorsal fin membrane attached to upper caudal fin ray; series of white bars present along sides; 3 anal spines:

WHITEBARRED PRICKLEBACK

membrane joining dorsal and caudal fins

8b (next page)   3 anal spines

* See comments on page 214.

8b Dorsal and caudal fins not joined; no white bars on sides; 1 anal spine:

SNAKE PRICKLEBACK

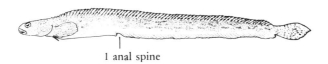

1 anal spine

9a *From 7a: gill membranes free from isthmus*
Two black spots in posterior half of dorsal fin; pelvic fins long, going into body depth at base of pectoral fins less than 1.5 times:

BLUEBARRED PRICKLEBACK

black spots

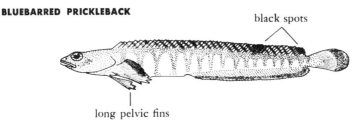

long pelvic fins

9b No black spots in dorsal fin as above; pelvic fins short, going into body depth at base of pectoral fins more than 2 times........ 10

10a Cheek area dark brown to black; sides with lateral lines branching vertically forming platelike divisions; pelvic soft-rays 4 (appearing as 5):

CRISSCROSS PRICKLEBACK

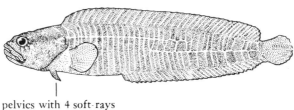

pelvics with 4 soft-rays

10b Cheek area cream colored; lateral lines not as in 10a above; pelvic soft-rays 3:

MASKED PRICKLEBACK

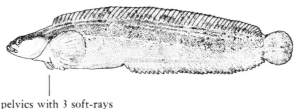

pelvics with 3 soft-rays

GUNNELS, Family Pholididae
(Principal sources: Hubbs, 1927; Schultz, 1936; Makushok, 1958; Clemens & Wilby, 1961; Rosenblatt, 1964; Peden, 1966b)

KELP GUNNEL, Ulvicola sanctaerosae. Guadalupe Isl. and on the mainland from Papalote Bay (south of Pt. Banda), Baja California, to Pacific Grove (CF&G collection, 1971). Length to 11.25 in. Kelp canopy to 40 ft. Uniform yellowish-tan to brown, and red-brown. Uncommon. D XCVII; A I,40; Pect. absent; Pelvic absent; Vert. 105–107.

PENPOINT GUNNEL, Apodichthys flavidus. Santa Barbara Isl. to Kodiak Isl., Alaska. Length to 18 in. Intertidal. Green, yellow, to light brown, and red. Common. D XC–XCIV; A I,36–42; Pelvic absent; GR 3 + 10-13 = 13–16; Vert. 96–101.

ROCKWEED GUNNEL, Xererpes fucorum. Pt. Escarpada, Baja California (SIO H 52-208), to Vancouver Isl., B.C. Length to 9 in. Intertidal to 30 ft. Greenish to red. Common. D LXXXII–LXXXVII; A I,29–38; Pelvic absent; GR 1-2 + 6-9 = 8–11; Vert. 84–93.

RED GUNNEL, Pholis schultzi. Diablo Cove, San Luis Obispo Co. (CF&G collection), to Tofino, Vancouver Isl., B.C. Length to 5 in. Intertidal and subtidal. Usually pinkish-red but occasionally light brown; vague bars and mottling on sides; 16–22 marks along base of dorsal fin. Uncommon. D LXXX–LXXXIX; A II,40-44; Pect. 11–12; Pelvic I,1; GR 1-2 + 7-10 = 8–12; Vert. 89–93.

SADDLEBACK GUNNEL, Pholis ornata. South end of Carmel Beach (CAS 63688) to Bering Sea and Sea of Japan. Length to 12 in. Intertidal to 120 ft. Olive-green to brown above, yellowish to red below. Uncommon. D LXXIV–LXXIX; A II,34–38; Pelvic I,1; Vert. 83–86.

CRESCENT GUNNEL, Pholis laeta. 1 mi. NW Crescent City (UCLA W 54-277) to Bering Sea. Length to 10 in. Intertidal to 240 ft. Yellowish-green. Uncommon. D LXXIV–LXXX; A II,34-37; Pelvic I,1; Vert. 84-85.

KEY TO THE GUNNELS, Family Pholididae:

1a Pectoral fins absent:

KELP GUNNEL

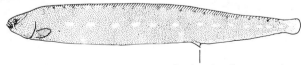

pectoral and pelvic
fins absent

1b Pectoral fins present........ 2

2a Pelvic fins present........ 4 (next page)

2b Pelvic fins absent........ 3

3a Pectoral fin about 2 times eye diameter; anal spine deeply concave (grooved on outer surface), and about 2 times longer than snout length:

PENPOINT GUNNEL

anal spine deeply grooved
on outer surface

3b (next page)

3b Pectoral fin about equal to diameter of eye; anal spine round, and about same
length as snout:

ROCKWEED GUNNEL

pectoral fin about
same length as eye
diameter

anal spine not grooved

4a *From 2a: pelvic fins present*
Anal soft-rays 40-44; anal fin with numerous dark narrow bars (bars rarely
absent); 16–22 bars or V shaped marks along base of dorsal fin:

RED GUNNEL

white bar below eye

anal fin usually with vertical bars

4b Anal soft-rays 34-38; anal fin plain or rarely with a few faint bars; 10-15 V
or ( ) shaped marks along base of dorsal fin 5

5a Markings on back V shaped; pectoral fin large, 1.8-2.3 into head length:

SADDLEBACK GUNNEL

5b Markings on back ( ) shaped; pectoral fins small, 2.4-3.0 into head length:

CRESCENT GUNNEL

GRAVELDIVER, SANDLANCE, PROWFISH, SLEEPER, and RAGFISH
(Principal source: Clemens & Wilby, 1961)

GRAVELDIVER, *Scytalina cerdale*. Family SCYTALINIDAE
Diablo Cove, San Luis Obispo Co., to Bering Sea. Length to 6 in. Intertidal to
subtidal. Body pinkish with purplish mottling. Uncommon, rarely seen. D 41–51;
A 36–41; Pelvic absent; LL absent.

PACIFIC SANDLANCE, *Ammodytes hexapterus*. Family AMMODYTIDAE
Balboa Isl., Orange Co. (CAS 48237), to Bering Sea, Arctic Alaska, and to Sea of
Japan. Length to 8 in. Depth, surface to 60 ft. Metallic blue on back, silvery
below. Common in northern California. D 54–59; A 24–30; Pelvic absent; GR
3–5 + 16–22 = 20–26; Vert. 65–70.

PROWFISH, *Zaprora silenus*. Family ZAPRORIDAE
Bodega Bay to Aleutian Isls., Alaska, and to Japan. Length to 2 ft. 10.5 in. Depth
96 to 1170 ft. Gray to dark green above, pale below; yellowish to orange on
cheeks and behind pectoral fin. Rare. D LIV–LVII; A O–III,24–27; Pect. 20–22;
Pelvic absent; LLs about 200; GR 8 + 20.

PACIFIC FAT SLEEPER, *Dormitator latifrons*. Family ELEOTRIDAE
Guayaquil, Ecuador, to Palos Verdes, Los Angeles Co., including Gulf of California. Length recorded to 12 in., reported to 24 in. Shallow inshore areas. Dark
olive with dark brown bars. One California record. D VII–VIII + I,8; A I,8–9;
Pect. I,13–15; Pelvic I,5, LLs 30–35.

RAGFISH, *Icosteus aenigmaticus*. Family ICOSTEIDAE
Pt. Loma, San Diego Co. (SIO 62–554), to S.E. Alaska and to Japan. Length to
6 ft. 10 in. Depth 270 to 1200 ft. Dark chocolate-brown in adult; young light
brown, with spotting and mottling. Adult fish has a forked tail, juvenile has a
rounded tail. Uncommon. D 52–56; A 34–44; Pelvic I,5 (occasionally I,4, absent
in adult); scales absent in adult; GR 1 + 6 = 7; Vert. 68.

GRAVELDIVER   body deepest posterior to vent

no pelvic fins   vent

PACIFIC SANDLANCE   lateral line adjacent to dorsal fin

no pelvic fins   fold of skin along sides near midventral line

dorsal fin entirely of spines

PROWFISH

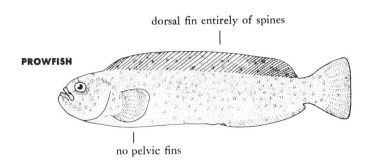

no pelvic fins

large, rounded tail

PACIFIC FAT SLEEPER

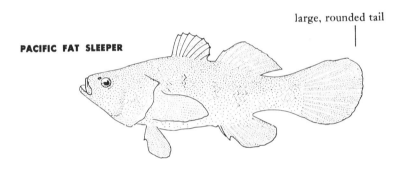

no spines in dorsal fin

body soft and flabby

RAGFISH

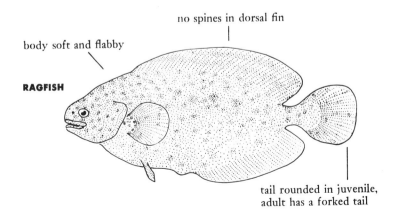

tail rounded in juvenile,
adult has a forked tail

GOBIES, Family Gobiidae

(Principal sources: Hubbs, 1926; Clemens & Wilby, 1961; Lillian Dempster [*1];
John Fitch [*2])

CHAMELEON GOBY. *Tridentiger trigonocephalus.* Los Angeles Harbor and in San Francisco Bay, inadvertently introduced from Orient. Length to 3.5 in. Shallow bay areas. Brownish-gray with dark mottling and spots. This fish has the ability to change color patterns rapidly between bars and stripes.[*1] Common. D VI + I,11–12; A I,10–11; midlateral scales 50–58.

BLACKEYE GOBY, *Coryphopterus nicholsii.* South of Pt. Rompiente, Baja California (LACM 32053), to Skidegate Channel, Queen Charlotte Isl., B.C. Length to 6 in. Depth 5 to 80 ft. (juv. reported in deep water). Tan to olive with brownish and green speckling; black on outer edge of first dorsal fin. Common. D V–VI + I–II,9–14; A O–I,11–12; midlateral scales 25–28; Vert. 26.

BLUEBANDED GOBY, *Lythrypnus dalli.* Gulf of California to Morro Bay (California State University at Long Beach C 484), including Guadalupe Isl. Length to 2.25 in. Intertidal to 210 ft. Red with bright blue bands. Common. D VI + 16–17; A 12–14; Pect. 17–18; midlateral scales 40.

ZEBRA GOBY, *Lythrypnus zebra.* Clarion Isl., Mexico, to Lion Rock, San Luis Obispo Co., including Guadalupe Isl. (SIO H 46–147). Length to 2.25 in. Subtidal to 318 ft. Red with bright blue bands. Common. D VI + 11–12; A O–I,9.

BLIND GOBY, *Typhlogobius californiensis.* Magdalena Bay, Baja California (SIO 58–154), to cove north of San Simeon Pt. (UCLA W 62–92). Length to 3.25 in. Intertidal to 25 ft., and possibly deeper. Uniform pink. Uncommon. D II–III + 12; A I,8–10; Vert. 30–32.

KELP GOBY, *Lethops connectens.* Cape Colnett, Baja California, to Carmel. Length to 2.5 in. Intertidal to 60 ft. Uniform tan. Uncommon. D VI + 14; A 12–13.

TIDEWATER GOBY, *Eucyclogobius newberryi.* Carlsbad Bird Sanctuary, San Diego Co. (UCLA W 53–235), to Stone Lagoon, Humboldt Co. (CAS 13641). Length to 2 in. Shallow areas of bays. Olive-brown with darker mottling. Common. D VI–VII + I,9–12; A I,8–11; LLs about 60–70; GR 1–2 + 7–8 = 8–10; Vert. 33–35.

KEY TO THE GOBIES, Family Gobiidae:

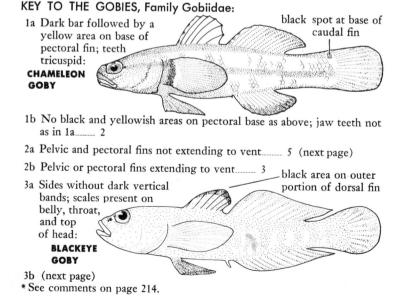

1a Dark bar followed by a yellow area on base of pectoral fin; teeth tricuspid: **CHAMELEON GOBY**
    black spot at base of caudal fin

1b No black and yellowish areas on pectoral base as above; jaw teeth not as in 1a........ 2

2a Pelvic and pectoral fins not extending to vent........ 5 (next page)

2b Pelvic or pectoral fins extending to vent........ 3

3a Sides without dark vertical bands; scales present on belly, throat, and top of head: **BLACKEYE GOBY**
    black area on outer portion of dorsal fin

3b (next page)

* See comments on page 214.

3b Sides with dark vertical bands; no scales on belly, throat, and top of head...... 4

4a Body with 2–6 bands; anal soft-rays 12–14:

BLUEBANDED GOBY

4b Body with 12–16 bands;
   anal soft-rays 9:

ZEBRA GOBY

5a *From 2a: pectoral and
   pelvic fins not reaching
   vent* Body with scales...... 7

5b Body without scales........ 6

6a First dorsal fin with 3 spines; eyes vestigial or absent:

BLIND GOBY   wide space between fins   8 to 10 soft-rays

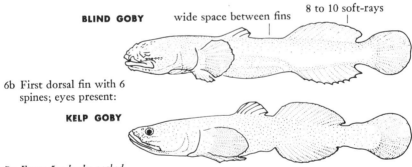

6b First dorsal fin with 6
   spines; eyes present:

KELP GOBY

7a *From 5a: body scaled*
   Insertion of uppermost pectoral ray above gill opening; a pair of pores present
   between eyes in interorbital space:

TIDEWATER GOBY   pores between eyes

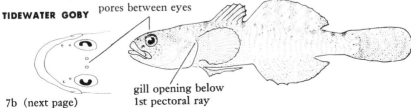

                              gill opening below
7b (next page)   1st pectoral ray

GOBIES, Family Gobiidae (continued)

LONGTAIL GOBY, *Gobionellus longicaudus.* Guaymas, Mexico, to San Diego. Length to 8 in. Shallow areas, lagoons. Light yellow-brown; black blotches on sides. Rare. D VI + 13–14; A 13; midlateral scales 66.

LONGJAW MUDSUCKER, *Gillichthys mirabilis.* Gulf of California to Tomales Bay (CAS 22071). Length to 8 in. Shallow areas of bays, mudflats. Dark olive-brown; belly yellow. Common. D IV–VIII + I–III,9–14; A I–III,8–14; GR 1-4 + 9–12; Vert. 31–33.

BAY GOBY, *Lepidogobius lepidus..* Cedros Isl., Baja California,* to Vancouver Isl., B.C. Length to 4 in. Shallow bays to 200 ft. Light olive with reddish mottling. Common. D VII–VIII + O–I,14–18; A O–I,13–16; midlateral scales about 86; GR 2-3 + 8–11; Vert. 37–38.

YELLOWFIN GOBY, *Acanthogobius flavimanus.* Elkhorn Slough (California State University at San Jose ES-39), to Tomales Bay (CAS 14405). Length to 9.5 in. Shallow bays. Light gray with black speckling and bars. Common. D VIII + 14; A 11–12; midlateral scales 44–50.

CHEEKSPOT GOBY, *Ilypnus gilberti.* Gulf of California to Walker Cr., Tomales Bay (CAS 24175). Length to 2.5 in. Mud flats of bays. Tan to light gray; a blue-black spot on operculum. Common. D V + O–I,13–17; A O–I,12–16; Vert. 32–34.

ARROW GOBY, *Clevelandia ios.* Gulf of California * to Vancouver Isl., B.C. Length to 2 in. Shallow areas of bays. Light olive with darker mottling. Common. D IV–VI + O–I,14–17; A O–I,14–17; midlateral scales about 70; GR 1-3 + 5–7 = 7–9; Vert. 36–37.

SHADOW GOBY, *Quietula y-cauda.* Gulf of California to Morro Bay (CAS 25468). Length to 2.75 in. Mud flats. Dark to light brown with darker blotches; a Y-shaped mark on caudal peduncle. Common. D IV–V + I,13–15; A O–I,12–15; midlateral scales about 50; GR 2-4 + 8–10 = 11–13; Vert. 33–34.

7b Insertion of uppermost pectoral ray below gill opening; no pores in inter-orbital space _____ 8

8a Mouth inferior; tail longer than head by 1.5 eye diameters or more:

LONGTAIL GOBY

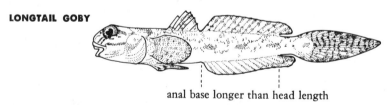

anal base longer than head length

8b Mouth terminal; tail shorter than head (rarely a large **YELLOWFIN GOBY** may have a tail longer than head, but by less than an eye diameter)_____ 9

9a Interorbital width greater than eye diameter (may be equal to or slightly less in fish under 1 in.); upper jaw extends beyond preopercle in fish longer than about 2¾ inches:

LONGJAW MUDSUCKER

preopercle

upper jaw

anal base shorter than head length

9b (next page)

* See comments on page 214.

9b Eye diameter greater than interorbital width; upper jaw not extending beyond preopercle........ 10

10a First dorsal spines 4-6; no scales on nape........ 12

10b First dorsal spines 7-8; scales present on nape........ 11

11a First dorsal spines 7 (rarely 8); eye diameter 1.0–1.2 into snout; wide space between dorsal fins:

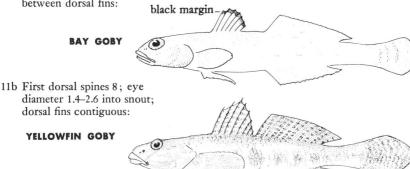

black margin

BAY GOBY

11b First dorsal spines 8; eye diameter 1.4–2.6 into snout; dorsal fins contiguous:

YELLOWFIN GOBY

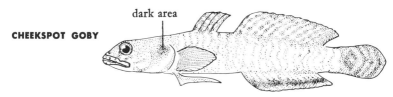

12a *From 10a: 1st dorsal with 4–6 spines*
Mouth not extending beyond eye; conspicuous blue-black blotch on operculum:

dark area

CHEEKSPOT GOBY

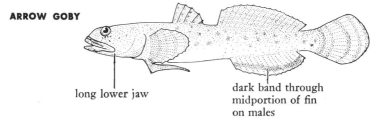

12b Mouth extending well beyond eye; no conspicuous blotch on operculum..... 13

13a Dorsal fins separated by a distance greater than eye diameter; body pale with brownish reticulation, no midline stripe; no groove across nape:

ARROW GOBY

long lower jaw

dark band through midportion of fin on males

13b Dorsal fins separated by a distance equal to or less than eye diameter; body with faint horizontal stripe along midline; groove present across nape:

groove across nape   Y-shaped blotch

SHADOW GOBY

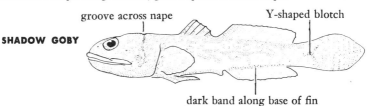

dark band along base of fin

CUTLASSFISHES* and SNAKE MACKERELS
(Principal sources: Tucker, 1956; Fitch and Gotshall, 1972)

PACIFIC CUTLASSFISH, *Trichiurus nitens*. Family TRICHIURIDAE
Worldwide in warmer seas; in eastern Pacific from Paita, Peru, to San Pedro,
including Galapagos Isls. and Gulf of California. Length to 44 in. Depth 18 to
1260 ft. Silvery-brown. Uncommon. D 118–128 ray elements*; A I–II (one
embedded), 95–105; GR 7–11 + 12–24 = 19–35; Vert. 141–155.

RAZORBACK SCABBARDFISH, *Assurger anzac*. Family TRICHIURIDAE
Worldwide; in eastern Pacific north to Pt. Dume. Length to 70 in. Bathypelagic.
Uniform silver. Rare. D 116–119 ray elements*; A II (one embedded), 74–76;
Pect. 12; GRt 13; Vert. 127.

PACIFIC SCABBARDFISH, *Lepidopus xantusi*. Family TRICHIURIDAE
Mazatlan, Mexico, to Eureka. Recorded length to 35.5 in., reported to 40 in.
Adults blackish; young silver. Uncommon. D 78–81 ray elements*; A III (one
embedded), 42–47; Pect. 12; GR 6–14 + 10–26 = 16–40; Vert. 82–87.

SNAKE MACKEREL, *Gempylus serpens*. Family GEMPYLIDAE
Worldwide in warm seas; in eastern Pacific from Chile to San Pedro. Length
to 5 ft. Surface to at least 3300 ft. Blackish. Uncommon. D XXV–XXXII +
O–I,12 + 5–7 finlets; A I–II,10–12 + 6–7 finlets; Pelvic I,5 (sometimes I,4 in largest
fish); GRt 18; Vert. 49–53.

OILFISH, *Ruvettus pretiosus*. Family GEMPYLIDAE
In all warm seas; north to Encinitas on our coast. Length to 6 ft. 8 in. Depth
360 to 2400 ft. Blackish to dark brown. Rare. D XII–XV + 16–18 + 2 finlets; A
16–18 + 2 finlets; GR rudimentary, small paired spines present; Vert. 32.

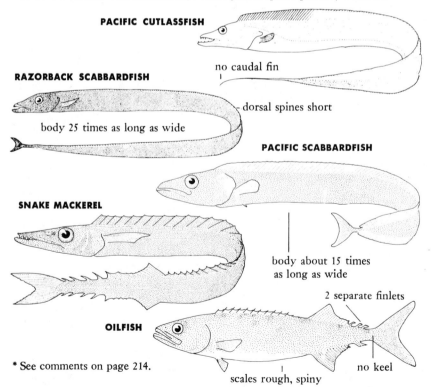

PACIFIC CUTLASSFISH

no caudal fin

RAZORBACK SCABBARDFISH

dorsal spines short

body 25 times as long as wide

PACIFIC SCABBARDFISH

SNAKE MACKEREL

body about 15 times
as long as wide

2 separate finlets

OILFISH

no keel

scales rough, spiny

* See comments on page 214.

MACKERELS, Family Scombridae

(Principal sources: Godsil & Byers, 1944; Fraser-Brunner, 1950; Godsil, 1954; Gosline & Brock, 1960; Fitch & Roedel, 1962; Collette & Gibbs, 1963)

ESCOLAR, *Lepidocybium flavobrunneum*.* Worldwide in warm seas; in eastern Pacific from Peru to Washington. Length to 62.25 in. Mesopelagic. Uniform dark brown. Rare. D VIII–XII + 16–18 + 4-6 finlets; A 13–15 + 4-5 finlets; Pect. 15–17; GR none or as minute spines.

PACIFIC MACKEREL, *Scomber japonicus*. Transpacific; in eastern Pacific from Chile to Gulf of Alaska. Length to 25 in., and wt. to 6.36 lbs. Depth from surface to 150 ft. Head dark blue, back with dark wavy lines, silver-green below. Common. D VIII–XI + I,9-14 + 4-6 finlets; A I + I or II,9-12 + 4-6 finlets; GR 11-14 + 27-29 = 38-43; Vert. 30-32.

FRIGATE MACKEREL, *Auxis thazard*. Worldwide in warm seas; in eastern Pacific from Peru to Santa Catalina Isl., including Galapagos Isls. and Gulf of California. Length to 24 in. Epipelagic. Dark above, silvery below; fine wavy lines on back. Rare. D X–XI + 10–12 + 8 finlets; A 9 – 13 + 7 finlets; GRt 37-47; Vert. 39.

KEY TO THE TUNAS, Family Scombridae:

1a Lateral line greatly undulating (see figure); gill rakers absent or represented by minute spines; anterior dorsal spines not elevated:

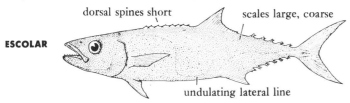

dorsal spines short   scales large, coarse

ESCOLAR

undulating lateral line

1b Lateral line not as above; gill rakers present; anterior dorsal spines elevated 2

2a Space between dorsal fins less than snout length....... 5 (next page)

2b Space between dorsal fins more than snout length........ 3

3a Vermiculations on back extend onto head; 4–6 finlets:

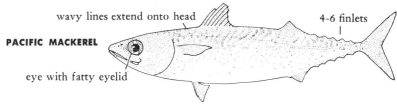

wavy lines extend onto head   4-6 finlets

PACIFIC MACKEREL

eye with fatty eyelid

3b Vermiculations on back not reaching head; 7–8 finlets........ 4

4a Corselet 1–4 scale rows in width under origin of 2nd dorsal fin; thin wavy lines on back:

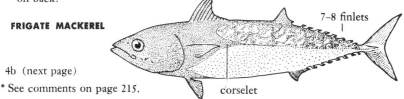

7–8 finlets

FRIGATE MACKEREL

4b (next page)

corselet

* See comments on page 215.

MACKERELS, Family Scombridae (continued)

BULLET MACKEREL, *Auxis rochei.* Worldwide in warm seas; in eastern Pacific from Callao, Peru, to Redondo Beach. Length to 20 in. Epipelagic. Dark anteriorly, silvery below; wide bars on back. Uncommon. GRt 40–49; Vert. 39.

SIERRA, *Scomberomorus sierra.* Paita, Peru, to Santa Monica, including Galapagos Isls. Length to 32 in., and wt. to 11 lbs. A nearshore fish. Dark blue above, silvery below; yellowish spots on sides. Rare. D XVI–XVIII + 15–18 + 8–9 finlets; A II,15–18 + 7–9 finlets; LLp 165; GR 3–5 + 10–13; Vert. 47–49.

MONTEREY SPANISH MACKEREL, *Scomberomorus concolor.* Gulf of California to Soquel. Length to 28.5 in., and wt. to 6.25 lbs. A nearshore pelagic fish. Bluish above, silver below; occasionally with yellow spots. Rare. D XVI–XVII + 16–18 + 8–9 finlets; A I–II,16–20 + 7–8 finlets; GR 5–9 + 15–20; Vert. 47–48.

SKIPJACK, *Euthynnus pelamis.* Worldwide in warm seas; in eastern Pacific from Peru to Vancouver Isl., B.C. Length to 40 in. Epipelagic. Dark on back, silver below; stripes on ventral surface. Common. D XV–XVI + 12–16 + 7–8 finlets; A II,12–16 + 6–8 finlets; GR 16–22 + 35–43 = 53–63; Vert. 41.

WAVYBACK SKIPJACK, *Euthynnus affinis.* An Indo-Pacific species; north to Los Angeles Harbor on our coast. Length to about 30 in. Epipelagic. Dark above, silvery below; black spots below pectoral base. Rare. XIV–XV + 11–13 + 8 finlets; A 12–14 + 6–7 finlets; GR 7–9 + 22–26.

BLACK SKIPJACK, *Euthynnus lineatus.* Colombia to San Simeon, including Galapagos Isls. Weight to 12 lbs. Epipelagic. Dark above, silver below; black spots below pectoral fin. Rare. D XIII–XV + 11–12 + 8 finlets; A III,9–10 + 7 finlets; GR 7–11 + 25–30 = 32–41; Vert. 37.

PACIFIC BONITO, *Sarda chiliensis.* Chile to Gulf of Alaska. Length to 40 in. Epipelagic. Dark blue above, silvery below. Common. D XVIII–XIX + I,12–15 + 6–9 finlets; A II,10–13 + 6–7 finlets; GR 7–10 + 11–18; Vert. 44–46.

4b Corselet with 6 or more (min. of 6 worldwide, in eastern Pacific min. of 13) scale rows under origin of 2nd dorsal; wide, nearly vertical bands on back:

BULLET MACKEREL

wide space between dorsal fins

5a *From 2a: space between dorsal fins less than snout length*
Corselet present; head length into total length about 4 times or less 7

5b Corselet absent; head length into total length at least 5 times 6

6a Gill rakers 10–13 on lower limb of 1st gill arch: **SIERRA**

body with golden spots on sides

6b Gill rakers 15–20 on lower limb of 1st gill arch:

MONTEREY SPANISH MACKEREL
7a (next page)

spots on sides usually absent

7a *From 5a: corselet present*
Body fully scaled, with enlarged scales in corselet area and along lateral line
.... 10
7b Scales present in corselet, absent posterior of corselet except on lateral line
.... 8
8a Back without longitudinal stripes; bright longitudinal stripes on ventral surface;
no black spots between pectoral and pelvic fins:

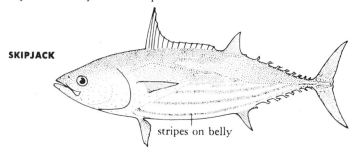

SKIPJACK

stripes on belly

8b Back with stripes; ventral surface with faint lines, or none; black spots present
between pectoral and pelvic fins........ 9

9a Wavy oblique lines on back; no faint longitudinal stripes on ventral suface:

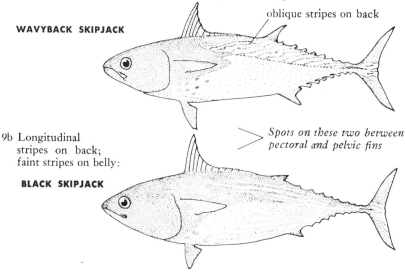

oblique stripes on back

WAVYBACK SKIPJACK

9b Longitudinal
stripes on back;
faint stripes on belly:

*Spots on these two between
pectoral and pelvic fins*

BLACK SKIPJACK

10a *From 7a: body fully scaled*
Dark oblique lines on back; teeth large, usually widely spaced:

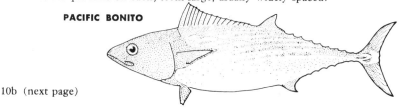

PACIFIC BONITO

10b (next page)

MACKERELS, Family Scombridae (continued)

SLENDER TUNA, *Allothunnus fallai.* Warm seas, mostly in southern hemisphere; north to Los Angeles Harbor. Length to 38 in., and wt. to 15 lbs. Inshore pelagic. One California record. D XVII + 12 + 7 finlets; A 12 + 7 finlets; Pect. 25; GR 23 + 48–51; Vert. 39.

ALBACORE, *Thunnus alalunga.* Worldwide in warm seas; in eastern Pacific from Guadalupe Isl. to S.E. Alaska. Length to 5 ft., and wt. to 93 lbs. (Calif. wt. to 76 lbs.) Epipelagic. Dark gray above, gray below. Common. D XIII–XIV + 0–II,13–16 + 7–8 finlets; A II,12–15 + 7–8 finlets; Pect. 31–34; GR 7–10 + 18–22 = 25–31; Vert. 39.

BIGEYE TUNA, *Thunnus obesus.* Worldwide in warmer seas; in eastern Pacific from Peru to Iron Springs, Washington, including Galapagos Isls. Length to about 80 in., and wt. to 300 lbs. Epipelagic. Dark blue above, gray below. Rare. D XIV–XVI + II,11–14 + 8–10 finlets; A II,10–15 + 8–9 finlets; GR 8–13 + 18–25; Vert. 39.

BLUEFIN TUNA, *Thunnus thynnus.* In all but coldest seas; in eastern Pacific from Peru to Shelikof Strait, Alaska, and over to the Kuril Isls., including Guadalupe Isl. Weight to 297 lbs. in Pacific, in Atlantic to 1500 lbs. Epipelagic. Dark blue above, gray below. Common. D XII–XV + 13–15 + 7–10 finlets; A O–I,12–15 + 7–9 finlets; GR 10–14 + 21–25 = 32–39; Vert. 39.

YELLOWFIN TUNA, *Thunnus albacares.* Transpacific; in eastern Pacific from Chile to Pt. Buchon, including Guadalupe Isl. Weight to 450 lbs. Epipelagic. Dark blue above, gray below. Common. D XII–XIV + 14–16 + 8–9 finlets; A 14–16 + 7–9 finlets; GR 8–11 + 19–24 = 27–34; Vert. 39.

10b No dark lines on back (faint lines present on juveniles of some); teeth minute, forming a tight continuous band on jaws........ 11

11a No teeth on palatines; 48–51 rakers on lower limb of 1st gill arch:

SLENDER TUNA

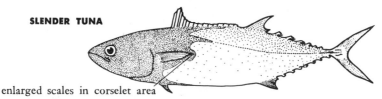

enlarged scales in corselet area

11b Palatines with teeth; 25 or less rakers on lower limb of 1st gill arch........ 12

12a Pectoral fin not extending to insertion of anal fin........ 14 (next page)

12b Pectoral fin extends beyond insertion of anal fin........ 13

13a Greatest body depth posterior to or at about midbody; posterior edge of caudal fin whitish; ventral surface of liver heavily striated:

ALBACORE   long pectoral fin

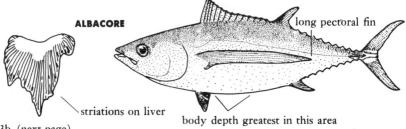

striations on liver

13b (next page)   body depth greatest in this area

13b Greatest body depth anterior to midbody, near pectoral fin base; posterior edge
    of caudal fin not whitish; striations present only on ventral edges of liver:

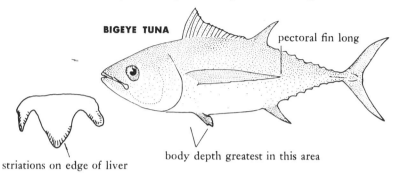

BIGEYE TUNA   pectoral fin long

striations on edge of liver   body depth greatest in this area

14a *From 12a: pectoral not extending to anal fin insertion*
    Pectoral fin less than 80% (more than 1.2) of head in length, not reaching be-
    yond origin of 2nd dorsal fin:

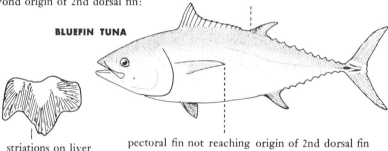

BLUEFIN TUNA

striations on liver   pectoral fin not reaching origin of 2nd dorsal fin

14b Pectoral fin length more than 80% (less than 1.2) of head length, extending
    beyond origin of 2nd dorsal fin........ 15

15a No striations on ventral surface of liver; 2nd dorsal fin about same height as
    1st dorsal in fish up to about 100 pounds, becoming greatly elongated in larger
    fish; pectoral fin length is relatively shorter with age, but never becomes as
    long as that of ALBACORE or juvenile BIGEYE TUNA:

2nd dorsal fin becomes elongate in large fish

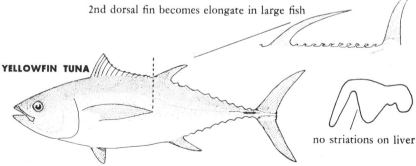

YELLOWFIN TUNA

no striations on liver

15b Striations present on ventral edges of liver; 2nd dorsal fin about same height as
    1st dorsal at all ages; pectoral fin length varys considerably with age, in large
    fish is about the same relative length as YELLOWFIN but is similar to
    ALBACORE in juveniles: BIGEYE TUNA (see 13b for figure)

SWORDFISH, Family Xiphiidae, and BILLFISHES, Family Istiophoridae
(Principal sources: Nakamura, 1955; Gosline & Brock, 1960;
Howard & Ueyanagi, 1965)

SWORDFISH, *Xiphias gladius.* Worldwide in warm seas; in eastern Pacific from Chile to Oregon. Length to 14 ft. 11.25 in., and wt. to 1182 lbs. Depth, surface to at least 2000 ft. Dark gray to black above, gray to yellowish below. Common. D total elements 22–40 + 4 (Nakamura gives III,9,XXVI + 4); A 8–18 + 4 (Nakamura gives II,7,IX–X + 4); Pelvic absent; GR none; Vert. 26.

SHORTBILL SPEARFISH, *Tetrapturus angustirostris.* Throughout tropical Pacific; in eastern Pacific from Chile to 40 miles W of Cape Mendocino. Length to 6 ft., and weight to 60 lbs. Epipelagic. Bluish above, white below. Rare. D III,11–13, XXXV–XXXVII + 6; A II,12 + 7; Pelvic I,2; Vert. 24.

SAILFISH, *Istiophorus platypterus.* In eastern Pacific from Chile to San Diego. Weight to 182 lbs. Epipelagic. Dark blue above, silver below. Rare. D XLI–L + 7; A XIV–XX + 6–7; GR none; Vert. 24.

BLACK MARLIN, *Makaira indica.* In most warm seas; in eastern Pacific from South America to off southern California. Length to 11.5 ft., and wt. to 1250 lbs. Epipelagic. Rare. D III,10–12,XXIII- XXV + 7; A II,10–11 + 7; Vert. 24.

BLUE MARLIN, *Makaira nigricans.* Tropical Pacific and Atlantic, north to southern California on our coast. Length to 11 ft., and wt. to 1400 lbs. Epipelagic. Dark blue above, silver below; dark bars on sides. Rare. D III,14–16,XXIII–XXVII + 7; A II,14 + 7; Pelvic I,2; Vert. 24.

STRIPED MARLIN, *Tetrapturus audax.* Throughout warmer waters of Pacific; in eastern Pacific from Chile to Pt. Conception. Length to 12 ft., and wt. to 350 lbs. in California, world record is 573 lbs. Dark blue above, silvery below; dark blue bars on sides. Common. D III,12–15,XXII–XXV + 6; A II,12–13 + 6; Pelvic I,2; Vert. 24.

KEY TO THE SWORDFISH, Family Xiphiidae, and BILLFISHES, Family Istiophoridae:

1a Pelvic fins absent:

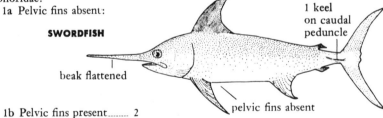

SWORDFISH

1 keel
on caudal
peduncle

beak flattened

1b Pelvic fins present........ 2

pelvic fins absent

2a Distance from nostril to posterior edge of operculum greater than length of pectoral fin or sword, measured from nostril to tip:

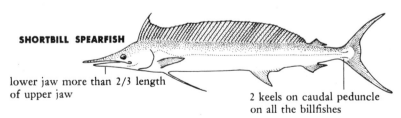

SHORTBILL SPEARFISH

lower jaw more than 2/3 length
of upper jaw

2 keels on caudal peduncle
on all the billfishes

2b Distance from nostril to posterior edge of operculum less than length of pectoral fin or of sword, measured from nostril to tip........ 3 (next page)

3a Middle dorsal rays longer than greatest body depth, and longer than anterior rays:

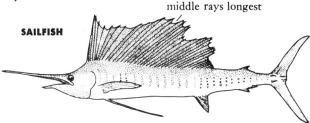

middle rays longest

SAILFISH

3b Middle dorsal rays shorter than greatest body depth, and shorter than anterior rays 4

4a Pectoral fins rigid, not moveable; sides without bars:

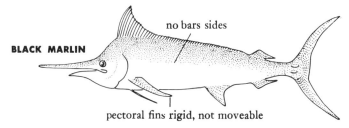

no bars sides

BLACK MARLIN

pectoral fins rigid, not moveable

4b Pectoral fins capable of being folded back along sides; sides with bars 5

5a Length of longest dorsal rays less than greatest body depth; body not laterally compressed at origin of anal fin:

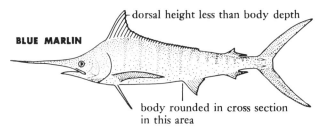

dorsal height less than body depth

BLUE MARLIN

body rounded in cross section
in this area

5b Length of longest dorsal rays equal to or greater than greatest body depth; body laterally compressed at origin of anal fin:

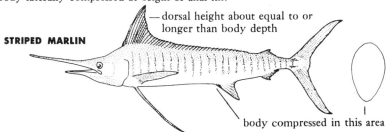

dorsal height about equal to or
longer than body depth

STRIPED MARLIN

body compressed in this area

LOUVAR, MEDUSAFISH, SQUARETAIL, and BUTTERFISH
(Principal sources: Clemens & Wilby, 1961; Haedrich, 1967;
Fitch & Lavenberg, 1968; Horn, 1970)

LOUVAR, Luvarus imperialis. Family LUVARIDAE
Worldwide; in eastern Pacific from Chile to Newport, Oregon. Length to 6 ft.
2 in., and wt. to 305 lbs. Depth, surface into mesopelagic zone. Pink (silver when
dead); fins red. Uncommon. D XIII; A XIV; GR 4 + 12 = 16; Vert. 22–23.

MEDUSAFISH, Icichthys lockingtoni. Family CENTROLOPHIDAE
In eastern Pacific from central Baja California to Gulf of Alaska and to Japan.
Length to 16 in. Depth, surface to 300 ft. Adult uniform brown; juvenile blue
above, white below. Common. D III,34–42; A III,20–29; Pect. 18–21; LLs 115–
121; GR 4–6 + 8–14; Vert. 50–62.

SMALLEYE SQUARETAIL, Tetragonurus cuvieri. Family TETRAGONURIDAE
Worldwide; in eastern Pacific from Cedros Isl., Baja California, to Aleutian Isls.
and to Japan. Length to 24.5 in. Depth, surface to 120 ft., but usually in greater
depths well offshore. Uniform dark brown to black. Rare D XV–XVIII +
10–13; A O–II,9–13; Pect. 16–17; LLp 98–103; LLs 93–126; GR 0–6 + 7–14; Vert.
52–58.

PACIFIC BUTTERFISH, Peprilus simillimus. Family STROMATEIDAE
Magdalena Bay, Baja California, to mouth of Fraser River, British Columbia; including one specimen taken inside the Gulf of California. Length to 11 in. Depth
30 to 300 ft. Bright metallic silver on sides, greenish on back. Common. D II–IV,
41–48; A II–III,35–44; Pect. 19–23; Pelvic absent; GRt 23–26; Vert. 29–31.

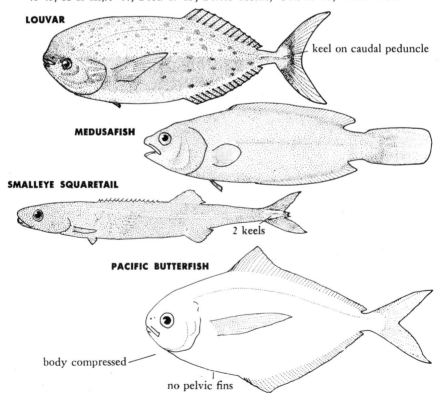

LOUVAR

keel on caudal peduncle

MEDUSAFISH

SMALLEYE SQUARETAIL

2 keels

PACIFIC BUTTERFISH

body compressed

no pelvic fins

FLATFISHES, Families Cynoglossidae, Bothidae, and Pleuronectidae*
(Principal sources: Norman, 1934, Taylor, 1957; Clemens &
Wilby, 1961; Fitch, 1963)

CALIFORNIA TONGUEFISH, *Symphurus atricauda*. Family Cynoglossidae
Cape San Lucas, Baja California, to Big Lagoon, Humboldt Co. Length to 8.25
in. Depth 5 to 276 ft. Gray to light brown, finely mottled. Common in southern
California. D .95–106; A 77–90; midlateral scales 100–110; Vert. 50–52.

CALIFORNIA HALIBUT, *Paralichthys californicus*. Family Bothidae
Gulf of California (isolated population), and from Magdalena Bay, Baja California, to Quillayute River, B.C. Length to 5 ft., and wt. to 72 lbs. Depth, surface to
300 ft. Uniform dark to black above. Common. D 66–76; A 49–59; Pect. 10–13;
LLs about 100; GR 7–11 + 18–23 = 25–32; Vert. 34–36.

PACIFIC HALIBUT, *Hippoglossus stenolepis*. Family Pleuronectidae
Santa Rosa Isl. to Bering Sea and Sea of Japan. Weight of males to 123 lbs., of
females to 495 lbs. Depth 20 to 3600 ft. Dark brown to black above, with fine
mottling. Uncommon. D 89–109; A 64–81; Pelvic 6; LLs 150+; Vert. 49–51.

---

* Fin ray counts for paired fins are for ocular side.

KEY TO THE FLATFISHES:

1a Caudal fin absent;
   lateral line absent:
CALIFORNIA TONGUEFISH

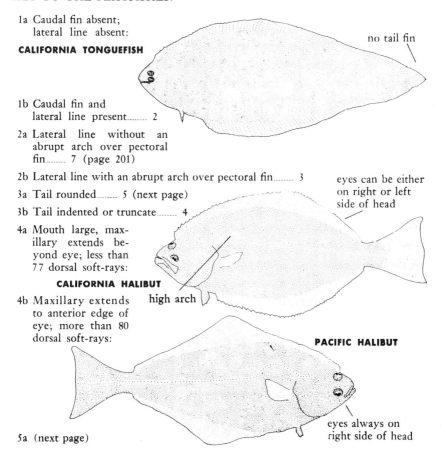

no tail fin

1b Caudal fin and
   lateral line present........ 2

2a Lateral line without an
   abrupt arch over pectoral
   fin........ 7 (page 201)

2b Lateral line with an abrupt arch over pectoral fin........ 3

3a Tail rounded........ 5 (next page)

3b Tail indented or truncate........ 4

eyes can be either
on right or left
side of head

4a Mouth large, max-
   illary extends be-
   yond eye; less than
   77 dorsal soft-rays:
CALIFORNIA HALIBUT

high arch

4b Maxillary extends
   to anterior edge of
   eye; more than 80
   dorsal soft-rays:

PACIFIC HALIBUT

5a (next page)

eyes always on
right side of head

FLATFISHES (continued)

ROCK SOLE, *Lepidopsetta bilineata*. Family Pleuronectidae
Tanner Bank (SIO 65-6) to Bering Sea and Sea of Japan. Length to 22.5 in.
Depth 50 to 480 ft. Light to dark brown, mottled with yellow and red. Common.
D 67–82; A 51–64; Pect. 10–12; Pelvic 6; LLp 72–85; GR 3 + 5–8; Vert. 38–41.

FANTAIL SOLE, *Xystreurys liolepis*. Family Bothidae
Gulf of California to Monterey Bay. Length to 20 in. Depth 15 to 260 ft. Uniform brown above. Uncommon. D 73–80; A 57–62; Pect. 13; LLs 120–123; GR
2 + 6–7; Vert. 37–38.

BIGMOUTH SOLE, *Hippoglossina stomata*. Family Bothidae
Gulf of California to Monterey Bay, including Guadalupe Isl. Length to 15.7 in.
Depth 100 to 450 ft. Brown with blue speckling; several dark blotches above. Uncommon. D 63–70; A 47–55; Pect. 11–12; Pelvic 6; LLs about 80; GR 4–6 +
11–15 = 15–21; Vert. 37–39.

CURLFIN TURBOT, *Pleuronichthys decurrens*. Family Pleuronectidae
San Quintin Bay, Baja California, to N.W. Alaska. Length to 14.5 in. Depth 60
to 1146 ft. Reddish-brown with darker brown or gray mottling above. Common.
D 67–79; A 45–53; Pect. 9–14; Pelvic 4–7; LLp 82–96; GR 3–4 + 6–9 = 9–13;
Vert. 37–40.

HORNYHEAD TURBOT, *Pleuronichthys verticalis*. Family Pleuronectidae
Gulf of California (isolated), and from Magdalena Bay, Baja California, to Pt.
Reyes. Length to 14.5 in. Depth 30 to 612 ft. Dark brown with gray blotches.
Common. D 65–75; A 44–51; Pect. 10–12; Pelvic 6; LLp 88–103; GR 2–3 +
6–9 = 9–11; Vert. 36–38.

SPOTTED TURBOT, *Pleuronichthys ritteri*. Family Pleuronectidae
Magdalena Bay, Baja California, to Pt. Conception. Length to 11.5 in. Depth 4
to 150 ft. Brown to gray with light speckling; usually with 3 dark spots. Common. D 61–70; A 43–49; Pect. 9–11; LLp 83–98; GR 3–5 + 8–12 = 12–17; Vert.
34–36.

5a *From 3a; tail rounded*
   Lateral line with a dorsal branch
   extending posteriorly:

ROCK SOLE

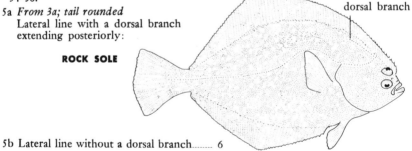

dorsal branch

5b Lateral line without a dorsal branch...... 6

6a Pectoral fin longer than head; anal soft-rays 57–62; maxillary into head about
   2.5 times:

FANTAIL SOLE

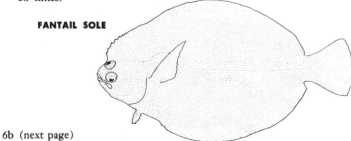

6b (next page)

6b Pectoral fin shorter than head; anal soft-rays 47–55; maxillary into head about 2 times:

BIGMOUTH SOLE

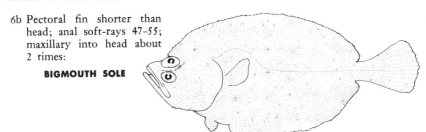

7a *From 2a: lateral line without an abrupt arch over pectoral fin*
   None or no more than 2 anteriormost dorsal rays extend onto blind side........ 11
   (next page)

7b Four to 10 anteriormost dorsal rays extend onto blind side........ 8

8a At least 9 rays extend onto blind side, the 1st reaching below a line between upper corner of mouth and base of pectoral fin:

CURLFIN TURBOT

blind side

spine between eyes

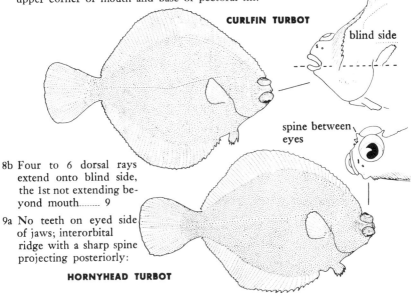

8b Four to 6 dorsal rays extend onto blind side, the 1st not extending beyond mouth........ 9

9a No teeth on eyed side of jaws; interorbital ridge with a sharp spine projecting posteriorly:

HORNYHEAD TURBOT

9b A single row of minute teeth on eyed side of jaws; interorbital ridge without a strong, sharp spine projecting posteriorly........ 10

10a One or 2 black spots on midlateral line; caudal peduncle 4.4–5.6 into body depth:

SPOTTED TURBOT

blind side

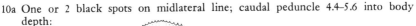
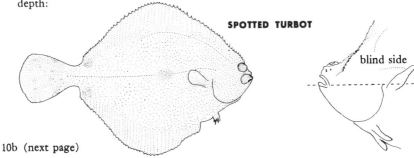

10b (next page)

FLATFISHES (continued)

C-O TURBOT, *Pleuronichthys coenosus*. Family PLEURONECTIDAE
Cape Colnett, Baja California, to S.E. Alaska. Length to 14 in. Shallow water to 210 ft. Dark brown above mottled with light brown. Common. D 65–78; A 46–56; Pect. 9–12; Pelvic 6; LLp 77–92; GR 3–4 + 8–11 = 11–15; Vert. 37–39.

SAND SOLE, *Psettichthys melanostictus*. Family PLEURONECTIDAE
Port Hueneme to northern Gulf of Alaska. Length to 21 in. Depth 5 to 27 ft. Dark gray above with whitish speckling. Common. D 72–90; A 53–66; Pect. 10–12; Pelvic 6; LLs 98–112; GR 5–7 + 14–18 = 20–25; Vert. 37–41.

DIAMOND TURBOT, *Hypsopsetta guttulata*. Family PLEURONECTIDAE
Gulf of California (isolated population), and from Magdalena Bay, Baja California, to Cape Mendocino. Length to 18 in. Depth 5 to 150 ft. Dark gray with bright blue round spots. Common. D 66–75; A 48–54; Pect. 11–13; LLs 83–95; GR 1–2 + 5–6 = 6–8; Vert. 35–36.

ENGLISH SOLE, *Parophrys vetulus*. Family PLEURONECTIDAE
San Cristobal Bay, Baja Calfornia, to N.W. Alaska. Length to 22.5 in. Depth 60 to 1000 ft. Uniform dark to light brown. Common. D 71–93; A 52–70; Pect. 10–12; Pelvic 6; LLs 89–105; GR 4–6 + 10–13 = 14–18; Vert. 41-47.

BUTTER SOLE, *Isopsetta isolepis*. Family PLEURONECTIDAE
Ventura * to Bering Sea. Length to 21.75 in. Shallow to 480 ft. Dark to light brown with mottling; fins edged with yellow. Common. D 78–92; A 58–69; Pect. 11–13; Pelvic 6; LLs 78–90; GR 7–8 on lower limb; Vert. 42.

HYBRID SOLE, *Inopsetta ischyra*. Family PLEURONECTIDAE (not illustrated)
This form is considered a hybrid and is probably not a true species. It is considered a cross between the STARRY FLOUNDER and ENGLISH SOLE. Eureka to Bering Sea. Length to 18 in. Moderated depths. Olive-brown with lighter mottling; often with dusky bars on fins. Rare. D 65–76; A 49–57; Pelvic 6; LLs 76–86; GR 10–12 on lower limb; Vert. 41.

10b No black spots as in 10a; caudal peduncle 3.8–4.4 into body depth:

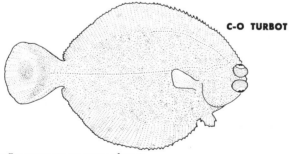

C-O TURBOT

11a *From 7a: none or no more than 2
dorsal rays extend onto blind side*
No dorsal branch to lateral line
.... 16 (Page 204)

11b Dorsal branch of lateral line present........ 12 (next page)

* See comments on page 215.

12a First 4 to 5 dorsal rays free:

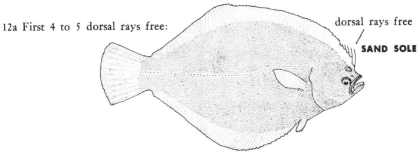

dorsal rays free

SAND SOLE

12b First 4–5 dorsal rays joined by membranes over most of length........ 13

13a Dorsal branch of lateral line extends posteriorly more than ½ distance to caudal fin; light blue spotting on pigmented side:

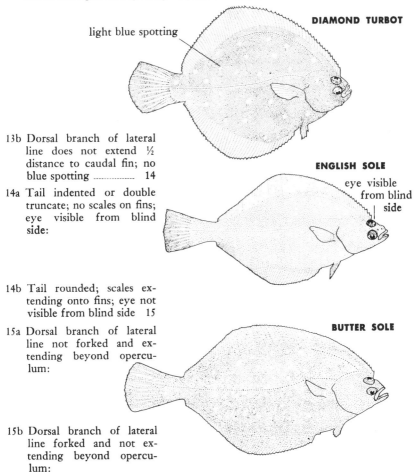

DIAMOND TURBOT

light blue spotting

13b Dorsal branch of lateral line does not extend ½ distance to caudal fin; no blue spotting 14

14a Tail indented or double truncate; no scales on fins; eye visible from blind side:

ENGLISH SOLE

eye visible from blind side

14b Tail rounded; scales extending onto fins; eye not visible from blind side 15

15a Dorsal branch of lateral line not forked and extending beyond operculum:

BUTTER SOLE

15b Dorsal branch of lateral line forked and not extending beyond operculum:

HYBRID SOLE (not illustrated, same body form as in 15a above)

16a (next page)

FLATFISHES (continued)

STARRY FLOUNDER, *Platichthys stellatus*. Family PLEURONECTIDAE
Santa Barbara to Arctic Alaska and Sea of Japan. Length to 3 ft. and wt. to 20 lbs. Depth 2 to 900 ft. Dark brown; alternated white to orange and black bars on dorsal and anal fins. Common. D 52–64; A 38–47; Pelvic 6; LLp 63–78; GR 0–3 + 6–8 = 6–11; Vert. 34–37.

LONGFIN SANDDAB, *Citharichthys xanthostigma*. Family BOTHIDAE
Costa Rica (UCLA W 54-95) to Monterey Bay, including Gulf of California. Length to 10 in. Depth 8 to 444 ft. Uniform dark brown; pectoral fin black. Common, but rare north of Santa Barbara. D 79–89; A 61–69; Pect. 10; LLs 50; GR 6–7 + 10–12 = 17–18; Vert. 36–38.

PACIFIC SANDDAB, *Citharichthys sordidus*. Family BOTHIDAE
Cape San Lucas, Baja California, to Bering Sea. Length to 16 in. Depth 30 to 1800 ft. Light brown mottled with yellow and orange. Common. D 86–102; A 67–81; Pect. 12; Pelvic 6; LLs 61–70; GR 6–9 + 12–16; Vert. 39–40.

SPECKLED SANDDAB, *Citharichthys stigmaeus*. Family BOTHIDAE
Magdalena Bay, Baja California, to Montague Isl., Alaska. Length to 6.7 in. Depth 10 to 1200 ft. Brown or tan with black speckling. Common. D 75–97; A 58–77; Pect. 12; Pelvic 6; LLs 52–58; GR 3–5 + 8–10; Vert. 34–39.

REX SOLE, *Glyptocephalus zachirus*. Family PLEURONECTIDAE
San Diego Trough (SIO 54–122) to Bering Sea. Length to 23.25 in. Depth 60 to 2100 ft. Uniform brown; pectoral fins black. Common below 200 ft. D 87–110; A 78–93; Pect. 11–13; Pelvic 6; LLs 132–138; GR 0–4 + 5–8; Vert. 62–66.

DEEPSEA SOLE, *Embassichthys bathybius*. Family PLEURONECTIDAE
Santa Catalina Isl. to Pratt Seamount, Gulf of Alaska. Length to 18.25 in. Depth 1140 to 4700 ft. Dark gray with blue mottling. Uncommon. D 109–117; A 94–98; Pect. 11; Pelvic 5–6; LLs about 165; GR 8–9 + 14–16 = 22–25; Vert. 60–65.

16a *From 11a: lateral line without a dorsal branch*
Dark and light bars in dorsal, anal, and caudal fins; patches of rough scales on pigmented side:

STARRY FLOUNDER

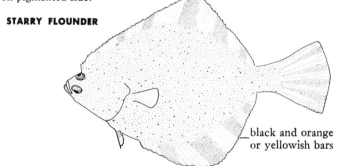

black and orange
or yellowish bars

16b No alternate dark and light bars in fins; no rough patches of scales as above........ 17

17a Eyes on right side of body; pelvic fins symmetrical (one fin on either side of ventral ridge)........ 20 (next page)

17b Eyes on left side of body; pelvic fins assymetrical (fin of eyed side attached directly on ventral ridge) .... 18 (next page)

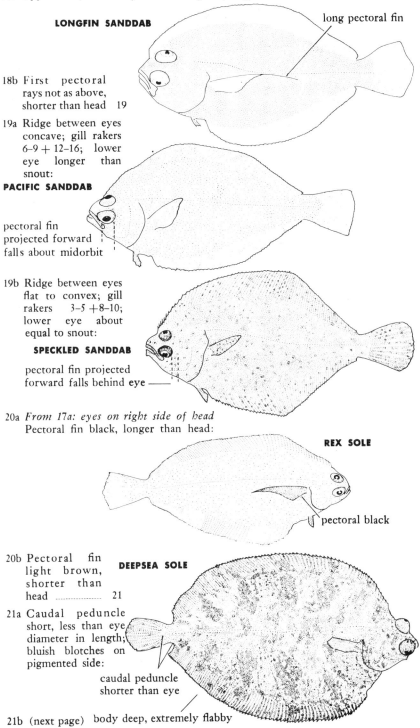

18a Uppermost pectoral rays much elongated, longer than head:

LONGFIN SANDDAB   long pectoral fin

18b First pectoral
    rays not as above,
    shorter than head   19

19a Ridge between eyes
    concave; gill rakers
    6–9 + 12–16; lower
    eye longer than
    snout:

PACIFIC SANDDAB

pectoral fin
projected forward
falls about midorbit

19b Ridge between eyes
    flat to convex; gill
    rakers   3–5 +8–10;
    lower eye about
    equal to snout:

SPECKLED SANDDAB

pectoral fin projected
forward falls behind eye ——

20a *From 17a: eyes on right side of head*
    Pectoral fin black, longer than head:

REX SOLE

pectoral black

20b Pectoral fin
    light brown,   **DEEPSEA SOLE**
    shorter than
    head 21

21a Caudal peduncle
    short, less than eye
    diameter in length;
    bluish blotches on
    pigmented side:

caudal peduncle
shorter than eye

21b (next page) body deep, extremely flabby

FLATFISHES (continued)

GREENLAND HALIBUT, *Reinhardtius hippoglossoides*. Family PLEURONECTIDAE
8 mi. south of Mexico border to Bering Sea and Sea of Japan, and in N. Atlantic.
Length to 3 ft. Depth 48 to 2100 ft. Uniform dark brown; pigment also on blind
side. Uncommon. D 83–105; A 63–79; Pect. 13–15; LLp about 110; LLs about
160; GR 10–12 on lower limb.

ARROWTOOTH FLOUNDER, *Atheresthes stomias*. Family PLEURONECTIDAE
10.5 mi. east of San Pedro light (UCLA W 70-17) to Bering Sea and Chukchi
Sea. Length to 2 ft. 9 in. Depth 60 to 2400 ft. Uniform dark brown. Uncommon.
D 93–115; A 81–99; Pect. 14–15; Pelvic 6; LLs about 135; GR 4 + 11–13;
Vert. 47–49.

DOVER SOLE, *Microstomus pacificus*. Family PLEURONECTIDAE
San Cristobal Bay, Baja California, to Bering Sea. Length to 30 in. Depth 90 to
3000 ft. Uniform brown; fins black. Common. D 88–116; A 75–96; Pect. 8–12;
Pelvic 5–6; LLs 137–146; GR 5–8 + 8–11; Vert. 50–55.

SLENDER SOLE, *Lyopsetta exilis*. Family PLEURONECTIDAE
Cedros Isl., Baja California, to Alsek Canyon, Alaska. Length to 13.25 in. Depth
250 to 1700 ft. Uniform light olive-brown. Uncommon. D 72–88; A 57–66; Pect.
10; Pelvic 6; LLs 65–73; GR 2–3 + 9–11 = 11–13; Vert. 42–47.

FLATHEAD SOLE, *Hippoglossoides elassodon*. Family PLEURONECTIDAE
Pt. Reyes (CAS 27083) to Bering Sea and Sea of Japan. Length to 18 in. Depth
20 to 1800 ft. Dark brown. Uncommon. D 72–90; A 57–71; Pect. 10–12; Pelvic
6; LLs 87–120; GR on lower limb 14–19; LLs 87–94; Vert. 42–46.

PETRALE SOLE, *Eopsetta jordani*. Family PLEURONECTIDAE
Los Coronados Isls., Baja California (SIO H 50-254), to northern Gulf of Alaska.
Length to 2 ft. 3.5 in. Depth 60 to 1500 ft. Uniform dark to light brown. Common. D 82–103; A 62–80; Pect. 13; Pelvic 6; LLs 88–100; GR 15–17 on lower
limb; Vert. 42–44.

21b Caudal peduncle longer than eye diameter; no blue blotches on dark
    side...... 22

22a Maxillary not extending posteriorly beyond eye; tail rounded, pointed, or
    double truncate, not forked ...... 24 (next page)

22b Maxillary extends beyond eye; tail deeply forked (middle rays shortest)...... 23

23a Teeth in a row in each jaw; blind side pigmented; anal soft-rays 63–79:

GREENLAND HALIBUT

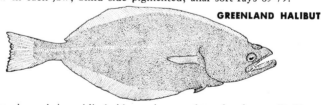

23b Teeth in 2 rows in each jaw; blind side unpigmented; anal soft-rays 81–99:

ARROWTOOTH FLOUNDER

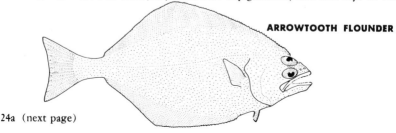

24a (next page)

24a *From 22a: tail rounded or truncate*
Opercular opening small, not extending above pectoral fin; edge of eye visible from blind side:

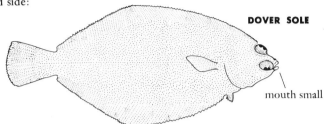

DOVER SOLE

mouth small

24b Opercular opening extends dorsally above pectoral fin; eye not visible from blind side........ 25

25a Total length more than 3 times body depth; tail rounded:

SLENDER SOLE

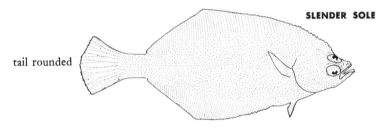

tail rounded

25b Total length less than 3 times body depth; tail double truncate or pointed 26

26a Membranes of caudal fin clear; pores present on preoperculum; 1 row of large, white teeth on each side of upper jaw:

FLATHEAD SOLE

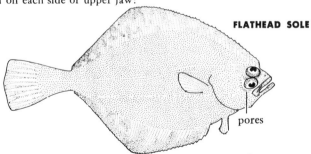

pores

26b Membranes of caudal fin pigmented; no pores on preoperculum; 2 rows of small, arrow-shaped teeth on each side of upper jaw:

PETRALE SOLE

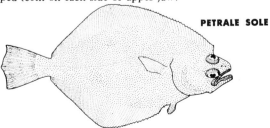

TRIGGERFISHES, PUFFERS, and PORCUPINEFISHES
(Principal source: Berry and Baldwin, 1966)

FINESCALE TRIGGERFISH, *Balistes polylepis*. Family BALISTIDAE
Chile to Pt. St. George, Del Norte Co., including Galapagos Isls. and Gulf of
California. Length to 2.5 ft. Near surface to 1680 ft. (trawl catch). Brownish;
blue speckling on head. Rare. D III + 26-28; A 24-26; Pect. 13-15; GRt 29-37;
Vert. 18.

BLACK TRIGGERFISH, *Melichthys niger*. Family BALISTIDAE
Worldwide in tropical seas; in eastern Pacific from Malpelo Isls., Colombia, to
off San Diego (reported in late 1800's). Recorded length to about 14 in. in
eastern Pacific; reported to 20 in. Near surface, usually around offshore islands.
Black, white to bluish lines along base of dorsal and anal fins. Rare. D III +
31-34; A 27-30; Pect. 14-16; midlateral scales 52-54; GRt 33-39; Vert. 18-19.

REDTAIL TRIGGERFISH, *Xanthichthys mento*. Family BALISTIDAE
Clipperton Isl. to Ventura, including Easter Isl. and Hawaiian Isls. Length to 10
in. Epipelagic. Body violet; stripes in cheek area. Rare. D III + 28-33; A 25-29;
Pect. 12-13; midlateral scales 42-43; GRt 40-47; Vert. 18.

OCEANIC PUFFER, *Lagocephalus lagocephalus*. Family TETRAODONTIDAE
Worldwide in warmer seas; in eastern Pacific from Galapagos Isls. to Alder
Creek Beach, Mendocino Co., including Gulf of California. Length to 24 in.
Epipelagic. White, with black spotting and bars. Rare. D 0-I,12-15; A 0-I,12-14;
Pect. 14; Vert. 18.

BULLSEYE PUFFER, *Sphoeroides annulatus*. Family TETRAODONTIDAE
Peru to San Diego, including Galapagos Isls. and Gulf of California. Length to
about 15 in. Shallow inshore areas. Dark brown above, white below; dark, round
spots on back. Rare. D 0-I,7-8; A 0-I,6-8; GR 8 on upper limb; Vert. 18-19.

PACIFIC BURRFISH, *Chilomycterus affinis*. Family DIODONTIDAE
Tropical Pacific, in eastern Pacific from Galapagos Isls. to San Pedro. Length
to about 20 in. Shallow inshore areas. Bluish above, whitish below; dark spots
on upper parts. Rare. D 13; A 12; Pect. 21; Pelvic absent; caudal 10.

SPOTTED PORCUPINEFISH, *Diodon hystrix*. Family DIODONTIDAE
Warm seas of world; in eastern Pacific from Chile to San Diego, including
Galapagos Isls. and Gulf of California. Length to 36 in. Shallow inshore areas.
Whitish to light brown. Rare. D 12-15; A 14-15; Pect. 22-23; GRt 6 (rudi-
ments); Vert. 20.

FINESCALE TRIGGERFISH

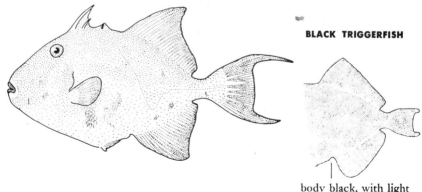

BLACK TRIGGERFISH

body black, with light
areas at base of fins

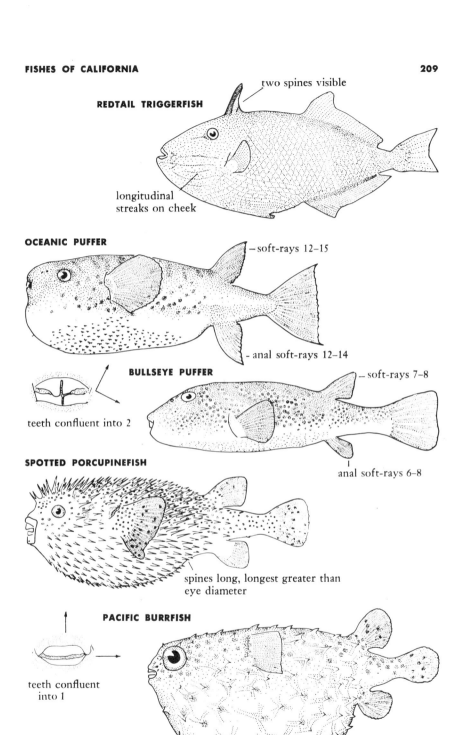

two spines visible

REDTAIL TRIGGERFISH

longitudinal
streaks on cheek

OCEANIC PUFFER

— soft-rays 12–15

- anal soft-rays 12–14

BULLSEYE PUFFER

— soft-rays 7–8

teeth confluent into 2

anal soft-rays 6–8

SPOTTED PORCUPINEFISH

spines long, longest greater than
eye diameter

PACIFIC BURRFISH

teeth confluent
into 1

spines short, bases 3 parted

BOXFISH and MOLAS
(Principal sources: Fraser-Brunner, 1951; Fitch, 1969)

SPINY BOXFISH, *Ostracion diaphanum.* Family OSTRACIIDAE
A tropical Indo-Pacific species; in eastern Pacific from Galapagos Isls. to Santa Barbara, including the Gulf of California. Length to 10 in. Depth, surface to 90 ft. Uniform tan or light brown. Rare. D 9; A 9–10; Vert. 15.

COMMON MOLA, *Mola mola.* Family MOLIDAE
Warm and temperate seas of the world; north to at least British Columbia, reported from S.E. Alaska but not verified. Length to 13.1 ft., and wt. to 3300 lbs. Epipelagic. Gray-blue on back, metallic silver on sides. Common. D 17–18; A 14–18; Pect. 12–13; Pelvic absent; scales absent; GR concealed; Vert. 17–18.

SLENDER MOLA, *Ranzania laevis.* Family MOLIDAE
Tropical Pacific; in eastern Pacific from Chile to Oceano, San Luis Obispo Co. Length to 18 in. Epipelagic. Dusky on back, silvery on sides, with dusky bars and oblique bands. Rare. D 17–19; A 18–19; Pect. 13; Pelvic absent; Vert. 18–19.

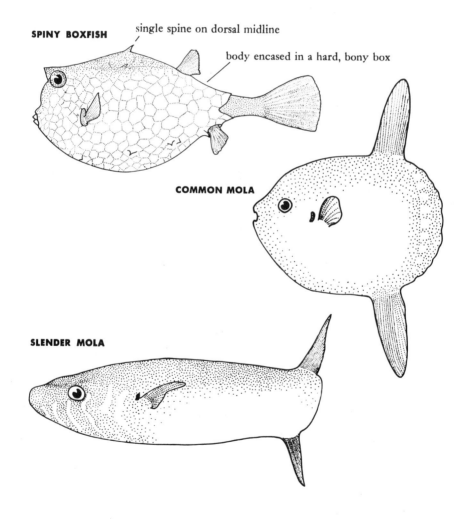

SPINY BOXFISH single spine on dorsal midline

body encased in a hard, bony box

COMMON MOLA

SLENDER MOLA

APPENDIX
Taxonomic Comments and Personal Communications Citations

Page 32

Included are 3 of the 5 California species of hagfishes, family Myxinidae. Carl L. Hubbs, Scripps Institution of Oceanography, La Jolla, is presently revising this family and is describing another species of *Myxine* and another *Eptatretus*, both of which are found in southern California.

Page 34

Several **PRICKLY SHARK,** *Echinorhinus cookei,* have been taken off Moss Landing at depths of 60 to 420 ft. (D. H. Varoujean, Moss Landing Marine Laboratory, unpbl. thesis.)

Page 36

The **WHALE SHARK,** *Rhincodon typus,* has not been landed in California but John E. Fitch, CF&G, reports several sightings, probably of the same individual, from San Diego north to Torrey Pines.

Page 40

A **PELAGIC WHITETIPPED SHARK,** *Carcharhinus longimanus,* was landed on a SIO research vessel off Cortez Bank (Carl L. Hubbs, SIO, pers. comm.).

Page 44

1. Particular attention was given to the Rajidae resulting in basically new identification criteria. Emphasis is placed upon ventral sensory pore patterns, with a de-emphasis of characters previously used such as concavity or convexity of the anterior edge of the disc, and numbers and placement of spines. While ventral pore patterns are presented in this publication, a synoptic study has not been made of these structures. We observed some variation within each species but the overall patterns remained distinct at the specific level. Further work on ventral sensory pores may reveal significant relationships between the taxa in this family.

2. Carl L. Hubbs, SIO, supplied considerable information on California skates, including use of photographs, specimens, and data recorded by himself and by Reizo Ishiyama, Tokyo Univ. of Fisheries, Japan.

3. We use **SANDPAPER SKATE** as the common name for *R. kincaidii* as this species is never black and has a uniformly rough, denticulated dorsal surface. **BLACK SKATE** is used for *R. trachura* because this is the only black colored California skate. The American Fisheries Society (Bailey et al, 1970) listed black skate for *R. kincaidii* and roughtail skate for *R. trachura.*

4. Carl L. Hubbs, SIO, (pers. comm., March 3, 1972) considers *Raja microtrachys* Osburn and Nichols as a junior synonym of *R. trachura* Gilbert thus provisionally extending the southern range limit of *R. trachura* to north of Guadalupe Isl., where the only specimen of *R. microtrachys* was collected.

Page 46

The **WHITE SKATE** was described as *Psammobatis spinosissima* Beebe and Tee-Van, 1941. Carl L. Hubbs, SIO, (pers. comm.) considers this species in the genus *Bathyraja.* Because of its weak rostral cartilage which characterizes *Bathyraja*, we provisionally follow Hubbs.

Page 52

1. The **RATFISH,** *Hydrolagus colliei,* has been taken in and near Sebastian Viscaino Bay, Baja California, by the CF&G research vessel ALASKA. Specimens were collected off Pt. Canoas (71A5-39), and a RATFISH vertebral column was taken from the stomach of a giant sea bass, *Stereolepis gigas*, caught inside Sebastian Viscaino Bay.

2. John E. Fitch, (CF&G), reports that the BONEFISH, *Albula vulpes*, in the eastern Pacific never reaches the large sizes it does elsewhere in the world.

APPENDIX

Page 54

We follow Svetovidov (1952) in considering all Pacific species of *Sardinops* under *S. sagax* and relegate *caeruleus* to subspecific status. John E. Fitch, CF&G, considers *caeruleus* as a distinct species using otolith and other differences. Until a definitive study is published to challenge Svetovidov's work, we retain *S. sagax caeruleus*.

Page 72

The **PLAINFIN MIDSHIPMAN, *Porichthys notatus*,** has been taken at Gorda Bank off the tip of Baja California (Robert J. Lavenberg, Los Angeles County Museum of Nat. Hist., pers. comm.) indicating the Gulf population may not be isolated.

Page 74

Briggs (1955) states for the genus *Gobiesox*: "Add two to both dorsal and anal ray counts if these fins are not dissected." We have arbitrarily subtracted 2 rays from Briggs' counts for *rhessodon*, *papillifer*, and *maeandricus*, these given in parentheses. For *G. eugrammus*, Greenfield and Wiley (1968) ". . . do not include the two extra rays added to the counts by Briggs." For this species the counts in parentheses are from their study. In all the California Gobiesocidae the pelvic counts are I,4, (spine embedded), and body scales and lateral line pores are absent.

Page 78

Shelly R. Johnson, University of Southern California, supplied data on eelpouts.

Page 80

Bruce B. Collette, U. S. National Museum, Washington, D. C. (pers. comm.), gives Mazatlan for the southern range limit of *Hyporhamphus rosae*.

Page 86

The **HIGHBROW CRESTFISH, *Lophotus cristatus*,** off Ventura was reported by John E. Fitch, CF&G.

Page 89

1. The pipefishes, family Syngnathidae, are a complicated group currently being studied. We recognize the species presented on page 89 as the only California syngnathids. Carl L. Hubbs, SIO (pers. comm., July 5, 1972), considers two other forms, *Dermatostethus punctipinnis* and *Siphostoma exile*, as valid California species; however, Herald (1940) considered both these species conspecific with *Syngnathus californiensis*. Until a synoptic review is published to remove these species from synonymy giving diagnostic features for identification, we follow Herald. The SPOTFIN PIPEFISH, *Dermatostethus punctipinnis*, is known only from the type series, 4 specimens, from San Diego, California. Hubbs (pers. comm., July 5, 1972) refers *D. punctipinnis* to the genus *Syngnathus*, and reports the specimens have dark spotting in the fins whereas none of the other California pipefishes of the genus *Syngnathus* have such spotting. Hubbs (pers. comm., July 5, 1972) refers *Siphostoma exile* Osburn and Nichols also to the genus *Syngnathus*, and reports this form ranges from Santa Maria Bay, Baja California, to Del Monte and attains a length of 10 in.
2. W. I. Follett, CAS (pers. comm.), states that *Syngnathus leptorhynchus* receives priority over *S. griseolineatus* in that *leptorhynchus* appeared first in print.

Page 116

Hexagrammos superciliosus, the **ROCK GREENLING**, was synonymized with *H. lagocephalus* by Jay C. Quast (1964); however, due to the length of orbital cirri and other features in California specimens, we follow Rass (1962) and Carl L. Hubbs, SIO, and W. I. Follett, CAS, (pers. comm.), in using *H. superciliosus*.

APPENDIX

Page 118

Forty-two members of family Cottidae are presented on pages 118 to 133. There are two other known cottoid fishes in California waters: an undescribed species of *Icelinus* taken by skindivers off La Jolla, and a deepwater cottoid taken by commercial trawlers off Eureka.

The new *Icelinus* is being described by Carl L. Hubbs (pers. comm.) and Conrad Limbaugh, SIO. It has the appearance of a deep-bodied *Artedius*, but has 2 pelvic soft-rays.

Five California specimens of the undescribed deepwater cottoid have been landed at Eureka over the past 3 years, one in 1969, and four in 1972. The first specimen was collected by Paul Gregory, CF&G. This species is being studied by fishery workers in the Pacific northwest where it also has been taken. The California specimens range in size from about 3 to 20 lbs., and were taken in depths from 2700-4350 ft. General description: Skin loose, flesh flabby, bones weak and pliable. Ventral surface flat; dorsal surface broadly and evenly rounded. Head much wider than deep and wider than body giving the fish a tadpolelike shape. Body color uniform pinkish-gray; fins dusky. About 30 small whitish widely spaced cirri on head and nape. Pelvics with three soft-rays.

We include *Rhamphocottus* in family Cottidae, although it has been placed in family Rhamphocottidae by some workers.

Page 134

1. A **SMOOTH ALLIGATORFISH,** *Anoplagonus inermis*, was taken for the first time in California off Pt. Arena on August 15, 1972, in a CF&G collection. The specimen, 43.4 mm TL (1.7 in.), was identified by Robert N. Lea and has been deposited at CAS (CAS 15049). This record was received too late for inclusion in the agonid section, thus a species description is given here: Pt. Arena to Aleutian Isls., and to Korea. Length to 6 in. Depth 30 to 334 ft. Body dark brown to blackish (Calif. specimen was nearly jet-black); fins black, caudal with two whitish areas laterally of mid-caudal rays, pectoral with whitish area on rays near base. Is distinguished from all other California agonids by having only one dorsal fin. Other characters: plates without spines; gill membranes united and joined to isthmus but with a narrow free fold across isthmus; rostral spines absent. D (spinous dorsal absent) 5-6; A 4-5; Pect. 10; Pelvic I,2; caudal 11; branchiostegals 6; LLp 41-44; Vert. 43.

2. Rolf L. Bolin, Professor emeritus, Stanford University, prepared a key to the poachers, family Agonidae, in the late 1940's (unpubl. mimeo.) from which we obtained key characters.

3. The **KELP POACHER, Agonomalus** sp., is being described by Norman J. Wilimovsky, Inst. of Fisheries, University of British Columbia, Vancouver, B. C.

Page 136

John E. Fitch, CF&G, reported **BLACKFIN STARNOSE, Bathyagonus nigripinnis,** off Eureka.

Page 140

We follow Whitehead and Wheeler (1967) in the use of the genus *Roccus*, instead of *Morone*, for the striped bass, *Roccus saxatilis*.

Page 148

A **CREVALLE JACK, Caranx hippos,** (SIO 72-69) caught in south San Diego Bay on March 16, 1972, was identified by Richard H. Rosenblatt, Scripps Inst. of Oceanography.

Page 150

A review of the family Bramidae by Giles Mead (1972) came to our attention too late for incorporation into the text. Mead gives five species of Bramidae for California: *Brama japonica*, *Taractichthys steindachneri* (formerly *Taractes longipinnis* of Calif.), *Pteraclis aesticola* (formerly *P. velifera* of Calif.), *Taractes asper*, and *Brama orcini* (formerly *Collybus drachme* of Calif.). On page 150 we include only the first three listed, and have incorporated the name changes and some of the meristic counts Mead presents for those.

APPENDIX

Page 152

Bernard J. Zahuranec and Carl L. Hubbs, SIO, have completed a study of the *genus Eucinostomus.* Hubbs (pers. comm.) reports that the specimen of *E. gracilis* listed for California (Bailey et al, 1970) is to receive a new name, because the name *E. gracilis* is identified with *E. californiensis elongatus*.

Page 160

All California marine species of Embiotocidae are included; however, the one freshwater member of the family, the **TULEPERCH, Hysterocarpus traskii,** is not included in the key to the surfperches. The **TULEPERCH** has 15 or more dorsal spines compared to 12 or less dorsal spines in marine surfperches.

Page 168

The **CALIFORNIA SHEEPHEAD, Pimelometopon pulchrum,** was reported from the Gulf of California by Richard H. Rosenblatt, Scripps Institution of Oceanography, La Jolla.

Page 172

1. John S. Stephens, Occidental College, supplied information on family Blenniidae and cited the northern range limit of *H. jenkinsi* as Coal Oil Pt., Santa Barbara Co.
2. Carl L. Hubbs, SIO, supplied information on *Hypsoblennius jenkinsi.*

Page 173

The **ORANGETHROAT PIKEBLENNY, Chaenopsis alepidota,** at Anacapa Isl. was identified by John S. Stephens, Occidental College, from an underwater photo by the late Charles H. Turner, CF&G.

Page 178

The **SIXSPOT PRICKLEBACK, Askoldia** ? sp., is a rare stichaeid taken only in Department sample poisonings at Diablo Cove, San Luis Obispo Co. The species description is being prepared by John E. Fitch, CF&G, and Robert J. Lavenberg, L.A. Co. Museum.

Page 180

The **MASKED PRICKLEBACK, Stichaeopsis** ? sp., is being described by W. I. Follett, Calif. Academy of Sciences, San Francisco. Information on this species was supplied by Boyd W. Walker, University of California at Los Angeles, and by W. I. Follett.

Page 186

1. Lillian J. Dempster, California Academy of Sciences, San Francisco, supplied information on the gobies, family Gobiidae, and discovered the phenomenon which resulted in changing the common name of *Tridentiger trigonocephalus* from trident goby to **CHAMELEON GOBY.** This species has the ability to change rapidly its color pattern (within seconds) to either stripes or bars.
2. John E. Fitch, CF&G, prepared an unpublished field key for the gobies from which we derived several key characters.

Page 188

The **BAY GOBY, Lepidogobius lepidus,** was reported from Cedros Island, Baja California, and the **ARROW GOBY, Clevelandia ios,** was reported from the Gulf of California by Doug Hoese, SIO (pers. comm. to Lillian J. Dempster, CAS).

Page 190

Dorsal ray elements of Trichiuridae are difficult to differentiate into spines and soft-rays. All have spines anteriorly, but they are flexible and often appear to be unsegmented soft-rays. Since these rays cannot be differentiated without magnification we have not separated the dorsal fin counts into spines and soft-rays.

APPENDIX

Page 191

The **ESCOLAR, Lepidocybium flavobrunneum,** has been placed in either family Gempylidae or Scombridae by various workers, and the problem is still unresolved. We have provisionally placed it in Scombridae based on evidence supplied by John E. Fitch, CF&G, (pers. comm.) on the structure of otoliths and other characters. Most ichthyologists place the **ESCOLAR** in Gempylidae mainly because the caudal rays do not cover the hypural bones. In Scombridae the caudal rays invariably cover the hypural structures.

Page 202

The **BUTTER SOLE, Isopsetta isolepsis,** was reported from Ventura by John E. Fitch, CF&G.

LITERATURE CITED

Bailey, Reeve M., John E. Fitch, Earl S. Herald, Ernest A. Lachner, C. C. Lindsey, C. Richard Robins and W. B. Scott. 1970. A list of common and scientific names of fishes from the United States and Canada. 3rd ed. Am. Fish. Soc., Spec. Publ., (6):1–150.

Baird, Ronald Clay. 1971. The systematics, distribution, and zoogeography of the marine hatchetfishes (family Sternoptychidae). Harvard Mus. Comp. Zool., Bull., 142(1):1–128.

Barnhart, Percy Spencer. 1936. Marine fishes of southern California. Univ. Calif. Press, Berkeley. 209 p.

Barsukov, V. V. 1964. Taxonomy of fishes of the family Scorpaenidae. Pac. Sci.- Res. Inst. Mar. Fish. Oceanog., Trans., (3):233–266. English transl. by Edith Roden, ed. by Richard H. Rosenblatt. U.S. Bur. Comm. Fish., Ichthyol. Lab., U.S. Nat. Mus., Transl., (47):1–44.

Bayliff, William H. 1959. Notes on the taxonomy and distribution of certain zoarcid fishes in the northeastern Pacific. Copeia, (1):78–80.

Beebe, William, and John Tee-Van. 1941. Eastern Pacific Expeditions of the New York Zoological Society. 25. Fishes from the tropical eastern Pacific. Pt. 2, Sharks. Zoologica 26(2):93–122.

Berg, Leo Semenovitch. 1940. Classification of fishes, both recent and fossil. Russian and English texts. Trudy Zool. Inst. AN SSSR, 5(2):87–517. Reprinted by Edwards Brothers Inc., Ann Arbor, Michigan, 1942. 517 p.

Berry, Frederick H., and Wayne J. Baldwin. 1966. Triggerfishes (Balistidae) of the eastern Pacific. Calif. Acad. Sci., Proc., 34(9):429–474.

Berry, F. H., and H. C. Perkins. 1966. Survey of pelagic fishes of the California Current area. U.S. Fish and Wild. Serv., Fish. Bull., 65:625–682.

Bigelow, Henry B., and William C. Schroeder. 1948. Sharks, p. 59–546. *In* Fishes of the western North Atlantic. Pt. 1. Sears Found. Mar. Res., Mem., (1):1–576.

Bolin, Rolf L. 1938. *Bathylagus wesethi*, a new argentinid fish from California. Calif. Fish and Game, 241(1):66–68.

———— 1939. A review of the myctophid fishes of the Pacific coast of the United States and of lower California. Stanford Ichthyol. Bull., 1(4):89–156.

———— 1940. A redescription of *Luvarus imperialis* Rafinesque based upon a specimen from Monterey, California. Calif. Fish and Game, 26(3):282–284.

———— 1944. A review of the marine cottid fishes of California. Stanford Ichthyol. Bull., 3(1):1–135.

———— 1950. Remarks on cottid fishes occasioned by the capture of two species new to California. Copeia, (3):195–202.

Briggs, John C. 1955. A monograph of the clingfishes (order Xenopterygii). Stanford Ichthyol. Bull., 6:1–224.

Bruun, Anton Fr. 1935. Flying-fishes (Exocoetidae) of the Atlantic: systematic and biological studies. Dana Rept. (6):1–106.

Burke, Victor. 1930. Revision of the fishes of the family Liparidae. U.S. Nat. Mus., Bull., (150):1–204.

Chen, Lo-Chai. 1971. Systematics, variation, distribution, and biology of rock-fishes of the subgenus *Sebastomus* (Pisces, Scorpaenidae, *Sebastes*). Scripps Inst. Oceanogr., Bull., 18:1–107.

Clemens, W. A., and G. V. Wilby. 1961. Fishes of the Pacific coast of Canada. 2nd. ed. Fish. Res. Bd. Can., Bull., (68):1–443.

Clothier, Charles R. 1950. A key to some southern California fishes based on vertebral characters. Calif. Div. Fish and Game, Fish. Bull., (79):1–83.

Cohen, Daniel M. 1956. The synonymy and distribution of *Leuroglossus stilbius* Gilbert, a north Pacific bathypelagic fish. Stanford Ichthyol. Bull., 7(2):19–23.

———— 1958. A revision of the fishes of the subfamily Argentininae. Florida St. Mus., Bull., 3(3):93–173.

———— 1966. The north Pacific deepsea fish name *Bathylagus milleri* Gilbert, a senior synonym of *Bathylagus alascanus* Chapman. Copeia, (4):877–878.

Collette, Bruce B., and Robert H. Gibbs, Jr. 1963. Preliminary field guide to the mackerel and tuna-like fishes of the Indian Ocean: (Scombridae). Smithsonian Inst., Wash. D. C. 55 p.

Fitch, John E. 1951. Notes on the squaretail, *Tetragonurus cuvieri*. Calif. Fish and Game, 37(1):55–59.

——— 1963. A review of the fishes of the genus *Pleuronichthys*. Los Angeles Co. Mus., Contrib. Sci., (76):1–33.

——— 1964. The ribbonfishes (family Trachipteridae) of the eastern Pacific Ocean, with a description of a new species. Calif. Fish and Game, 50(4):228–240.

——— 1966. The poacher *Asterotheca infraspinata* (Gilbert) added to California's marine fauna, and a key to Californian Agonidae (Pisces). Calif. Fish and Game, 52(2):121–124.

——— 1967. The tapertail ribbonfish (*Trachipterus fukuzakii* Fitch) added to the marine fauna of California. Calif. Fish and Game, 53(4):298–299.

——— 1969. A second record of the slender mola *Ranzania laevis* (Pennant), from California. So. Calif. Acad. Sci., Bull., 68(2):115–118.

Fitch, John E., and Lloyd Barker. 1972. The fish family Moridae in the eastern north Pacific with notes on morid otoliths, caudal skeletons, and the fossil record. U.S. Fish and Wild. Serv., Fish. Bull., 70(3):559–578.

Fitch, John E., and Daniel Gotshall. 1972. First record of the black scabbardfish, *Aphanopus carbo*, from the Pacific Ocean with notes on other Californian trichiurid fishes. So. Calif. Acad. Sci., Bull., 71(1):12–18.

Fitch, John E., and Robert J. Lavenberg. 1968. Deep-water teleostean fishes of California. Univ. of Calif. Press, Berkeley. 155 p.

——— 1971. Marine food and game fishes of California. Univ. of Calif. Press, Berkeley. 179 p.

Fitch, John E., and P. M. Roedel. 1962. A review of the frigate mackerels (genus *Auxis*) of the world. FAO World Sci. Meet., Biol. Tunas and Related Species, La Jolla, Calif., Exp. Pap., (18):1–16.

Follett, W. I. 1952. Annotated list of fishes obtained by the California Academy of Sciences during six cruises of the *U.S.S. Mulberry* conducted by the United States Navy off central California in 1949 and 1950. Calif. Acad. Sci., Proc., 27(16):399–432.

——— 1970. Benthic fishes cast ashore by giant waves near Point Joe, Monterey County, California. Calif. Acad. Sci., Proc., 37(15):473–488.

Follett, W. I., and Lillian J. Dempster. 1960. First records of the echeneidid fish *Remilegia australis* (Bennett) from California, with meristic data. Calif. Acad. Sci., Proc., 31(7):169–184.

——— 1963. Relationships of the percoid fish *Pentaceros richardsoni* Smith, with description of a specimen from the coast of California. Calif. Acad. Sci., Proc., 32(10):315–338.

Follett, W. I., D. Gotshall and J. G. Smith. 1960. Northerly occurrences of the scorpid fish *Medialuna californiensis* (Steindachner), with meristic data, life history notes, and discussion of the fisheries. Calif. Fish and Game, 46(2):165–175.

Forrester, C. R., and A. L. Pritchard. 1944. The identification of the young of five species of Pacific salmon, with notes on the freshwater phase of their life-history. Brit. Columbia, Prov. Fish. Dept., Rept. for 1943:86–97.

Fraser-Brunner, A. 1950. The fishes of the family Scombridae. Ann. Mag. Nat. Hist., ser. 12, 3:131–163.

——— 1951. The ocean sunfishes (family Molidae). Brit. Mus. Nat. Hist., Bull.: Zool., 1(6):87–121.

Godsil, Harry C. 1954. A descriptive study of certain tuna-like fishes. Calif. Dept. Fish and Game, Fish Bull., (97):1–185.

Godsil, Harry C., and R. D. Byers. 1944. A systematic study of the Pacific tunas. Calif. Div. Fish and Game, Fish Bull., (60):1–131.

Gosline, William A., and Vernon E. Brock. 1960. Handbook of Hawaiian fishes. Univ. of Hawaii Press, Honolulu. 372 p.

Greenfield, David W., and James W. Wiley. 1968. Geographic variation in the clingfish, *Gobiesox eugrammus* Briggs. San Diego Soc. Nat. Hist., Trans., 15 (10):141–147.

Greenwood, P. Humphry, Donn E. Rosen, Stanley H. Weitzman and George S. Myers. 1966. Phyletic studies of teleostean fishes, with a provisional classification of living forms. Am. Mus. Nat. Hist., Bull., 131(4):341–455.

Gudger, E. W. 1930. The opah or moonfish, *Lampris luna*, on the eastern coast of North America. Am. Nat., 64(691):168–177.

Haedrich, Richard L. 1967. The stromateoid fishes: systematics and a classification. Harvard Mus. Comp. Zool., Bull., 135(2):31–139.

Hallock, Richard J., and Donald H. Fry, Jr. 1967. Five species of salmon, *Oncorhynchus*, in the Sacramento River, California. Calif. Fish and Game, 53 (1):5–22.

Hedgepeth, Joel W. 1957. Classification of marine environments, p. 17–28. *In* Treatise on marine ecology and paleoecology, vol. 1. Geol. Soc. Am. Mem. (67): 2 vol.

Herald, Earl Stannard. 1940. A key to the pipefishes of the Pacific American coasts with descriptions of new genera and species. Alan Hancock Pac. Exped., 9(3):51–64.

———— 1941. A systematic analysis of variation in the western American pipefish, *Syngnathus californiensis*. Stanford Ichthyol. Bull., 2(3):49–88.

Hildebrand, Samuel F. 1943. A review of the American anchovies (family Engraulidae). Bingham Oceanogr. Coll., Bull., 8(2):1–165.

Horn, Michael H. 1970. Systematics and biology of the stomatoid fishes of the genus *Peprilus*. Harvard Mus. Comp. Zool., Bull., 140(5):165–262.

Howard, Gerald V. 1954. A study of populations of the anchoveta, *Cetengraulis mysticetus*, based on meristic characters. Inter-Am. Trop. Tuna Comm., Bull., 1(1):1–24.

Howard, John K., and Shoji Ueyanagi. 1965. Distribution and relative abundance of billfishes (Istiophoridae) of the Pacific Ocean. Stud. Trop. Oceanogr. (2) :1–134.

Hubbs, Carl L. 1925. Racial and seasonal variation in the Pacific herring, California sardine and California anchovy. Calif. Fish and Game Comm., Fish. Bull., (8):1–23.

———— 1926. Notes on the goboid fishes of California, with descriptions of two new genera. Univ. Mich. Mus. Zool., Occas. Pap., (169):1–6.

———— 1927. Notes on the blennioid fishes of western North America. Mich. Acad. Sci. Arts Lett., Pap., 7:351–394.

———— 1967. Occurrence of the Pacific lamprey, *Entosphenus tridentatus*, off Baja California and in streams of southern California; with remarks on its nomenclature. San Diego Soc. Nat. Hist., Trans., 14(21):301–312.

Hubbs, Carl L., and Sam D. Hinton. 1963. The giant sea horse returns. Pac. Discov., 16(5):12–15.

Hubbs, Carl L., and Karl F. Lagler. 1958. Fishes of the Great Lakes region. Univ. of Mich. Press, Ann Arbor. 213 p.

Hubbs, Carl L., and Andreas B. Rechnitzer. 1958. A new fish, *Chaetodon falcifer*, with notes on related species. Calif. Acad. Sci., Proc., 29(8):273–313.

Hubbs, Carl L., and Leonard P. Schultz. 1934. The reef liparid fishes inhabiting the west coast of the United States. Pan-Pac. Res. Inst., J., 9(4):2–7.

———— 1939. A revision of the toadfishes referred to *Porichthys* and related genera. U.S. Nat. Mus., Proc., 86(3060):473–496.

Hubbs, Carl L., and Norman J. Wilimovsky. 1964. Distribution and synonymy in the Pacific Ocean, and variation, of the Greenland halibut, *Reinhardtius hippoglossoides* (Walbaum). Fish. Res. Bd. Can., J., 21(5):1129–1154.

Hubbs, Clark. 1952. A contribution to the classification of the blennoid fishes of the family Clinidae, with a partial revision of the eastern Pacific forms. Stanford Ichthyol. Bull., 4(2):41–165.

—— 1953. Revision and systematic position of the blennoid fishes of the genus *Neoclinus*. Copeia, (1):11–23.

Jordan, David Starr, and Barton Warren Evermann. 1896-1900. The fishes of North and Middle America. U.S. Nat. Mus., Bull., (47):4 vol.

Kanazawa, Robert H. 1952. Variations in the wolf eel, *Anarrhichthys ocellatus* Ayres, a fish inhabiting the north Pacific Ocean. Calif. Fish and Game, 38(4): 567–574.

Kato, Susumu, Stewart Springer and Mary H. Wagner. 1967. Field guide to eastern Pacific and Hawaiian sharks. U.S. Fish and Wild. Serv., Circ., (271): 1–47.

Lachner, Ernest A. 1966. Order Echeneida, family Echeneidae: diskfishes, p. 74-80. *In* Leonard P. Schultz, Loren P. Woods and Ernest A. Lachner, Fishes of the Marshall and Marianas Islands, vol. 3. U.S. Nat. Mus., Bull., (202):3 vol.

Lane, David E. 1962. A review of the genus *Caranx* from the tropical east Pacific. Ms. Thesis. Univ: Brit. Columbia. 77 p.

Limbaugh, Conrad. 1955. Fish life in the kelp beds and effects of harvesting. Univ. Calif. Inst. Mar. Res., IMR Ref., (55-9):1–156.

Makushok, V. M. 1958. The morphology and classification of the northern blennoid fishes (Stichaeoidae, Blennioidei, Pisces). Akad. Nauk S.S.S.R., Zool. Inst., Trudy, 25:3–129. English Transl. by Alice R. Gosline. U.S. Bur. Comm. Fish., Ichthyol. Lab., U.S. Nat. Mus.

McAllister, D. E. 1963. A revision of the smelt family, Osmeridae. Nat. Mus. Can., Bull., (191):1–53.

McPhail, J. D. 1958. Key to the croakers (Sciaenidae) of the eastern Pacific. Univ. Brit. Columbia, Inst. Fish., Mus. Contrib., (2):1–20.

Mead, Giles W. 1972. Bramidae. Dana Rept., (81):1–166.

Meek, Seth E., and Samuel F. Hildebrand. 1923-1928. The marine fishes of Panama. Field Mus. Nat. Hist., Zool. ser., 15:3 pts.

Miller, Robert Rush, and Carl L. Hubbs. 1969. Systematics of *Gasterosteus aculeatus*, with particular reference to intergradation and introgression along the Pacific coast of North America: a commentary on a recent contribution. Copeia, (1):52–69.

Moser, H. Geoffrey, and Elbert H. Ahlstrom. 1970. Development of lanternfishes (family Myctophidae) in the California current. Pt. 1. Species with narrow-eyed larvae. Los Angeles Co. Mus. Nat. Hist., Bull.: Sci., (7):1–145.

Nakamura, Hiroshi. 1955. Report of an investigation of the spearfishes of Formosan waters. U.S. Fish and Wild. Serv., Spec. Sci. Rept.–Fish., (153):1–46.

Norman, J. R. 1934. A systematic monograph of the flatfishes (Heterosomata). Brit. Mus. Nat. Hist., London. 459 p. (Reprinted, 1966, Johnson Reprint Corp., New York)

Paxton, J. R. 1967. A distributional analysis for the lanternfishes (family Myctophidae) of the San Pedro Basin, California. Copeia, (2):422–440.

Peden, Alex E. 1966a. Reexamination of two species in the stichaeid genus, *Anoplarchus*. Copeia, (2):340–345.

—— 1966b. Occurrences of the fishes *Pholis schultzi* and *Liparis mucosus* in British Columbia. Fish. Res. Bd. Can., J., 23(2):313–316.

Peterson, Clifford L. 1956. Observations on the taxonomy, biology and ecology of the engraulid and clupeid fishes in the Gulf of Nicoya, Costa Rica. Inter-Amer. Trop. Tuna Comm., Bull., 1(5):139–280.

Phillips, Julius B. 1957. A review of the rockfishes of California (family Scorpaenidae). Calif. Dept. Fish and Game, Fish Bull., (104):1–158.

—— 1966. Skilfish. *Erilepis zonifer* (Lockington), in Californian and Pacific northwest waters. Calif. Fish and Game, 52(3):151–156.

Quast, Jay C. 1964. Meristic variation in the hexagrammid fishes. U.S. Fish and Wild. Serv., Fish. Bull., 63(3):589–609.

—— 1965. Osteological characteristics and affinities of the hexagrammid fishes, with a synopsis. Calif. Acad. Sci., Proc., 31(21):563–600.

Radford, Keith W., and Witold L. Klawe. 1965. Biological observation on the whalesucker, *Remilegia australis*, Echeneiformes:Echeneidae. San Diego Soc. Nat. Hist., Trans., 14(6):65–72.

Rass, T. S. (Ed.) 1962. Greenlings: taxonomy; biology; interoceanic transplantation. Akad. Nauk S.S.S.R., Inst., Okeanol., Trudy, 59:1–208. (English translation, 1970. Nat. Sci. Found. and U.S. Dept. Int., Wash., D.C.)

Roedel, Phil M. 1953. Common ocean fishes of the California coast. Calif. Dept. Fish and Game, Fish Bull., (91):1–184.

Roedel, Phil M., and Wm. Ellis Ripley. 1950. California sharks and rays. Calif. Dept. of Fish and Game, Fish Bull., (75):1–88.

Rosenblatt, Richard H. 1964. A new gunnel, *Pholis clemensi*, from the coast of western North America. Fish. Res. Bd. Can., J., 21(5):933–939.

Rosenblatt, Richard H., and Terrence D. Parr. 1969. The Pacific species of the clinid fish genus *Paraclinus*. Copeia, (1):1–20.

Rosenblatt, Richard, and B. Zahuranec. 1967. The eastern Pacific groupers of the genus *Mycteroperca;* including a new species. Calif. Fish and Game, 53(4): 228–245.

Rounsefell, George A. 1962. Relationships among North American Salmonidae. U.S. Fish and Wild. Serv., Fish. Bull., 62(209):235–270.

Schultz, Leonard P. 1936. Keys to the fishes of Washington, Oregon and closely adjoining regions. Univ. Wash., Publ. Biol., 2(4):103–228.

—— 1961. Revision of the marine silver hatchetfishes (family Sternoptychidae). U.S. Nat. Mus., Proc., 112(3449):587–649.

Shmidt, P. Yu. 1950. Fishes of the Sea of Okhotsk. Acad. Sci. USSR., Trans. Pac. Comm., 6:1–392. (English translation, 1965. Nat. Sci. Found., Wash., D.C.)

Smith, C. Lavett 1971. A revision of the American groupers: *Epinephelus* and lalied genera. Am. Mus. Nat. Hist., Bull., 146(2):6–241.

Starks, E. C. 1918. The herrings and herring-like fishes of California. Calif. Fish and Game, 4(2):58–65.

Stephens, John S., Robert K. Johnson, Gerald S. Key and John E. McCosker. 1970. The comparative ecology of three sympatric species of California blennies of the genus *Hypsoblennius* Gill (Teleostomi, Blenniidae). Ecol. Monogr., 40(2):213–233.

Strasburg, Donald W. 1964. Further notes on the identification and biology of echeneid fishes. Pac. Sci., 18(1):51–57.

Svetovidov, A. N. 1948. Fishes: Gadiformes, 9(4):1–304. *In* E. N. Pavlovskii and A. A. Shatkel'berg (eds.) Fauna of U.S.S.R., Zool. Inst. Akad. Nauk S.S.S.R., n.s. 34. (English translation, 1962. Nat. Sci. Found., Wash., D.C.)

—— 1952. Fishes: Clupeidae, 2(1):1–428. *In* Fauna of U.S.S.R., Zool. Inst. Akad. Nauk S.S.S.R. n.s. 48. (English translation, 1963. Nat. Sci. Found., Wash., D.C.)

Tarp, Fred Harald. 1952. A revision of the family Embiotocidae (the surfperches). Calif. Dept. Fish and Game, Fish Bull., (88):1–99.

Taylor, Frederick H. C. 1957. Variations and populations of four species of Pacific coast flatfish. Ph.D. Thesis. Univ. Calif. Los Angeles. 376 p.

Tsuyuki, H., and S. J. Westrheim. 1970. Analyses of the *Sebastes aleutianus—S. melanostomus* complex, and description of a new scorpaenid species, *Sebastes caenaematicus*, in the northeast Pacific Ocean. Fish. Res. Bd. Can., J., 27(12): 2233–2254.

Tucker, Denys W. 1956. Studies on the trichiuroid fishes. 3. A preliminary revision of the family Trichiuridae. Brit. Mus. (Nat. Hist.), Bull.: Zool., 4(3):73–130.

Vladykov, Vadim D., and W. I. Follett. 1958. Redescription of *Lampetra ayresii* (Gunther) of western north America, a species of lamprey (Petromyzontidae) distinct from *Lampetra fluviatilis* (Linneaus) of Europe. Fish. Res. Bd. Can., J., 15(1):47–77.

Walford, Lionel A. 1937. Marine game fishes of the Pacific coast from Alaska to the equator. Univ. Calif. Press, Berkeley. 205 p.

Walker, Boyd W., (Ed). 1961. The ecology of the Salton Sea, California, in relation to the sportfishery. Calif. Dept. Fish and Game, Fish. Bull., (113):1–204.

Whitehead, P. J. P., and A. C. Wheeler. 1966–1967. The generic names used for sea basses of Europe and N. America (Pisces: Serranidae). Mus. Civ. St. Nat. Genova, Ann., 76:23–41.

Wilimovsky, Norman J. 1958. Provisional keys to the fishes of Alaska. U.S. Fish and Wild. Serv., Juneau Fish. Res. Lab. 113 p. (mimeo.)

GENERAL REFERENCES

Bailey, Reeve M., John E. Fitch, Earl S. Herald, Ernest A. Lachner, C. C. Lindsey, C. Richard Robins and W. B. Scott. 1970. A list of common and scientific names of fishes from the United States and Canada. 3rd ed. Am. Fish. Soc., Spec. Publ., (6):1–150.

Baxter, John L. 1966. Inshore fishes of California. 3rd rev. Calif. Dept. Fish and Game, Sacramento. 80 p.

Berdegue, Julio A. 1956. Peces de importancia commercial en la casta non-occidental de Mexico. Sec. de Marina, Comm. Bara el Fomento de la Piscicaltura Rural, Mexico City. 345 p.

Bolin, Rolf L. 1954. Key to the intertidal fishes, p. 313-322. *In* S. F. Light, Intertidal invertebrates of the central California coast, rev. by Ralph I. Smith, Frank A. Pitelka, Donald P. Abbott, Frances M. Weasner and others. Univ. Calif. Press, Berkeley. 446 p.

Bohlke, James E., and Charles C. G. Chaplin. 1968. Fishes of the Bahamas and adjacent tropical waters. Publ. by Livingston Pub. Co., Wynnewood, Pa., for Acad. Nat. Sci. Phila. 771 p.

Clemens, W. A., and G. V. Wilby. 1961. Fishes of the Pacific coast of Canada. 2nd ed. Fish. Res. Bd. Can., Bull., (68):1–443.

Fitch, John E. 1969. Offshore fishes of California. 4th rev. Calif. Dept. Fish and Game, Sacramento. 80 p.

Fitch, John E., and Robert J. Lavenberg. 1968. Deep-water teleostean fishes of California. Univ. Calif. Press, Berkeley. 155 p.

——— 1971. Marine food and games fishes of California. Univ. of Calif. Press, Berkeley. 179 p.

Gosline, William A., and Vernon E. Brock. 1960. Handbook of Hawaiian fishes. Univ. Hawaii Press, Honolulu. 372 p.

Herald, Earl S. 1961. Living fishes of the world. Doubleday and Co., Inc., New York. 304 p.

——— 1972. Fishes of North America. Doubleday and Co., Inc., New York. 254 p.

Hiyama, Yosio. 1937. Marine fishes of the Pacific coast of Mexico. Nisson Fish. Inst. & Co., Ltd., Odawara, Japan. 75 p.

Hubbs, Carl L., and Karl F. Lagler. 1958. Fishes of the Great Lakes region. Univ. of Mich. Press, Ann Arbor. 213 p.

Kimsey, J. B., and Leonard O. Fisk. 1960. Keys to the freshwater and anadromous fishes of California. Calif. Fish and Game, 46(4):453–479.

Lagler, Karl F., John E. Bardach and Robert R. Miller. 1962. Ichthyology. Univ. of Mich. Press, Ann Arbor. 545 p.

Leim, A. H., and W. B. Scott. 1966. Fishes of the Atlantic coast of Canada. Fish. Res. Bd. Can., Bull., (155):1–485.

Marshall, N. B. 1965. The life of fishes. Weidenfeld and Nicolson, London. 402 p.

Norman, J. R., and P. H. Greenwood. 1963. A history of fishes. Ernest Benn Ltd., London. 398 p.

Radovich, John. 1961. Relationships of some marine organisms of the northeast Pacific to water temperatures, particularly during 1957 through 1959. Calif. Dept. Fish and Game. Fish Bull., (112):1–62.

Smith, J. L. B. 1965. The sea fishes of southern Africa. 5th ed. Central News Agency, Ltd., Capetown. 580 p.

Turner, Charles H., and Jeremy C. Sexsmith. 1964. Marine baits of California. Calif. Dept. Fish and Game, Sacramento. 71 p.

INDEX TO COMMON NAMES

INDEX TO SCIENTIFIC NAMES

C

Calamus brachysomus, 152–153
Carangidae, 26, 146–149
Caranx caballus, 148–149
Caranx hippos, 148–149, 213
Carcharhinidae, 33, 38–41
Carcharhinus leucas, 40–41
Carcharhinus longimanus, 40, 211
Carcharhinus obscurus, 40–41
Carcharhinus remotus, 40–41
Carcharodon carcharias, 38
Careproctus melanurus, 138
Caulolatilus princeps, 143
Cebidichthyidae, 17, 177
Cebidichthys violaceus, 177
Centriscidae, 20, 88
Centrolophidae, 23, 198
Cephaloscyllium ventriosum, 36–37
Ceratiidae, 15, 84–85
Cetengraulis mysticetus, 56
Cetorhinidae, 33, 36–37
Cetorhinus maximus, 36–37
Chaenopsis alepidota, 173, 214
Chaetodipterus zonatus, 152–153
Chaetodon falcifer, 158–159
Chaetodon humeralis, 158–159
Chaetodontidae, 26, 158–159
Chauliodontidae, 20, 68–69
Chauliodus macouni, 68–69
Cheilotrema saturnum, 156–157
Chilara taylori, 72–73
Chilomycterus affinis, 208–209
Chimaeridae, 20, 52
Chirolophis nugator, 180
Chitonotus pugetensis, 124–125
Chlamydoselachidae, 32, 34
Chlamydoselachus anguineus, 34
Chloroscombrus orqueta, 148–149
Chromis punctipinnis, 167
Citharichthys sordidus, 204–205
Citharichthys stigmaeus, 204–205
Citharichthys xanthostigma, 204–205
Clevelandia ios, 188–189, 214
Clinidae, 29, 30, 173–176
Clinocottus acuticeps, 132
Clinocottus analis, 130–131
Clinocottus embryum, 132–133
Clinocottus globiceps, 9, 132–133
Clinocottus recalvus, 132–133
Clupea harengus pallasii, 54–55
Clupeidae, 18, 54–55
Collybus drachme, 213
Cololabis saira, 82
Congridae, 16, 52–53
Coryphaena hippurus, 150–151
Coryphaenidae, 23, 150–151

Coryphaenoides acrolepis, 76
Coryphopterus nicholsii, 186
Cottidae, 15, 23, 30, 118–133, 213
Cryptacanthodidae, 17, 177
Cryptopsaras couesii, 84–85
Cryptotrema corallinum, 174–175
Cyclothone acclinidens, 64
Cymatogaster aggregata, 162–163
Cymatogaster gracilis, 162–163
Cynoglossidae, 199
Cynoscion nobilis, 154
Cynoscion parvipinnis, 154–155
Cynoscion xanthulus, 154–155
Cyprinodontidae, 17, 82–83
Cypselurus californicus, 80–81
Cypselurus heterurus, 80–81

D

Damalichthys vacca, 166
Danaphos oculatus, 64
Dasyatididae, 42, 50–51
Dasyatis dipterura, 50–51
Dasyatis violacea, 50–51
Decapterus hypodus, 146
Delolepis gigantea, 177
Dermatostethus punctipinnis, 212
Desmodema polysticta, 87
Diaphus theta, 70
Diodon hystrix, 208–209
Diodontidae, 14, 208–209
Dormitator latifrons, 184–185
Dorosoma petenense, 54

E

Echeneididae, 22, 144–145
Echeneis naucrates, 144
Echinorhinus cookei, 34–35, 211
Eleotridae, 26, 184–185
Elopidae, 18, 52–53
Elops affinis, 52–53
Embassichthys bathybius, 204–205
Embiotoca jacksoni, 160
Embiotoca lateralis, 164–165
Embiotocidae, 26, 160–166, 214
Embryx crotalina, 78–79
Engraulididae, 18, 56–57
Engraulis mordax, 56–57
Enophrys bison, 120–121
Enophrys taurina, 122
Eopsetta jordani, 206–207
Ephippidae, 28, 152–153
Epinephelus analogus, 140–141
Epinephelus niveatus, 140–141
Eptatretus, 211
Eptatretus deani, 32
Eptatretus stoutii, 32

ADDENDUM

This supplement for the guide includes 246 additions or changes for 170 species, and a listing of eight additions to the coastal California marine fish fauna. Several other species new to California waters have been recorded since 1972, but these have been deepwater fishes not covered by this work. This supplement contains an alphabetical listing by genus or family of new information and changes for species previously included, a listing of additional species not included in the first printing, and literature references to new material or to information inadvertently overlooked in preparation of the first printing.

Additional changes of size, depth distribution, and meristic characters have been reported, but confirmation of these requires literature search and correspondence. These additions, when confirmed, will be included in future addenda or a revision of the guide.

Changes are accompanied by the name of the person who either collected or observed the fish or confirmed the new information. In a series of data wherein several counts are given, such as when depicting the number of fin rays, the new information is underlined. In the case of range and depth extensions and length changes, only the new information is listed. New literature references are listed in this addendum; references already appearing in the guide are not repeated here. Museum and organizational symbols are: CAS — California Academy of Sciences, San Francisco; CF&G — California Department of Fish and Game; LACM — Los Angeles County Museum of Natural History; MLML — Moss Landing Marine Laboratories; NMFS — United States National Marine Fisheries Service, Department of Commerce; SIO — Scripps Institution of Oceanography, La Jolla; UCLA — University of California at Los Angeles.

We are indebted to many conscientious fishery scientists for reporting new information to us and to the fishermen who brought to the attention of fishery workers "odd looking" species to have them checked out. John Fitch of the Department of Fish and Game has kept detailed records of many of the entries, and our deep appreciation is offered for the use of his data. Eric Anderson and Gregor Cailliet of Moss Landing Marine Laboratories have been helpful in searching for new records and information, as have the staffs of natural history museums. Camm Swift, LACM, has informed us of many new records entering the LACM files as has Lillian Dempster, CAS, and John Bleck, formerly of UCLA, when new information became available to them. This supplement is the result of the continuing work of many fishery workers along the Pacific coast and we are thankful for the extreme cooperation we have received.

Daniel J. Miller
Robert N. Lea

Additions and Changes

Acanthogobius flavimanus (page 188). Northern range limit: Estero Americano, Sonoma Co. (James Carlton, CAS). Inadvertently introduced from the Orient.

Allosmerus elongatus (page 62). Common in deeper water; an offshore species (John Fitch, CF&G).

Ammodytes hexapterus (page 184). Depth: (max.) to 156 ft. (E.A. Best, Seattle).

Amphistichus rhodoterus (page 160). Depth: to 60 ft. (John Fitch, CF&G).

Anarrhichthys ocellatus (page 170). Depth: (max.) to 738 ft. (Grinols, 1965).

Anisotremus davidsonii (page 152). Color: Has a bright yellow or golden phase (John Fitch, CF&G).

Anoplopoma fimbria (page 113). Depth: (max.) to 6000 ft. (Gregor Cailliet, MLML).

Apristurus brunneus (page 36). Depth: (max.) to 3120 ft. (Hart, 1973).

Aprodon cortezianus (page 78). Depth: (min.) 240 ft. (Love and Lee, 1974). D 105-113. A 89-93 (William Bayliff, La Jolla). Pect. 18-21. GRt 16-17 (Hart, 1973).

Argentina sialis (page 64). Length: to 8.4 in. (Richard Parrish, CF&G).

Artedius creaseri (page 126). Northern range limit: Monterey breakwater (Eric Anderson, MLML).

Artedius harringtoni (page 128). Length: to 5.0 in. (Eric Anderson, MLML).

Artedius lateralis (page 126). Depth: (max.) to 30 ft. (CF&G collection, Pt. Arena). D VII-X + 15-17 (Hart, 1973).

Ascelichthys rhodorus (page 118). Southern range limit: Pillar Pt., San Mateo Co. (Margaret Bradbury, Calif. State Univ., San Francisco). D VII-X, 17-20 (Hart, 1973).

Askoldia ? sp. (page 178). Letter from John Bleck, UCLA (27 May 1973):"The sixspot prickleback has been taken by (Boyd) Walker at San Simeon. Our specimens are as follows: W 71-11, 1 specimen; W 66-67, 5; W 64-82, 4; and we also have one from Jade Cove, W 70-16, 1. In addition, we have a specimen from George Barlow that he collected at the mouth of the Carmel River, 400 m offshore (85') and later one of his students collected another specimen in the same area (45') which she kept alive in the marine tank. The specimen from George Barlow has only 5 ocelli, but ours have six."

Bleck also noted that one of the Barlow specimens increased the maximum size to 5.4 in.

Six juvenile specimens (CAS 27696) were collected 0.5 mi. N of Mendocino City at Jack Peters Gulch (Ident. by R. N. Lea from collection made by Rofen, CAS 27696).

One specimen taken in CF&G collection at Arena Cove, April 7, 1973. Synopsis of new information: *Askoldla* ? sp. Diablo Cove, San Luis Obispo Co. to 0.5 mi. N of Mendocino City. Length to 5.4 in. Intertidal to 85 ft. Uncommon.

Asterotheca (page 136). Should read: *Bathyagonus Infrasplnatus* and *Bathyagonus pentacanthus* (Fitch, 1973a).

Aulorhynchus flavidus (page 88). D XXIV-XXVII + 9-11 (Hart, 1973).

Auxis thazard (page 191). Uncommon (Stephen Crooke, CF&G).

Bathophilus flemingi (page 68). Pect. 4-7. Vert. 44-49 (Hart, 1973).

Benthalbella dentata (page 68). Length: to 9.25 in. (Hart, 1973).

Bothragonus swanll (page 134). Length to 3.5 in. D II-V + 4-5 (Hart, 1973).

Bothrocara brunneum (page 78). Length: to 26.1 in. D 107-117. A 92-100. Pect. 13-17. Pelvic absent. Vert. 111-116 (William Bayliff, La Jolla).

Bothrocara molle (page 78). D 100-112 (William Bayliff, La Jolla). A 89-101 (Hart, 1973). Pect. 13-14. Vert. 110-113 (William Bayliff, La Jolla).

Brosmophycis marginata (page 72). Reported to 20 in. but largest recorded recently in California is 16 in. (John Fitch, CF&G). D 98-110. Follett (1970) noted that the 92 dorsal ray count was erroneous and should have been 100; he reported the 110 count, and unpublished counts by C. Clothier (CF&G) yielded the 98 rays.

Carcharodon carcharias (page 38). Size: Randall (1973) has reviewed all size records and remeasured the jaws of the white shark that was erroneously determined to be 36.5 ft. His conclusion: The largest reliably measured is a 21-ft. specimen from Cuba. Largest estimated from bites on whales may be as much as 25 to 26 ft. in length.

Chaetodipterus zonatus (page 152). Shallow inshore areas to 150 ft. Length reported to 25.5 in., but largest recorded in north Pacific is 10.0 in. (John Fitch, CF&G).

Chaetodon falcifer (page 158). Depth: (max.) to 492 ft. (Freihofer, 1966).

Citharichthys xanthostigma (page 204). Depth: (max.) to 660 ft. (Love and Lee, 1974).

Clinocottus analis (page 130). Length: to 7.4 in. (MLML collection, Pigeon Pt., San Mateo Co.).

Coryphopterus nicholsii (page 186). Depth: (min.) Intertidal (Steven Schultz, CF&G); (max.) 348 ft. (John Fitch, CF&G).

Damalichthys vacca (page 166). Depth: (max.) 240 ft. (Love and Lee, 1974).

Echinorhinus cookei (page 34). Depth: to 1800 ft. (Osada and Cailliet, 1975).

Elops affinis (page 52). Northern range limit: Ventura, California. Largest recently recorded size from eastern Pacific is 3 lbs. (John Fitch, CF&G).

Embryx crotalina (page 78). Length: to 17.2 in. D 120-128. Pect. 14-17. Vert. 127 (William Bayliff, La Jolla).

Eopsetta jordani (page 206). Southern range limit: 25 mi. NNE Cedros Island, Baja California, 28°47.5′N; 114°57.0′W (NMFS Cruise Rept., R/V EKVATOR).

Epinephelus niveatus (page 140). Northern range limit: Pt. Piedras Blancas, San Luis Obispo Co. (Steven Schultz, CF&G). Max. size: John Fitch reports an Atlantic specimen at approx. 45 in. and the largest Pacific record at 31.5 in. Depth to 1500 ft.; deepest Pacific depth record is 426 ft. (John Fitch, CF&G). D XI, 14-16. A 8-10. Vert. 24 (Smith, 1971).

Eptatretus deani (page 32). Length: to 25 in. (Hart, 1973).

Eptatretus stoutii (page 32). Depth: (max.) to 3096 ft. (Hart, 1973).

Erilepis zonifer (page 113). Northern range limit: to SE Alaska, Kamchatka, and Japan. LLs 122-134. Vert. 57 (Hart, 1973).

Eucyclogobius newberryi (page 186). Southern range limit: Agua Hedionda Cr., Carlsbad, San Diego Co. Northern range limit: Lake Earl, Del Norte Co. (Camm Swift, LACM).

Euthynnus lineatus (page 192). Uncommon (Stephen Crooke, CF&G).

Gadus macrocephalus (page 76). D 10-16 + 13-21 + 14-21 (Hart, 1973).

Genyonemus lineatus (page 156). Depth: (max.) to 420 ft. (Eric Anderson, MLML). Length: to 16.3 in. (Mike McCorkle, Santa Barbara).

Glyptocephalus zachirus (page 204). Southern range limit: 20.5 mi. NNW Cedros Isl., Baja California, 28°42.8′N; 115°19.3′W (NMFS Cruise Rept., R/V EKVATOR).

Gobiesox maeandricus (page 74). Intertidal and kelp canopy to 26 ft. (CF&G collection at Pt. Arena).

Gobiesox papillifer (page 74). Rare (Carl Hubbs, SIO; only one specimen has been recorded from California).

Gobiesox rhessodon (page 74). Northern range limit: Pismo Beach (Harry Fierstine, Calif. Polytech. Univ., San Luis Obispo).

Halichoeres semicinctus (page 168). Length: to 14 in. (John Fitch, CF&G).

Hemanthias peruanus (page 140). Length to 15.1 in. (John Fitch, CF&G; specimen at LACM).

Hemilepidotus hemilepidotus (page 120). Vert. 36 (Hart, 1973).

Hemilepidotus spinosus (page 120). Length: to 11.3 in. (James Hardwick, CF&G). Depth: (max.) to 318 ft. (CF&G collection in Gulf of the Farallones).

Heterodontus franclscl (page 34). Length: reported to 4 ft. but largest recorded is a 3 ft. 2.12 in., 22 lb. fish from Mexico (John Fitch, CF&G).

Hexanchus grlseus (page 34). Range: Cosmopolitan in temperate seas. Hart (1973) reports this species from Australia, Mediterranean, and Japan. Length to 14 ft., and wt. to 1280 lbs. (Richard Burge, CF&G.; note being prepared).

Hlppoglossina stomata (page 200). Depth: (min.) 40 ft. (John Fitch, CF&G).

Hlppoglossoides elassodon (page 206). A 55-71. GRt 16-24 (Hart, 1973).

Hlppoglossus stenolepls (page 199). Reported to 800 lbs.; documented at 507 lbs. (Skud, 1975).

Hypsoblennius gilberti (page 172). Length: to 6.75 in. (John Fitch, CF&G).

Icelinus quadriserlatus (page 122). Depth: (max.) to 660 ft. (Love and Lee, 1974). Length: to 3.4 in. (MLML collection).

Icosteus aenigmaticus (page 184). Depth: (min.) 60 ft. (Stephen Crooke, CF&G); (max.) 2400 ft. (Grinols, 1965).

Isopsetta isolepls (page 202). Depth: (max.) to 1200 ft. (Hart, 1973).

Istiophorus platypterus (page 196). Length: to 10 ft. 9 in.; wt. to 221 lbs. (LaMonte, 1958).

Lamna ditropis (page 38). Range: also extends to Japan (Hart, 1973).

Lampetra tridentata (page 32). Length: to 30 in. (McPhail and Lindsey, 1970).

Lampris regius (page 84). Pect. 20-24. Pelvic 14-17 (Hart, 1973).

Lepidogobius lepidus (page 188). Depth: (max.) to 660 ft. (Love and Lee, 1974).

Lepidopsetta bilineata (page 200). Length: to 23.5 in. Depth: (max.) 1200 ft. D 65-82. A 50-65. Pect. 10-13 (Hart, 1973).

Lestidium ringens (page 68). Length: to 8.25 in. (Hart, 1973).

Liparis fucensis (page 138). Depth: (min.) Intertidal (CF&G collection at Arena Cove).

Lycodapus flerasfer (page 78). Southern range limit: Gulf of California. Uncommon (Eric Anderson, MLML). D 82-91. A 70-81. Vert. 87-92 (William Bayliff, La Jolla).

Lycodapus mandibularis (page 78). D 86-92. A 72-78. Pect. 7-9 (Eric Anderson, MLML). Vert. 87-88 (William Bayliff, La Jolla).

Lycodes diapterus (page 78). Length: to 13.0 in. (Hart, 1973). Depth: (min.) 42 ft. D 104-124. Vert. 113-125 (William Bayliff, La Jolla).

Lycodopsis pacifica (page 78). Length: to 18 in. (Hart, 1973).

Lythrypnus zebra (page 186). Northern range limit: San Jose Beach, Monterey Co. (Eric Anderson, MLML; note being prepared).

Macrouridae (page 76). We have included only two of the eight species of this family found in California waters; most grenadiers are found in deeper water than considered in the guide. Iwamoto and Stein (1974) reviewed the macrourids of the eastern North Pacific Ocean and their work should be consulted for California species.

Makaira indica (page 196). Weight: to 1560 lbs. (LaMonte, 1958).

Makaira nigricans (page 196). Weight to 1805 lbs., from Hawaiian Isls. (Shomura and Williams, 1975).

Merluccius productus (page 76). D 10-13 + 37-44 (Hart, 1973).

Microstomus pacificus (page 206). Depth: (min.) 60 ft. (Carlisle, Turner, and Ebert, 1964).

Mugil cephalus (page 167). Is no longer common in the Salton Sea (John Fitch, CF&G).

Mustelus henlei (page 38). Depth: (max.) to 360 ft. (Eric Anderson, MLML).

Myliobatis californica (page 50). Width to 4 ft. 9 in. (Steven Schultz, CF&G).

Nematistius pectoralis (page 150). Northern range limit: San Clemente, Orange Co. (not San Clemente Isl.).

Notorynchus maculatus (page 34). Southern range limit in north Pacific: San Carlos Bay, Baja Calif. (Homer Moore, Long Beach; specimen at LACM).

Occella verrucosa (page 134). D VII-X + 6-9. Pect. 13-15 (Gruchy, 1969). This changes the key on page 135 to read: 5a Breast with large bony plates; pect. rays 13-15.

Odontaspis ferox (page 38). California specimens treated as *Odontaspis herbsti* (Garrick, 1974).

Odontopyxis trispinosa (page 136). Length: to 3.9 in. (MLML collection).

Oligocottus rimensis (page 128). Southern range limit: Baja California (Hart, 1973).

Oligocottus snyderi (page 130). Length: to 3.6 in. (CF&G collection, Pt. Arena).

Oncorhynchus keta (page 58). Southern range limit: San Diego Harbor (John Duffy, CF&G).

Oncorhynchus nerka (page 58). Southern range limit: Los Angeles Harbor (John Fitch, CF&G).

Ophichthus triserialis (page 52). Peru to Klamath River, Del Norte Co. Depth: Shallow waters to 72 ft. (Quirollo and Dinnel, 1975).

Ophichthus zophochir (page 52). Northern range limit: Humboldt Bay (Quirollo and Dinnel, 1975). Depth: (max.) to 210 ft. (Wintersteen, 1975).

Ophiodon elongatus (page 114). Length: approx. 52 in., and wt. to 54 lbs. in California (Julius B. Phillips, CF&G). D XXIV-XXVIII, 19-24 (Hart, 1973).

Oxyjulis californica (page 168). Northern range limit: Salt Pt., Sonoma Co. (Edmund Hobson, NMFS, Tiburon). Depth: (max.) to 240 ft. (Love and Lee, 1974).

Paraclinus integripinnis (page 173). Northern range limit (mainland): Serena Cove, Santa Barbara Co. D XXVII-XXXIII (Love and Lee, 1974).

Parophrys vetulus (page 202). Northern range limit: Bering Sea (E. A. Best, Seattle).

Pholis schultzi (page 182). Intertidal to 60 ft. (Steven Schultz, CF&G).

Platichthys stellatus (page 204). D 52-66 (Hart, 1973).

Pleurogrammus monopterygius (page 116). Southern range limit: Morro Bay (Steven Schultz, CF&G). Length: to 19.7 in. (Rass, 1962).

Pleuronichthys coenosus (page 202). Depth: (max.) 966 ft. (Hart, 1973).

Pleuronichthys decurrens (page 200). Southern range limit: 25 mi. NNE Cedros Isl., Baja California, 28°47.5"N; 114°57.0'W (NMFS, Cruise Rept., R/V EKVATOR). Depth: (min.) 25 ft. (Steven Schultz, CF&G).

Pleuronichthys ritteri (page 200). Northern range limit: Morro Bay (Fierstine, Kline, and Garman, 1973).

Pleuronichthys verticalis (page 200). Depth: (max.) to 660 ft. (Love and Lee, 1974).

Porichthys myriaster (page 72). Length: to 20 in. (CF&G collection, Santa Catalina Isl.).

Poromitra crassiceps (page 86). Pect. 13-14 (Hart, 1973).

Psettichthys melanostictus (page 202). Southern range limit: El Segundo, Los Angeles Co. (John Fitch, CF&G). Northern range limit: Bering Sea (E. A. Best, Seattle). Depth: (max.) to 312 ft. (Patrick Collier, CF&G).

Pseudopriacanthus serrula (page 143). Northern range limit to Monterey Bay. Length to 13 in. Depth: (min.) 30 ft. (Fitch and Lavenberg, 1975).

Radulinus asprellus (page 128). A 21-25 (Hart, 1973).

Raja binoculata (page 44). Southern range limit: 22 mi. NNW Cedros Isl., Baja California, 28°42.4'N; 115° 22.2'W (NMFS, Cruise Rept. R/V EKVATOR).

Raja rhina (page 44). Southern range limit: 20.5 mi. NNW of Cedros Isl., Baja California, 28°42.8'N; 115°19.3'W (NMFS, Cruise Rept. R/V EKVATOR).

Raja trachura (page 44). Depth: (min.) 1860 ft. (Richard Nitsos, CF&G). Length: to 35 in. (John Fitch, CF&G).

Reinhardtius hippoglossoides (page 206). D 83-108. A 62-79. GRt 14-20. Vert. 61-65 (Hart, 1973).

Rhincodon typus (page 36). Color: reddish or greenish brown above with white or yellow spots.

Rhombochirus osteochir (pages 144 and 145). **HARDFIN MARLINSUCKER** page 145: 5a Disc extending posteriorly beyond end of depressed pectoral fin (in fish over 65 mm SL).

Rimicola eigenmanni (page 74). Depth: (max.) 48 ft. (Fitch, 1952).

Salmo clarkii (page 58). GRt 14-22 (Hart, 1973).

Salmo gairdnerii (page 58). Largest sea run wt. is 43 lbs. (Hart, 1973).

Scytalina cerdale (page 184). Depth: (max.) 25 ft. (Steven Schultz, CF&G).

Sebastes auriculatus (page 94). Depth: (max.) to 420 ft. (Eric Anderson, MLML).

Sebastes aurora (page 106). Southern range limit: 22 mi. NNW Cedros Isl., Baja California, 28°42.4'N; 115°22.2'W (NMFS, Cruise Rept. R/V EKVATOR).

Sebastes babcocki (page 102). Length: to 25.0 in. (Hart, 1973). Depth: (min.) 300 ft. (Hart, 1973).

Sebastes borealis (page 108). Length to 38 in. (John Fitch, CF&G).

Sebastes brevispinis (page 92). Depth: (max.) to 1200 ft. (Hart, 1973).

Sebastes caurinus (page 92). Chen (1975) states: "With these additions, with another new species to be described by Lea and Fitch (personal communication), and with the placement of *S. vexillaris* in the synonymy of *S. caurinus* (Chen, in preparation), the number of known species of *Sebastes* in the eastern North Pacific is now 69."

When Chen's synonymy is published, the species will be referred to as *Sebastes caurinus,* and the information for *S. vexillaris* and *S. caurinus* on page 92 is to be integrated. We suggest **COPPER ROCKFISH** as the common name.

Sebastes constellatus (page 98). Length: to 18.0 in. (Miller and Gotshall, 1965).

Sebastes crameri (page 110). Depth: (max.) to 1800 ft. (Grinols, 1965). A III, 5-7 (Hart, 1973).

Sebastes dallii (page 92). Southern range limit: S. of Rompiente Pt., Baja California, LACM 32056-5 (Camm Swift, LACM).

Sebastes diploproa (page 106). Southern range limit: 22 mi. NNW Cedros Isl., Baja California, 28°42.4′N; 115°22.2′W (NMFS, Cruise Rept. R/V EKVATOR).

Sebastes entomelas (page 96). Depth: (max.) to 1200 ft. A III, 8-10 (Hart, 1973).

Sebastes flavidus (page 96). Depth: (max.) to 1800 ft. (Grinols, 1965).

Sebastes gilli (page 104). Southern range limit: Cape Colnett, Baja California, CAS 28496 (James Phelan, CF&G). Length: to 28 in. Depth: (max.) to 1230 ft. (Julius B. Phillips, CF&G).

Sebastes helvomaculatus (page 98). Depth: (min.) 390 ft. (James Hardwick, CF&G). Depth: (max.) 1800 ft. (Hart, 1973).

Sebastes jordani (page 102). Southern range limit: 7 mi. NW of Punta Baja, Baja California (Klingbeil and Knaggs, 1976).

Sebastes macdonaldi (page 108). Southern range limit: Morgan Bank, Baja California and in the Gulf of California (Moser, 1972). Depth: (min.) 300 ft. (A. Howe, Los Angeles). D XIII, 12-14. Pect. 18-20. GRt 36-42. Vert. 26 (Chen, 1975).

Sebastes melanops (page 96). Depth: (max.) to 1200 ft. (Hart, 1973).

Sebastes miniatus (page 110). Depth: (max.) to 900 ft. (Grinols, 1965).

Sebastes mystinus (page 96). Southern range limit: 2 mi. S of Punta Banda, Baja California (Klingbeil and Knaggs, 1976).

Sebastes proriger (page 108). Depth: (max.) to 1200 ft. (Hart, 1973).

Sebastes rosaceus (page 98). Length: to 14.2 in. (Miller and Gotshall, 1965).

Sebastes rosenblatti (page 100). Northern range limit: Monterey and probably to San Francisco (the confirmed Monterey specimen reported by Eric Anderson, MLML).

Sebastes rubrivinctus (page 102). Southern range limit: 4 mi. S of Cape San Quintin, Baja California (Klingbeil and Knaggs, 1976).

Sebastes saxicola (page 110). Southern range limit: Rompiente Pt., Baja California (Camm Swift, LACM).

Sebastes semicinctus (page 112). Southern range limit: San Pablo Pt., Baja California, LACM 32077-1 (Camm Swift, LACM).

Sebastes sp. (page 106). Should read: *Sebastes rufinanus* (ref. Lea and Fitch, 1972).

Sebastes umbrosus (page 100). Northern range limit: Pt. Pinos, Monterey Co. (John Geibel, CF&G).

Sebastes vexillaris (page 92). See *Sebastes caurinus,* this addendum.

Sebastes wilsoni (page 112). Depth: (max.) to 900 ft. (Hart, 1973).

Sebastolobus alascanus (page 91). Southern range limit: 22 mi. NNW of Cedros Isl., Baja California, 28°42.4'N; 115°22.2'W (NMFS, Cruise Rept. R/V EKVATOR).

Seriola dorsalis (page 146). Depth: (max.) 228 ft. (Stephen Crooke, CF&G).

Somniosus pacificus (page 34). Depth: (max.) to 3000 ft. (Osada and Cailliet, 1975).

Squalus acanthias (page 34). Depth: (max.) to 2400 ft. (Hart, 1973).

Stellerina xyosterna (pages 134 and 135). The fish drawing of the **PRICKLEBREAST POACHER** (page 135) is actually of a male *Occella verrucosa*. These forms are similar, except the pelvic fins of *Stellerina* are much shorter than on a male *Occella*. The underview drawings of these species showing the breast are correct.

Stichaeopsis ? sp. (page 180). Southern range limit: San Miguel Isl., SIO 54-191 (John Bleck, UCLA).

Symphurus atricauda (page 199). Depth: (max.) to 660 ft. (Love and Lee, 1974).

Synodus lucioceps (page 68). Depth: (max.) to 750 ft. (Love and Lee, 1974).

Tetrapturus angustirostris (page 196). Weight: to 114 lbs. (Shomura and Williams, 1975).

Thaleichthys pacificus (page 62). The 12 in. TL size given in the guide has not been verified. E. A. Best, Seattle, shipped a 10.0-in. specimen taken from the Bering Sea to John Fitch, CF&G. Hart (1973) gives a TL of 9 in.

Thunnus obesus (page 194). Wt. to 435 lbs. (Fish. Market News Rept., S-1. January 2, 1973).

Thunnus thynnus (page 194). Wt. to 448 lbs. (John Fitch, CF&G).

Trichodon trichodon (page 170). Depth: to 180 ft. (E. A. Best, Seattle). Pect. 21-22 (Hart, 1973).

Typhlogobius californiensis (pages 186 and 187). Figure of **BLIND GOBY** on page 187: the "8 to 10 soft-rays" refers to the anal fin, not the dorsal fin as shown.

Umbrina roncador (page 154). Length: to 20.13 in. (C.L. Hubbs, SIO).

Xeneretmus latifrons (page 136). Southern range limit: Cape Colnett, Baja California (Fitch and Lavenberg, 1968).

Xystreurys liolepis (page 200). Length: to 21 in. (Robert McAllister, CF&G).

Zalembius rosaceus (page 164). Northern range limit: 1.3 mi. SW of Salt Pt., Sonoma Co. (Lillian Dempster, CAS). Depth: (max.) to 750 ft. (Love and Lee, 1974). Common in deeper waters (John Fitch, CF&G).

Zaniolepis latipinnis (page 114). Depth: (max.) to 660 ft. (Love and Lee, 1974).

Zaprora silenus (page 184). Southern range limit: Monterey Bay. A O-IV, 24-27; Pect. 20-23 (Cailliet and Anderson, 1975).

Additions to the California Marine Fish Fauna

Anthias gordensis, **THREADFIN BASS** (Family Serranidae). At least from Cape San Lucas, Baja California, to Santa Catalina Isl. (Hobson, 1975). Length to about 11 in. Depth 132 to 660 ft. Reddish-orange with reticulations on body; tail yellow. One California record. D X,15; A III,7; Pect. 20; Pelvic I,5; LLs 48-50. The common name was suggested by Lillian Dempster, CAS.

Anoplarchus insignis, **SLENDER COCKSCOMB** (Family Stichaeidae). Arena Cove, Mendocino Co. (CF&G collection; note being prepared by Lea, Laurent, and Gotshall) to Attu Island. Length to 4 in. Intertidal to 100 ft. Dark brown to black with lighter patterns; thin bars on top of head. Uncommon. D LVII-LXIV; A 40-46; Pect. 9-10; Pelvic absent; Vert. 63-69.

Artedius meanyi, **PUGET SOUND SCULPIN** (Family Cottidae). Arena Cove, Mendocino Co. (Lea, 1974) to Graham Isl., British Columbia. Length to 2 in. Sublittoral to 269 ft. Green to cream with darker bars on back. Rare; nine specimens from California. D X + 15-17; A 11-12; Pect. 15-16; Pelvic I,2-3; LLs 35-37 + 1.

Chirolophis decoratus, **DECORATED WARBONNET** (Family Stichaeidae). South Jetty, Humboldt Bay (Robert Behrstock, Humboldt State University; note being prepared) to Bering Sea. Length to 16.5 in. Shallow subtidal to 300 ft. Pale brown with light mottling and bars, especially dorsal fin. One California record. D LXI-LXII; A I,44-51; Pect. about 14; Pelvic I,4.

Kyphosus analogus, **STRIPPED SEA CHUB** (Family Kyphosidae). Peru to Oceanside, Encina Power Plant (Crooke, 1973); including the Gulf of California. Length to 18 in. Sublittoral. Color: steel blue with bronze streaks along sides. Two California specimens. D XI,14; A III,12-14; scales below lateral line 70-80.

Paralabrax auroguttatus, **GOLDEN SPOTTED ROCK BASS** (Family Serranidae). John Fitch, CF&G, received a call from partyboat operator Dan Anderson, Redondo Beach, who described this specimen over the phone. The fisherman who caught the fish was reluctant to give it up, so we must be content with this verbal, unconfirmed record of its occurrence in California. Fitch considers the description "to fit no other species." This bass is similar in body form to the other *Paralabrax* (page 142). Its third dorsal spine is longer than the 4th or 5th; the head, fins, and body are covered with round or oblong orange spots. There is a distinct pale streak along the lateral line. California specimen was 18 in. TL and was taken in 200 ft. depth.

Pholis clemensi, **LONGFIN GUNNEL** (Family Pholididae). Arena Cove, Mendocino Co. (CF&G collection; note being prepared by Lea, Laurent, and Gotshall) to Walsh Cove, Strait of Georgia, British Columbia. Length to 5 in. Depth 24 to 210 ft. Reddish and silver with even spaced bars under dorsal fin. One California record. D LXXXVII-XC; A II,50-53; Pect. 13-14; Pelvic I,1.

Sphoeroides lobatus, **LONGNOSE PUFFER** (Family Tetraodontidae). Peru to Redondo Pier (Fitch, 1973b). Length to about 13.5 in. One California record. D 8; A 6-7. Differs from *S. annulatus* by having a black flap on back over pectoral fin base, and bony interorbital into snout more than 4.0. In *S. annulatus* bony interorbital into snout is 3.5 or less.

References

Cailliet, G. M., and M. E. Anderson. 1975. Occurrence of the prowfish, *Zaprora silenus* Jordan, 1896 in Monterey Bay, California. Calif. Fish and Game, 61(1):60-62.

Carlisle, J. G., Jr., C. H. Turner, and E. E. Ebert. 1964. Artificial habitat in the marine environment. Calif. Dept. Fish and Game, Fish Bull., (124): 1-93.

Chen, L. 1975. The rockfishes, genus *Sebastes* (Scorpaenidae), of the Gulf of California, including three new species, with a discussion of their origin. Calif. Acad. Sci., Proc., 40(6):109-141.

Crooke, S. L. 1973. The first occurrence of *Kyphosus analogus* in California. Calif. Fish and Game, 59(4):310-311.

Fierstine, H. L., K. F. Kline, and G. R. Garman. 1973. Fishes collected in Morro Bay, California between January 1968 and December 1970. Calif. Fish and Game, 59(1):73-88.

Fitch, J. E. 1952. Distributional notes on some Pacific coast marine fishes. Calif. Fish and Game, 38(4):557-564.

———. 1973a. The taxonomic status of genus *Asterotheca* and clarification of the distribution of *Bathyagonus pentacanthus* (Pisces: Agonidae). Copeia, (4):815-817.

———. 1973b. The longnose puffer, *Sphoeroides lobatus* (Steindachner) added to the marine fauna of California. So. Calif. Acad. Sci., Bull., 72(3):163.

Fitch, J. E., and R. J. Lavenberg. 1975. Tidepool and nearshore fishes of California. Univ. of Calif. Press, Berkeley. 156 p.

Freihofer, W. C. 1966. New distributional records of the butterflyfish *Chaetodon falcifer*. Stanford Ichthyol. Bull., 8(3):207.

Garrick, J. A. F. 1974. First record of an odontaspidid shark in New Zealand waters. New Zealand J. Mar. and Freshw. Res., 8(4):621-630.

Grinols, R. B. 1965. Check-list of the offshore marine fishes occurring in the northeastern Pacific ocean, principally off the coasts of British Columbia, Washington, and Oregon. M. S. Thesis, Univ. Wash. 217 p.

Gruchy, C. G. 1969. Canadian records of the warty poacher, *Occa verrucosa*, with notes on the standardization of plate terminology in Agonidae. Fish. Res. Bd. Can., J., 26(6):1467-1472.

Hart, J. L. 1973. Pacific fishes of Canada. Fish. Res. Bd. Can., Bull., (180):1-740.

Hobson, E. S. 1975. First California record of the serranid fish *Anthias gordenis* Wade. Calif. Fish and Game, 61(2):111-112.

Iwamoto, T., and D. L. Stein. 1974. A systematic review of the rattail fishes (Macrouridae: Gadiformes) from Oregon and adjacent waters. Calif. Acad. Sci., Occas. Pap., (111):1-79.

Klingbeil, R. A., and E. H. Knaggs. 1976. Southern range extensions of the blue rockfish, *Sebastes mystinus;* the flag rockfish, *S. rubrivinctus;* and the shortbelly rockfish, *S. jordani.* Calif. Fish and Game, 62(2): 160.

LaMonte, F. 1958. North American game fishes. Doubleday and Co., Inc., New York. 206 p.

Lea, R. N. 1974. First record of Puget Sound sculpin, *Artedius meanyi,* from California. Fish. Res. Bd. Can., J., 31(7):1242-1243.

Lea, R. N., and J. E. Fitch. 1972. *Sebastes rufinanus,* a new scorpaenid fish from Californian waters. Copeia, (3):423-427.

Love, M. S., and R. S. Lee. 1974. New geographic and bathymetric records for fishes from southern California. Calif. Fish and Game, 60(4):212-216.

McPhail, J. D., and C. C. Lindsey. 1970. Freshwater fishes of Northwestern Canada and Alaska. Fish. Res. Bd. Can., Bull., (173):1-385.

Miller, D. J., and D. Gotshall. 1965. Ocean sportfish catch and effort from Oregon to Point Arguello, California. Calif. Dept. Fish and Game, Fish Bull., (130):1-135.

Moser, G. 1972. Development and geographic distribution of the rockfish, *Sebastes macdonaldi* (Eigenmann and Beeson, 1893), family Scorpaenidae, off southern California and Baja California. U.S. Fish and Wild. Serv., Fish. Bull., 70(3):941-958.

Osada, E. K., and G. M. Cailliet. 1975. Trap-caught sablefish in Monterey Bay, California. Cal-Neva Wild. Trans., (1975):56-73. (Joint Meet. West. Soc. Wild. Soc. and Amer. Fish. Soc. Calif. - Nevada Chpt.)

Quirollo, L. F., and P. A. Dinnel. 1975. Latitudinal range extensions for yellow and spotted snake eels (genus *Ophichthus*). Calif. Fish and Game, 61(3):156-157.

Randall, J. E. 1973. Size of the great white shark *(Carcharodon)*. Science, 181:169-170.

Shomura, R. S., and F. Williams (Eds.). 1975. Species synopsis. *Pt. 3*. Proceedings of the International Billfish Symposium, Kailua-Kona, Hawaii, 9-12 August 1972. U.S. Nat. Mar. Fish. Serv., SSRF, (-675):pt. 3, 1-159.

Skud, B. E. 1975. The sport fishery for halibut: development, recognition and regulation. Intern. Pac. Halibut Comm., Tech. Rept., (13): 1-19.

Wintersteen, J. 1975. Occurrence and depth range extension of the yellow snake eel *(Ophichthus zophochir)* off southern California. Calif. Fish and Game, 61(3):157-158.